I0006162

Learning Ceph

A practical guide to designing, implementing, and managing your software-defined, massively scalable Ceph storage system

Karan Singh

BIRMINGHAM - MUMBAI

Learning Ceph

Copyright © 2015 Packt Publishing

All rights reserved. No part of this book may be reproduced, stored in a retrieval system, or transmitted in any form or by any means, without the prior written permission of the publisher, except in the case of brief quotations embedded in critical articles or reviews.

Every effort has been made in the preparation of this book to ensure the accuracy of the information presented. However, the information contained in this book is sold without warranty, either express or implied. Neither the author, nor Packt Publishing, and its dealers and distributors will be held liable for any damages caused or alleged to be caused directly or indirectly by this book.

Packt Publishing has endeavored to provide trademark information about all of the companies and products mentioned in this book by the appropriate use of capitals. However, Packt Publishing cannot guarantee the accuracy of this information.

First published: January 2015

Production reference: 1240115

Published by Packt Publishing Ltd.
Livery Place
35 Livery Street
Birmingham B3 2PB, UK.

ISBN 978-1-78398-562-3

www.packtpub.com

Credits

Author
Karan Singh

Reviewers
Zihong Chen
Sébastien Han
Julien Recurt
Don Talton

Commissioning Editor
Taron Pereira

Acquisition Editor
James Jones

Content Development Editor
Shubhangi Dhamgaye

Technical Editor
Pankaj Kadam

Copy Editors
Janbal Dharmaraj
Sayanee Mukherjee
Alfida Paiva

Project Coordinator
Harshal Ved

Proofreaders
Simran Bhogal
Amy Johnson
Kevin McGowan

Indexer
Tejal Soni

Graphics
Disha Haria

Production Coordinator
Melwyn D'sa

Cover Work
Melwyn D'sa

Foreword

We like to call Ceph the "future of storage", a message that resonates with people at a number of different levels. For system designers, the Ceph system architecture captures the requirements for the types of systems everyone is trying to build; it is horizontally scalable, fault-tolerant by design, modular, and extensible. For users, Ceph provides a range of storage interfaces for both legacy and emerging workloads and can run on a broad range of commodity hardware, allowing production clusters to be deployed with a modest capital investment. For free software enthusiasts, Ceph pushes this technical envelope with a code base that is completely open source and free for all to inspect, modify, and improve in an industry still dominated by expensive and proprietary options.

The Ceph project began as a research initiative at the University of California, Santa Cruz, funded by several Department of Energy laboratories (Los Alamos, Lawrence Livermore, and Sandia). The goal was to further enhance the design of petabyte-scale, object-based storage systems. When I joined the group in 2005, my initial focus was on scalable metadata management for the filesystem — how to distribute management of the file and directory hierarchy across many servers so that the system could cope with a million processors in a supercomputer, dumping files into the filesystem, often in the same directory and at the same time. Over the course of the next 3 years, we incorporated the key ideas from years of research and built a complete architecture and working implementation of the system.

When we published the original academic paper describing Ceph in 2006 and the code was open sourced and posted online, I thought my work was largely complete. The system "worked", and now the magic of open source communities and collaborative development could kick in and quickly transform Ceph into the free software I'd always wanted to exist to run in my own data center. It took time for me to realize that there is a huge gap between prototype and production code, and effective free software communities are built over time. As we continued to develop Ceph over the next several years, the motivation remained the same. We built a cutting-edge distributed storage system that was completely free (as in beer and speech) and could do to the storage industry what Linux did to the server market.

Building a vibrant user and developer community around the Ceph project has been the most rewarding part of this experience. While building the Inktank business to productize Ceph in 2012 and 2013, the community was a common topic of conversation and scrutiny. The question at that point in time was how do we invest and hire to build a community of experts and contributors who do not work for us? I believe it was a keen attention to and understanding of the open source model that ultimately made Inktank and Ceph a success. We sought to build an ecosystem of users, partners, and competitors that we could lead, not dominate.

Karan Singh has been one such member of the community who materialized around Ceph over the last several years. He is an early and active member of the e-mail- and IRC-based discussion forums, where Ceph users and developers meet online to conduct their business, whether it is finding help to get started with Ceph, discussing optimal hardware or software configuration options, sharing crash reports and tracking down bugs, or collaborating in the development of new features.

Although we have known each other online for several years now, I recently had the opportunity to meet Karan in person and only then discovered that he has been hard at work writing a book on Ceph. I find it fitting and a testament to the diversity and success of the community we have built that this book, the first published about Ceph, is written by someone with no direct ties to the original Ceph research team or the Inktank business that helped push it into the limelight. Karan's long background with Ceph and deep roots in the community gave him an ideal perspective on the technology, its impact, and the all-important user experience.

Sage Weil
Ceph Principal Architect, Red Hat

About the Author

Karan Singh is a curious IT expert and an overall tech enthusiast living with his beautiful wife, Monika, in Espoo, Finland. He holds a bachelor's (honors) degree in computer science and a master's degree in system engineering from BITS Pilani, India. In addition to this, he is a certified professional for technologies such as OpenStack, NetApp, and Oracle Solaris.

Karan is currently working as a system specialist of storage and platform for CSC – IT Center for Science Ltd. in Finland. He is actively involved in providing IaaS cloud solutions based on OpenStack and Ceph Storage at his workplace and has been building economic multipetabyte storage solutions using Ceph. Karan possesses extensive system administration skills and has excellent working experience on a variety of Unix environments, backup, enterprise storage systems, and cloud platforms.

When not working on Ceph and OpenStack, Karan can be found working with technologies such as Ansible, Docker, Hadoop, IoT, and other cloud-related areas. He aims to get a PhD in cloud computing and big data and wants to learn more about these technologies. He is an avid blogger at `http://karan-mj.blogspot.fi/`. You can reach him on Twitter as `@karansingh010` and Ceph and OpenStack IRC channels as `ksingh`. You can also e-mail him at `karan_singh1@live.com`.

I'd like to thank my wife, Monika, for providing encouragement and patience throughout the writing of this book.

In addition, I would like to thank my company, CSC- IT Center for Science Ltd., and my colleagues for giving me an opportunity to work on Ceph and other cloud-related areas. Without CSC and Ceph, the opportunity to write this book would never have been possible. A big thanks goes out to the Ceph community for developing, improving, and supporting Ceph, which is an amazing piece of software.

About the Reviewers

Zihong Chen earned his master's and bachelor's degrees in computer science from Xiamen University in 2014 and 2011, respectively. He worked as a software engineer intern at Intel, Taobao, Longtop, and China Mobile Limited. In 2013, he worked for Intel, where he was involved in the development of iLab-Openstack and Ceph benchmark projects. His research interests lie in distributed storage, hand gesture recognition, Android software development, and data mining.

> I would like to thank everybody, especially my family. Without their support and encouragement in these years, I couldn't achieve anything. I will try even harder in the future!

Sébastien Han is a 26-year-old French open source DevOps from Marseille, France. His involvement in the universe of open source software started while doing his bachelors, during which he had his very first taste of open source platforms. For Sébastien, this was a true revelation that radically changed his career prospects. This passion was fostered during his studies at SUPINFO, eventually leading to a position as a professor for first-, second-, and third-year students. Additionally, this led to him taking full responsibility for SUPINFO's Linux laboratory. He has gained a knack for organizing, has valuable communicational skills, and has learned how to formulate proposals to his fellow members and manage the site.

In order to complete his degree, he had to do a final year internship for a duration of 6 months. He moved to Utrecht, the Netherlands, and worked for Stone-IT (a Smile company). The purpose of the internship was to design and build their Cloud 2.0 infrastructure. Sébastien's principal focus was on two open source technologies called OpenStack and Ceph. He had to investigate the robustness, stability, scalability, and high availability of OpenStack. Finally, he migrated the entire current cloud to an OpenStack platform. The entire project was documented as an integral part of his master's thesis.

Sébastien is currently working for Smile Netherlands in Utrecht's office of eNovance Paris (a Red Hat company) as a cloud architect. His job is mainly focused on designing and architecting OpenStack and Ceph. However, he rotates between several positions, where he helps on consulting, presale, and coding. As part of a community engagement, he has been leading the effort on Ceph integration into OpenStack during each OpenStack Summit, along with Josh Durgin. He tries to do his best to evangelize Ceph and its integration in OpenStack. He devotes a third of his time to research and development around open cloud platform and open storage.

Apart from this, he writes several articles about Linux services, majorly focusing on performance, high availability, open source cloud (OpenStack), and open source storage (Ceph). Take a look at his blog at `http://www.sebastien-han.fr/blog/`. Enjoy!

Julien Recurt is an engineer who has worked in multiple roles, depending on the occasion. He started with working for SUPINFO (his school) to enhance a complex and multisite infrastructure and reduce global costs. He really started to work with Ceph at Cloud-Solution, a French start-up, to provide low cost, scalable storage. Currently, he is working at Waycom, an Internet and web services provider.

> I would like to thank everybody who contributed to open source software and also my coworkers for supporting me in this job.

Don Talton has made a career out of solving difficult IT challenges for over 20 years. A committed engineer and entrepreneur, Don is dedicated to working with bleeding-edge technology. He has contributed significantly to the Ceph and OpenStack communities, and is the author of Kraken, the first free Ceph dashboard with feature parity to Calamari.

Don is the owner of Merrymack, Inc., a company that specializes in training for cutting-edge open source software such as Ceph, OpenStack, and Docker. Over the span of his career, he has worked as a consultant for Wells Fargo, PayPal, and Cisco Systems.

> I would like to thank my lovely wife, Sarah, and my two children, Benjamin and Elizabeth, for allowing me the time to properly review this excellent book.

www.PacktPub.com

Support files, eBooks, discount offers, and more

For support files and downloads related to your book, please visit www.PacktPub.com.

Did you know that Packt offers eBook versions of every book published, with PDF and ePub files available? You can upgrade to the eBook version at www.PacktPub.com and as a print book customer, you are entitled to a discount on the eBook copy. Get in touch with us at service@packtpub.com for more details.

At www.PacktPub.com, you can also read a collection of free technical articles, sign up for a range of free newsletters and receive exclusive discounts and offers on Packt books and eBooks.

https://www2.packtpub.com/books/subscription/packtlib

Do you need instant solutions to your IT questions? PacktLib is Packt's online digital book library. Here, you can search, access, and read Packt's entire library of books.

Why subscribe?
- Fully searchable across every book published by Packt
- Copy and paste, print, and bookmark content
- On demand and accessible via a web browser

Free access for Packt account holders

If you have an account with Packt at www.PacktPub.com, you can use this to access PacktLib today and view 9 entirely free books. Simply use your login credentials for immediate access.

I dedicate this book to the loving memory of my grandparents, Late Rajeshwari and Harish Kumar Verma; without their support, I would have never existed in this world.

This book also goes to my adorable wife, my life, my lucky charm, Monika Shrestha Singh. I love you, MJ.

Table of Contents

Preface

Data — it's a simple word that stores the past, present, and future of the entire universe, and it's the most critical element of any system that exists today. We live in an era of technology that is generating enormous amount of data each second, and with time, this data growth will be unimaginable. However, how do we store this ever-growing data such that it remains secure, reliable, and future ready? This book is about one of the storage technology game-changers that will redefine the future of storage.

Ceph is an open source technology that is leading the way in providing software-defined storage. Ceph is an excellent package of reliability, unified nature, and robustness. It is more complete and economic than any other storage solution present today. Ceph has developed its own entire new way of storing data; it's distributed, massively scalable, with no single point of failure, and the best part is that it runs on commodity hardware, which makes it amazingly economic. It will give you power to break the knots of expensive vendor lock-in solutions and switch to enterprise-grade open source technology for all your storage needs.

Ceph has been enriched with enterprise-class features such as high degree of reliability, robustness, scalability, erasure coding, cache tiering, and many more. The maturity that Ceph has gained over the period of a decade makes it stand out in a crowd and lead the way to storage. It is the technology of today and the future; unified Ceph storage system is the solution for whatever requirements you have for data storage. Ceph is truly unified, that is, it has files, blocks, and objects in a single storage system; this makes Ceph extremely flexible and adaptable to all your data needs. It is the answer to all the data storage problems you have.

Cloud computing is the next paradigm shift, and a storage system such as Ceph is the most essential component of the cloud infrastructure. Ceph has its big footprint in the cloud storage area. It has been a leading open source software-defined storage choice for cloud platforms such as OpenStack and CloudStack. These cloud platforms leverage the features of Ceph and deliver robust, scalable, and exabyte-level public or private cloud infrastructures. In addition to this, virtualization platforms such as KVM and libvirt support Ceph big time, and support from proprietary virtualization solutions such as VMware and HyperV is on the way.

Ceph is surely the next big thing in the storage industry, which is backed by Inktank, now a part of Red Hat. Ceph has an amazing community presence and quick development cycles, making it more reliable a couple of times a year. Though Ceph is purely open source, one can enjoy enterprise-support subscriptions from Red Hat and their partner ecosystem, which is an advantage.

What this book covers

Chapter 1, *Introducing Ceph Storage*, covers the evolution, history, as well as the future of Ceph. This chapter explains common storage challenges and how Ceph deals with them and becomes the game-changer. It also covers a comparison of Ceph with other storage systems.

Chapter 2, *Ceph Instant Deployment*, covers instant, step-by-step practical approaches to deploy your first Ceph cluster. It includes a guided tour of creating the Ceph sandbox environment on VirtualBox as well as scaling it up.

Chapter 3, *Ceph Architecture and Components*, dives deep into the Ceph internal architecture, explaining each and every component in detail. Components are explained sequentially and practically for greater learning and correlation.

Chapter 4, *Ceph Internals*, covers how Ceph manages data; the practical content will help you understand every piece of it. It also covers CRUSH, placement groups, and pools in detail.

Chapter 5, *Deploying Ceph – the Way You Should Know*, covers hardware planning required for a production-grade Ceph cluster. It also includes practical approaches of building a Ceph cluster in both the manual and automated ways using ceph-deploy.

Chapter 6, *Storage Provisioning with Ceph*, includes practical hands-on approaches to explain files, blocks, and object type storage in Ceph and how to configure and provision each type. The chapter also covers snapshots, cloning, S3- and swift-compatible object storage, and much more.

Chapter 7, Ceph Operations and Maintenance, covers everything to manage and operate Ceph from a system admin point of view. It includes daily operations, scaling up and down, hardware replacement, and a detailed coverage on CRUSH management and its advanced concepts.

Chapter 8, Monitoring Your Ceph Cluster, makes you competent in monitoring your Ceph cluster and all of its components. It also covers open source Ceph monitoring dashboard projects such as Kraken and ceph-dash and their installation and configuration.

Chapter 9, Integrating Ceph with OpenStack, covers step-by-step practical approaches to set up your own test OpenStack environment and integrating it with Ceph. It explains how Ceph benefits OpenStack and how OpenStack components make use of Ceph.

Chapter 10, Ceph Performance Tuning and Benchmarking, covers advanced concepts of Ceph, such as performance tuning from both hardware and software points of view. It also includes hands-on approaches to erasure coding and cache tiering and discusses Ceph benchmarking tools.

What you need for this book

The various software components required to follow the instructions in the chapters are as follows:

- VirtualBox 4.0 or higher (`https://www.virtualbox.org/wiki/Downloads`)
- CentOS operating system 6.4 (`http://wiki.centos.org/Download`)
- Ceph software packages Version 0.78 or higher (`http://ceph.com/resources/downloads/`)
- S3 Client, typically S3cmd (`http://s3tools.org/download`)
- Python-swiftclient
- Kraken dashboard for monitoring (`https://github.com/krakendash`)
- The ceph-dash dashboard for monitoring (`https://github.com/Crapworks/ceph-dash`)
- OpenStack RDO (`http://rdo.fedorapeople.org/rdo-release.rpm`)

Who this book is for

This book targets IT and storage administrators who want to enter into the world of software-defined storage using Ceph. It also targets anyone who wishes to understand how to use Ceph and its workings to start developing and contributing to Ceph open source projects.

This book also provides valuable information for IT managers and professionals trying to understand the difference between traditional and software-defined cloud storage.

Conventions

In this book, you will find a number of styles of text that distinguish between different kinds of information. Here are some examples of these styles, and an explanation of their meaning.

Code words in text, database table names, folder names, filenames, file extensions, pathnames, dummy URLs, user input, and Twitter handles are shown as follows: "The disk zap subcommand will destroy the existing partition table and content from the disk."

A block of code is set as follows:

```
DEVICE=<correct device name of your second network interface,
check ifconfig -a>
ONBOOT=yes
BOOTPROTO=static
IPADDR=192.168.57.102
NETMASK=255.255.255.0
HWADDR= <correct MAC address of your second network interface,
check ifconfig -a >
```

Any command-line input or output is written as follows:

```
# ceph status
```

New terms and important words are shown in bold. Words that you see on the screen, for example, in menus or dialog boxes, appear in the text like this: "You can do this by selecting the **ceph-node1** VM from Oracle VM VirtualBox Manager, and then clicking on the **Start** button."

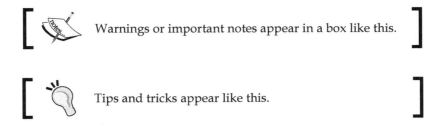

Warnings or important notes appear in a box like this.

Tips and tricks appear like this.

Reader feedback

Feedback from our readers is always welcome. Let us know what you think about this book — what you liked or may have disliked. Reader feedback is important for us to develop titles that you really get the most out of.

To send us general feedback, simply send an e-mail to feedback@packtpub.com, and mention the book title via the subject of your message.

If there is a topic that you have expertise in and you are interested in either writing or contributing to a book, see our author guide on www.packtpub.com/authors.

Customer support

Now that you are the proud owner of a Packt book, we have a number of things to help you to get the most from your purchase.

Downloading the example code

You can download the example code files for all Packt books you have purchased from your account at http://www.packtpub.com. If you purchased this book elsewhere, you can visit http://www.packtpub.com/support and register to have the files e-mailed directly to you.

Errata

Although we have taken every care to ensure the accuracy of our content, mistakes do happen. If you find a mistake in one of our books—maybe a mistake in the text or the code—we would be grateful if you would report this to us. By doing so, you can save other readers from frustration and help us improve subsequent versions of this book. If you find any errata, please report them by visiting http://www.packtpub. com/submit-errata, selecting your book, clicking on the **errata submission form** link, and entering the details of your errata. Once your errata are verified, your submission will be accepted and the errata will be uploaded to our website or added to any list of existing errata under the Errata section of that title.

To view the previously submitted errata, go to https://www.packtpub.com/books/ content/support and enter the name of the book in the search field. The required information will appear under the Errata section.

Piracy

Piracy of copyright material on the Internet is an ongoing problem across all media. At Packt, we take the protection of our copyright and licenses very seriously. If you come across any illegal copies of our works, in any form, on the Internet, please provide us with the location address or website name immediately so that we can pursue a remedy.

Please contact us at copyright@packtpub.com with a link to the suspected pirated material.

We appreciate your help in protecting our authors, and our ability to bring you valuable content.

Questions

You can contact us at questions@packtpub.com if you are having a problem with any aspect of the book, and we will do our best to address it.

1
Introducing Ceph Storage

In this chapter, we will cover the following topics:

- An overview of Ceph
- The history and evolution of Ceph
- Ceph and the future of storage
- The compatibility portfolio
- Ceph versus other storage solutions

An overview of Ceph

Ceph is an open source project, which provides software-defined, unified storage solutions. Ceph is a distributed storage system which is massively scalable and high-performing without any single point of failure. From the roots, it has been designed to be highly scalable, up to exabyte level and beyond while running on general-purpose commodity hardware.

Ceph is getting most of the buzz in the storage industry due to its open, scalable, and distributed nature. Today, public, private, and hybrid cloud models are the dominant strategies for the purpose of providing massive infrastructure, and Ceph is getting popular in becoming a cloud storage solution. Commodity hardware is what the cloud is dependent on, and Ceph makes the best use of this commodity hardware to provide you with an enterprise-grade, robust, and highly reliable storage system.

Ceph has been raised and nourished with an architectural philosophy which includes the following features:

- Every component must be scalable
- There can be no single point of failure
- The solution must be software-based, open source, and adaptable
- Ceph software should run on readily available commodity hardware
- Everything must self-manageable wherever possible

Ceph provides great performance, limitless scalability, power, and flexibility to enterprises, thereby helping them get rid of expensive proprietary storage silos. Ceph is an enterprise-class, software-defined, unified storage solution that runs on commodity hardware, which makes it the most cost-effective and feature-rich storage system. The Ceph universal storage system provides block, file, and object storage under one hood, enabling customers to use storage as they want.

The foundation of Ceph lies on objects, which are its building blocks. Any format of data, whether it's a block, object, or file, gets stored in the form of objects inside the placement group of a Ceph cluster. Object storage such as Ceph is the answer for today's as well as the future's unstructured data storage needs. An object-based storage system has its advantages over traditional file-based storage solutions; we can achieve platform and hardware independence using object storage. Ceph plays intelligently with objects, and replicates each object across clusters to improve reliability. In Ceph, objects are not tied to a physical path, making objects flexible and location-independent. This enables Ceph to scale linearly from the petabyte level to an exabyte level.

The history and evolution of Ceph

Ceph was developed at University of California, Santa Cruz, by Sage Weil in 2003 as a part of his PhD project. The initial project prototype was the Ceph filesystem, written in approximately 40,000 lines of C++ code, which was made open source in 2006 under a **Lesser GNU Public License** (**LGPL**) to serve as a reference implementation and research platform. Lawrence Livermore National Laboratory supported Sage's initial research work. The period from 2003 to 2007 was the research period of Ceph. By this time, its core components were emerging, and the community contribution to the project had begun at pace. Ceph does not follow a dual licensing model, and has no enterprise-only feature set.

In late 2007, Ceph was getting mature and was waiting to get incubated. At this point, DreamHost, a Los-Angeles-based web hosting and domain registrar company entered the picture. DreamHost incubated Ceph from 2007 to 2011. During this period, Ceph was gaining its shape; the existing components were made more stable and reliable, various new features were implemented, and future roadmaps were designed. Here, the Ceph project became bona fide with enterprise options and roadmaps. During this time, several developers started contributing to the Ceph project; some of them were Yehuda Sadeh, Weinraub, Gregory Farnum, Josh Durgin, Samuel Just, Wido den Hollander, and Loïc Dachary, who joined the Ceph bandwagon.

In April 2012, Sage Weil founded a new company, Inktank, which was funded by DreamHost. Inktank was formed to enable the widespread adoption of Ceph's professional services and support. Inktank is the company behind Ceph whose main objective is to provide expertise, processes, tools, and support to their enterprise-subscription customers, enabling them to effectively adopt and manage Ceph storage systems. Sage was the CTO and Founder of Inktank. In 2013, Inktank raised $13.5 million in funding. On April 30, 2014, Red Hat, Inc.—the world's leading provider of open source solutions—agreed to acquire Inktank for approximately $175 million in cash. Some of the customers of Inktank include Cisco, CERN, and Deutsche Telekom, and its partners include Dell and Alcatel-Lucent, all of which will now become the customers and partners of Red Hat for Ceph's software-defined storage solution. For more information, please visit www.inktank.com.

The term *Ceph* is a common nickname given to pet octopuses; Ceph can be considered as a short form for Cephalopod, which belongs to the mollusk family of marine animals. Ceph has octopuses as its mascot, which represents Ceph's parallel behavior to octopuses.

The word Inktank is somewhat related to cephalopods. Fishermen sometimes refer to cephalopods as inkfish due to their ability to squirt ink. This explains how cephalopods (Ceph) have some relation with inkfish (Inktank). Likewise, Ceph and Inktank have a lot of things in common. You can consider Inktank to be a *thinktank* for Ceph.

[Sage Weil is one of the cofounders of DreamHost.]

Ceph releases

During late 2007, when the Ceph project started, it was first incubated at DreamHost. On May 7, 2008, Sage released Ceph v0.2, and after this, its development stages evolved quickly. The time between new releases became short and Ceph now has new version updates every next month. On July 3, 2012, Sage announced a major release with the code name Argonaut (v0.48). The following are the major releases of Ceph, including **Long Term Support (LTS)** releases. For more information, please visit https://ceph.com/category/releases/.

Ceph release name	Ceph release version	Released in
Argonaut	v0.48 (LTS)	July 3, 2012
Bobtail	v0.56 (LTS)	January 1, 2013
Cuttlefish	v0.61	May 7, 2013
Dumpling	v0.67 (LTS)	August 14, 2013
Emperor	v0.72	November 9, 2013
Firefly	v0.80 (LTS)	May 2014
Giant	v0.87	(Future release)

Ceph release names follow alphabetical order; the next release will be named with the initial *I*.

Ceph and the future of storage

Enterprise storage requirements have grown explosively over the last few years. Research has shown that data in large enterprises is growing at a rate of 40 to 60 percent annually, and many companies are doubling their data footprint each year. IDC analysts estimated that there were 54.4 exabytes of total digital data worldwide in the year 2000. By 2007, this reached 295 exabytes, and by the end of 2014, it's expected to reach 8,591 exabytes worldwide.

Worldwide storage demands a system that is unified, distributed, reliable, high performance, and most importantly, massively scalable up to the exabyte level and beyond. The Ceph storage system is a true solution for the growing data explosion of this planet. The reason why Ceph is emerging at lightning pace is its lively community and users who truly believe in the power of Ceph. Data generation is a never-ending process. We cannot stop data generation, but we need to bridge the gap between data generation and data storage.

Ceph fits exactly in this gap; its unified, distributed, cost-effective, and scalable nature is the potential solution to today's and the future's data storage needs. The open source Linux community had foreseen Ceph's potential long back in 2008, and they had added support for Ceph in the mainline Linux kernel. This has been a milestone for Ceph as there is no other competitor to join it there.

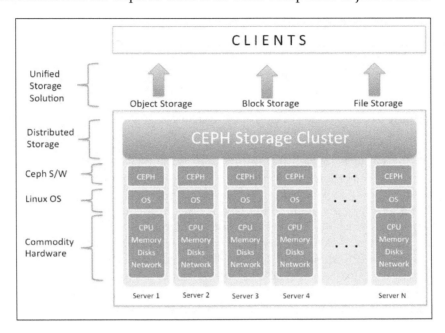

Ceph as a cloud storage solution

One of the most problematic areas in cloud infrastructure development is storage. A cloud environment needs storage that can scale up and out at low cost and which can be easily integrated with other components of that cloud framework. The need of such a storage system is a vital aspect to decide the **total cost of ownership (TCO)** of the entire cloud project. There are several traditional storage vendors who claim to provide integration to the cloud framework, but today, we need additional features beyond just integration support. These traditional storage solutions might have proven successful a few years back, but at present, they are not a good candidate for being a unified cloud storage solution. Also, traditional storage systems are too expensive to deploy and support in the long run, and scaling up and out is a gray area for them. Today, we need a storage solution that has been totally redefined to fulfill the current and future needs, a system that has been built upon open source software, and commodity hardware that can provide the required scalability in a cost-effective way.

Ceph has been rapidly evolving in this space to bridge this gap of a true cloud storage backend. It is grabbing center stage with every major open source cloud platform such as OpenStack, CloudStack, and OpenNebula. In addition to this, Ceph has built partnerships with Canonical, Red Hat, and SUSE, the giants in Linux space. These companies are favoring big time to Ceph—the distributed, reliable, and scalable storage clusters for their Linux and cloud software distributions. Ceph is working closely with these Linux giants to provide a reliable multifeatured storage backend for their cloud platforms.

Public and private clouds are gaining a lot of momentum due to the OpenStack project. OpenStack has proven itself as an end-to-end cloud solution. It has its internal core storage components named Swift, which provides object-based storage, and Nova-Volume, also known as Cinder, which provides block storage volumes to VMs.

Unlike Swift, which is limited only to object storage, Ceph is a unified storage solution of block, file, and object storage, and thus benefits OpenStack by providing multiple storage types from a single storage cluster. So, you can easily and efficiently manage storage for your OpenStack cloud. The OpenStack and Ceph communities have been working together for many years to develop a fully supported Ceph storage backend for the OpenStack cloud. Starting with Folsom, which is the sixth major release of OpenStack, Ceph has been fully integrated with it. The Ceph developers ensured that Ceph works well with the latest version of OpenStack, and at the same time, contribute to new features as well as bug fixes. OpenStack utilizes one of the most demanding feature of Ceph, the **RADOS block device (RBD)**, through its cinder and glance components. Ceph RBD helps OpenStack in rapid provisioning of hundreds of virtual machine instances by providing snapshotted-cloned volume, which are thin-provisioned, and hence less space hungry and ultra quick.

Cloud platforms with Ceph as a storage backend provide the much needed flexibility to service providers to build Storage-as-a-Service and Infrastructure-as-a-Service solutions, which they cannot achieve from other traditional enterprise storage solutions, as they are not designed to fulfill cloud needs. Using Ceph as a backend for cloud platforms, service providers can offer low-cost cloud services to their customers. Ceph enables them to offer relatively low storage prices with enterprise features compared to other storage providers such as Amazon.

Dell, SUSE, and Canonical offer and support deployment and configuration management tools such as Dell Crowbar and Juju for automated and easy deployment of Ceph storage for their OpenStack cloud solutions. Other configuration management tools such as Puppet, Chef, SaltStack, and Ansible are quite popular for automated Ceph deployment. Each of these tools has its open source, readymade Ceph modules that can be easily used for Ceph deployment. In a distributed environment such as Cloud, every component must scale. These configuration management tools are essential to quickly scale up your infrastructure.

Ceph is now fully compatible with these tools, allowing customers to deploy and extend a Ceph cluster instantly.

 Starting with the OpenStack Folsom release, the nova-volume component has become cinder; however, nova-volume commands still work with OpenStack.

Ceph as a software-defined solution

All the customers who want to save money on storage infrastructure are most likely to consider **Software-defined Storage (SDS)** very soon. An SDS can offer a good solution to customers with a large investment in legacy storage who are still not getting required flexibility and scalability. Ceph is a true SDS solution, which is an open source software, runs on any commodity hardware, hence no vendor lock in, and provides low cost per GB. An SDS solution provides the much needed flexibility with respect to hardware selection. Customers can choose any commodity hardware from any manufacturer and are free to design a heterogeneous hardware solution for their own needs. Ceph's software-defined storage on top of this hardware will take care of everything. It also provides all the enterprise storage features right from the software layer. Low cost, reliability, and scalability are its main traits.

Ceph as a unified storage solution

The definition of a unified storage solution from a storage vendor's perspective is comprised of file-based and block-based access from a single platform. The enterprise storage environment provides NAS plus SAN from a single platform, which is treated as a unified storage solution. NAS and SAN technologies were proven to be successful in the late 90's and early 20's, but if we think about the future, are we sure that NAS and SAN can manage storage needs 50 years down the line? Do they have enough potential to handle multiexabytes of data? Probably not.

In Ceph, the term *unified storage* is more meaningful than what existing storage vendors claim to provide. Ceph has been designed from the ground to be future ready; its building blocks are constructed such that they handle enormous amounts of data. Ceph is a true unified storage solution that provides object, block, and file storage from a single unified software layer. When we call Ceph as future ready, we mean to focus on its object storage capabilities, which is a better fit for today's mix of unstructured data than blocks or files. Everything in Ceph relies on intelligent objects, whether it's block storage or file storage.

Rather than managing blocks and files underneath, Ceph manages objects and supports block- and file-based storage on top of it. If you think of a traditional file-based storage system, files are addressed via the file path, and in a similar way, objects in Ceph are addressed by a unique identifier, and are stored in a flat addressed space. Objects provide limitless scaling with increased performance by eliminating metadata operations. Ceph uses an algorithm to dynamically compute where the object should be stored and retrieved from.

The next generation architecture

The traditional storage systems do not have a smarter way of managing metadata. Metadata is the information (data) about data, which decides where the data will be written to and read from. Traditional storage systems maintain a central lookup table to keep track of their metadata; that is, every time a client sends a request for a read or write operation, the storage system first performs a lookup to the huge metadata table, and after receiving the results, it performs the client operation. For a smaller storage system, you might not notice performance hits, but think of a large storage cluster; you would definitely be restricted by performance limits with this approach. This would also restrict your scalability.

Ceph does not follow the traditional architecture of storage; it has been totally reinvented with the next-generation architecture. Rather than storing and manipulating metadata, Ceph introduces a newer way, the CRUSH algorithm. CRUSH stands for Controlled Replication Under Scalable Hashing. For more information, visit http://ceph.com/resources/publications/. Instead of performing a lookup in the metadata table for every client request, the CRUSH algorithm, on demand, computes where the data should be written to or read from. By computing metadata, there is no need to manage a centralized table for metadata. Modern computers are amazingly fast and can perform a CRUSH lookup very quickly; moreover, a smaller computing load can be distributed across cluster nodes, leveraging the power of distributed storage. CRUSH does clean management of metadata, which is a better way than the traditional storage system.

In addition to this, CRUSH has a unique property of infrastructure awareness. It understands the relationship between the various components of your infrastructure, right from the system disk, pool, node, rack, power board, switch, and data center row, to the data center room and further. These are failure zones for any infrastructure. CRUSH stores the primary copy of the data and its replica in a fashion such that data will be available even if a few components fail in a failure zone. Users have full control of defining these failure zones for their infrastructure inside Ceph's CRUSH map. This gives power to the Ceph administrator to efficiently manage the data of their own environment.

CRUSH makes Ceph self managing and self healing. In the event of component failure in a failure zone, CRUSH senses which component has failed and determines the effect of this failure on the cluster. Without any administrative intervention, CRUSH does self managing and self healing by performing a recovery operation for the data lost due to failure. CRUSH regenerates the data from the replica copies that the cluster maintains. At every point in time, the cluster will have more than one copy of data that will be distributed across the cluster.

Using CRUSH, we can design a highly reliable storage infrastructure with no single point of failure. It makes Ceph a highly scalable and reliable storage system, which is future ready.

Raid – end of an era

Raid technology has been the fundamental building block for storage systems for many years. It has proven successful for almost every kind of data that has been generated in the last 30 years. However, all eras must come to an end, and this time, it's for RAID. RAID-based storage systems have started to show limitations and are incapable of delivering future storage needs.

Disk-manufacturing technology is getting mature over the years. Manufacturers are now producing larger-capacity enterprise disks at lower prices. We no longer talk about 450 GB, 600 GB, or even 1 TB disks as there are a lot of other options with larger-capacity, better performing disks available today. The newer enterprise disk specifications offer up to 4 TB and even 6 TB disk drives. Storage capacity will keep on increasing year by year.

Think of an enterprise RAID-based storage system that is made up of numerous 4 or 6 TB disk drives; in the event of disk failure, RAID will take several hours and even up to days to repair a single failed disk. Meanwhile, if another drive fails, that would be chaos. Repairing multiple large disk drives using RAID is a cumbersome process.

Moreover, RAID eats up a lot of whole disks as a spare disk. This again affects the TCO, and if you are running short of spare disks, then again you are in trouble. The RAID mechanism requires a set of identical disks in a single RAID group; you will face penalties if you change the disk size, RPM, and disk type. Doing this will adversely affect the capacity and performance of your storage system.

Enterprise RAID-based systems often require expensive hardware component also known as RAID cards, which again increases the overall costs. RAID can hit a dead end when it's not possible to grow its size that is no scale up or scale out feature after a certain limit. You cannot add more capacity even though you have the money. RAID 5 can survive a single disk failure and RAID 6 survives two-disk failure, which is the maximum for any RAID level. At the time of RAID recovery operations, if clients are performing an operation, they will most likely starve for I/O until the recovery operation finishes. The most limiting factor in RAID is that it only protects against disk failure; it cannot protect against failure of a network, server hardware, OS, switch, or regional disaster. The maximum protection you can get from RAID is survival for two-disk failures; you cannot survive more than two-disk failures in any circumstance.

Hence, we need a system that can overcome all these drawbacks in a performance- and cost-effective way. A Ceph storage system is the best solution available today to address these problems. For data reliability, Ceph makes use of the data replication method; that is, it does not use RAID, and because of this, it simply overcomes all the problems that can be found in a RAID-based enterprise system. Ceph is a software-defined storage, so we do not require any specialized hardware for data replication; moreover, the replication level is highly customized by means of commands; that is, the Ceph storage administrator can easily manage a replication factor as per their requirements and underlying infrastructure. In the event of one or more disk failures, Ceph's replication is a better process than that in RAID. When a disk drive fails, all the data that was residing on that disk at that point of time starts to recover from its peer disks. Since Ceph is a distributed system, all the primary copies and replicated copies of data are scattered on all the cluster disks such that no primary and replicated copy should reside on the same disk and must reside on a different failure zone defined by the CRUSH map. Hence, all the cluster disks participate in data recovery. This makes the recovery operation amazingly fast without performance bottlenecks. This recovery operation does not require any spare disk; data is simply replicated to other Ceph disks in the cluster. Ceph uses a weighting mechanism for its disks; hence, different disk sizes is not a problem. Ceph stores data based on the disk's weight, which is intelligently managed by Ceph and can also be managed by custom CRUSH maps.

In addition to the replication method, Ceph also supports another advance way of data reliability, by using the erasure-coding technique. Erasure-coded pools require less storage space compared to replicated pools. In this process, data is recovered or regenerated algorithmically by erasure-code calculation. You can use both the techniques of data availability, that is, replication as well as erasure coding, in the same Ceph cluster but over different storage pools. We will learn more about the erasure-coding technique in the coming chapters.

The compatibility portfolio

Ceph is an enterprise-ready storage system that offers support to a wide range of protocols and accessibility methods. The unified Ceph storage system supports block, file, and object storage; however, at the time of writing this book, Ceph block and object storage are recommended for production usage, and the Ceph filesystem is under QA testing and will be ready soon. We will discuss each of them in brief.

Ceph block storage

Block storage is a category of data storage used in the storage area network. In this type, data is stored as volumes, which are in the form of blocks and are attached to nodes. This provides a larger storage capacity required by applications with a higher degree of reliability and performance. These blocks, as volumes, are mapped to the operating system and are controlled by its filesystem layout.

Ceph has introduced a new protocol RBD that is now known as Ceph Block Device. RBD provides reliable, distributed, and high performance block storage disks to clients. RBD blocks are striped over numerous objects, which are internally scattered over the entire Ceph cluster, thus providing data reliability and performance to clients. RBD has native support for the Linux kernel. In other words, RBD drivers have been well integrated with the Linux kernel since the past few years. Almost all the Linux OS flavors have native support for RBD. In addition to reliability and performance, RBD also provides enterprise features such as full and incremental snapshots, thin provisioning, copy-on-write cloning, and several others. RBD also supports in-memory caching, which drastically improves its performance.

Ceph RBD supports images up to the size of 16 exabytes. These images can be mapped as disks to bare metal machines, virtual machines, or to a regular host machine. The industry-leading open source hypervisors such as KVM and Zen provide full support to RBD and leverage their features to their guest virtual machines. Other proprietary hypervisors such as VMware and Microsoft HyperV will be supported very soon. There has been a lot of work going on in the community for support to these hypervisors.

The Ceph block device provides full support to cloud platforms such as OpenStack, CloudStack, as well as others. It has been proven successful and feature-rich for these cloud platforms. In OpenStack, you can use the Ceph block device with the cinder (block) and glance (imaging) components; by doing this, you can spin 1,000s of VMs in very little time, taking advantage of the copy-on-write feature of the Ceph block storage.

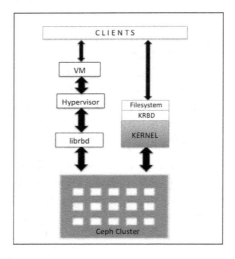

The Ceph filesystem

The Ceph filesystem, also known as CephFS, is a POSIX-compliant filesystem that uses the Ceph storage cluster to store user data. CephFS has support for the native Linux kernel driver, which makes CephFS highly adaptive across any flavor of the Linux OS. CephFS stores data and metadata separately, thus providing increased performance and reliability to the application hosted on top of it.

Inside a Ceph cluster, the Ceph filesystem library (libcephfs) works on top of the RADOS library (librados), which is the Ceph storage cluster protocol, and is common for file, block, and object storage. To use CephFS, you will require at least one Ceph **metadata server (MDS)** to be configured on any of your cluster nodes. However, it's worth keeping in mind that only one MDS server will be a single point of failure for the Ceph filesystem. Once MDS is configured, clients can make use of CephFS in multiple ways. To mount Ceph as a filesystem, clients may use native Linux kernel capabilities or can make use of the ceph-fuse (filesystem in user space) drivers provided by the Ceph community.

In addition to this, clients can make use of third-party open source programs such as Ganesha for NFS and Samba for SMB/CIFS. These programs interact with `libcephfs` to store user's data to a reliable and distributed Ceph storage cluster. CephFS can also be used as a replacement for **Apache Hadoop File System (HDFS)**. It also makes use of the `libcephfs` component to store data to the Ceph cluster. For its seamless implementation, the Ceph community provides the required `CephFS` Java interface for Hadoop and Hadoop plugins. The `libcephfs` and `librados` components are very flexible and you can even build your custom program that interacts with it and stores data to the underlying Ceph storage cluster.

CephFS is the only component of the Ceph storage system, which is not production-ready at the time of writing this book. It has been improving at a very high pace and is expected to be production-ready very soon. Currently, it's quite popular in the testing and development environment, and has been evolved with enterprise-demanding features such as dynamic rebalancing and a subdirectory snapshot. The following diagram shows various ways in which CephFS can be used:

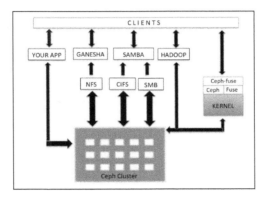

Ceph object storage

Object storage is an approach to storing data in the form of objects rather than traditional files and blocks. Object-based storage has been getting a lot of industry attention. Organizations that look for flexibility for their enormous data are rapidly adopting object storage solutions. Ceph is known to be a true object-based storage system.

Ceph is a distributed object storage system, which provides an object storage interface via Ceph's object gateway, also known as the RADOS gateway (radosgw). The RADOS gateway uses libraries such as `librgw` (the RADOS gateway library) and `librados`, allowing applications to establish a connection with the Ceph object storage. Ceph delivers one of the most stable multitenant object storage solutions accessible via a RESTful API.

The RADOS gateway provides a RESTful interface to the user application to store data on the Ceph storage cluster. The RADOS gateway interfaces are:

- **Swift compatibility**: This is an object storage functionality for the OpenStack Swift API

- **S3 compatibility**: This is an object storage functionality for the Amazon S3 API

- **Admin API**: This is also known as the management API or native API, which can be used directly in the application to gain access to the storage system for management purposes

To access Ceph's object storage system, you can also bypass the RADOS gateway layer, thus making accessibility more flexible and quicker. The librados software libraries allow user applications to directly access Ceph object storage via C, C++, Java, Python, and PHP. Ceph object storage has multisite capabilities; that is, it provides solutions for disaster recovery. Multisite object storage configuration can be achieved by RADOS or by federated gateways. The following diagram shows different API systems that can be used with Ceph:

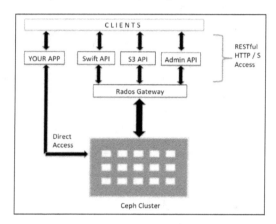

Ceph versus others

The storage market needs a shift; proprietary storage systems are incapable of providing future data storage needs at a relatively low budget. After hardware procurement, licensing, support, and management costs, the proprietary systems are very expensive. In contrast to this, the open source storage technologies are well proven for their performance, reliability, scalability, and lower TCO. Numerous organizations, government-owned as well as private, universities, research and healthcare centers, and HPC systems are already using some kind of open source storage solution.

However, Ceph is getting tremendous feedback and gaining popularity, leaving other open source as well as proprietary storage solutions behind. The following are some open source storage solutions in competition with Ceph. We will briefly discuss the shortcomings of these storage solutions, which have been addressed in Ceph.

GPFS

General Parallel File System (GPFS) is a distributed filesystem, developed and owned by IBM. This is a proprietary and closed source storage system, which makes it less attractive and difficult to adapt. The licensing and support cost after storage hardware makes it very expensive. Moreover, it has a very limited set of storage interfaces; it provides neither block storage nor RESTful access to the storage system, so this is very restrictive deal. Even the maximum data replication is limited to only three copies, which reduces system reliability in the event of more than one simultaneous failure.

iRODS

iRODS stands for Integrated Rule-Oriented Data System, which is an open source data-management software released under a 3-clause BSD license. iRods is not a highly reliable storage system as its iCAT metadata server is SPOF (single point of failure) and it does not provide true HA. Moreover, it has a very limited set of storage interfaces; it neither provides block storage nor RESTful access to the storage system, thus making it very restrictive. It's more suitable to store a small quantity of big files rather than both small and big files. iRods works in a traditional way, maintaining an index of the physical location, which is associated with the filename. The problem arises with multiple clients' request for the file location from the metadata server, applying more computing pressure on the metadata server, resulting in dependency on a single machine and performance bottlenecks.

HDFS

HDFS is a distributed scalable filesystem written in Java for the Hadoop framework. HDFS is not a fully POSIX-compliant filesystem and does not support block storage, thus making it less usable than Ceph. The reliability of HDFS is a question for discussion as it's not a highly available filesystem. The single NameNode in HDFS is the primary reason for its single point of failure and performance bottleneck problems. It's more suitable to store a small quantity of big files rather than both small and big files.

Lustre

Lustre is a parallel-distributed filesystem driven by the open source community and is available under GNU General Public License. In Lustre, a single server is responsible to store and manage metadata. Thus, the I/O request from the client is totally dependent on single server's computing power, which is quite low for an enterprise-level consumption. Like iRODS and HDFS, Lustre is suitable to store a small quantity of big files rather than both small and big files. Similar to iRODS, Lustre manages an index file that maintains physical addresses mapped with filenames, which makes its architecture traditional and prone to performance bottlenecks. Lustre does not have any mechanism for node failure detection and correction. In the event of node failure, clients have to connect to another node themselves.

Gluster

GlusterFS was originally developed by Gluster, which was then bought by Red Hat in 2011. GlusterFS is a scale-out network-attached filesystem. In Gluster, administrators have to determine which placement strategy to use to store data replica on different geographical racks. Gluster does not provide block access, filesystem, and remote replication as its intrinsic functions; rather, it provides these features as add-ons.

Ceph

If we make a comparison between Ceph and other storage solutions available today, Ceph clearly stands out of the crowd due to its feature set. It has been developed to overcome the limitations of existing storage systems, and it has proved to be an ideal replacement for old and expensive proprietary storage systems. It's an open source, software-defined storage solution on top of any commodity hardware, which makes it an economic storage solution. Ceph provides a variety of interfaces for the clients to connect to a Ceph cluster, thus increasing flexibility for clients. For data protection, Ceph does not rely on RAID technology as it's getting limited due to various reasons mentioned earlier in this chapter. Rather, it uses replication and erasure coding, which have been proved to be better solutions than RAID.

Every component of Ceph is reliable and supports high availability. If you configure Ceph components by keeping redundancy in mind, we can confidently say that Ceph does not have any single point of failure, which is a major challenge for other storage solutions available today. One of the biggest advantages of Ceph is its unified nature, where it provides out-of-the-box block, file, and object storage solutions, while other storage systems are still incapable of providing such features. Ceph is suitable to store both small as well as big files without any performance glitch.

Ceph is a distributed storage system; clients can perform quick transactions using Ceph. It does not follow the traditional method of storing data, that is, maintaining metadata that is tied to a physical location and filename; rather, it introduces a new mechanism, which allows clients to dynamically calculate data location required by them. This gives a boost in performance for the client, as they no longer need to wait to get data locations and contents from the central metadata server. Moreover, the data placement inside the Ceph cluster is absolutely transparent and automatic; neither the client nor the administrators have to bother about data placement on a different failure zone. Ceph's intelligent system takes care of it.

Ceph is designed to self heal and self manage. In the event of disaster, when other storage systems cannot provide reliability against multiple failures, Ceph stands rock solid. Ceph detects and corrects failure at every failure zone such as a disk, node, network, rack, data center row, data center, and even different geographies. Ceph tries to manage the situation automatically and heal it wherever possible without data outage. Other storage solutions can only provide reliability up to disk or at node failure.

When it comes to a comparison, these are just a few features of Ceph to steal the show and stand out from the crowd.

Summary

Ceph is an open source software-defined storage solution that runs on commodity hardware, thus enabling enterprises to get rid of expensive, restrictive, proprietary storage systems. It provides a unified, distributed, highly scalable, and reliable object storage solution, which is much needed for today's and the future's unstructured data needs. The world's storage need is exploding, so we need a storage system that is scalable to the multiexabyte level without affecting data reliability and performance. Ceph is future proof, and provides a solution to all these data problems. Ceph is in demand for being a true cloud storage solution with support for almost every cloud platform. From every perspective, Ceph is a great storage solution available today.

2
Ceph Instant Deployment

In this chapter, we will cover the following topics:

- Creating a sandbox environment with VirtualBox
- From zero to Ceph – deploying your first Ceph cluster
- Scaling up your Ceph cluster – monitor and OSD addition

Creating a sandbox environment with VirtualBox

We can test deploy Ceph in a sandbox environment using Oracle VirtualBox virtual machines. This virtual setup can help us discover and perform experiments with Ceph storage clusters as if we are working in a real environment. Since Ceph is an open source software-defined storage deployed on top of commodity hardware in a production environment, we can imitate a fully functioning Ceph environment on virtual machines, instead of real-commodity hardware, for our testing purposes.

Oracle VirtualBox is a free software available at http://www.virtualbox.org for Windows, Mac OS X, and Linux. We must fulfil system requirements for the VirtualBox software so that it can function properly during our testing. The Ceph test environment that we will create on VirtualBox virtual machines will be used for the rest of the chapters in this book. We assume that your host operating system is a Unix variant; for Microsoft windows, host machines use an absolute path to run the VBoxManage command, which is by default c:\Program Files\Oracle\ VirtualBox\VBoxManage.exe.

The system requirement for VirtualBox depends upon the number and configuration of virtual machines running on top of it. Your VirtualBox host should require an x86-type processor (Intel or AMD), a few gigabytes of memory (to run three Ceph virtual machines), and a couple of gigabytes of hard drive space. To begin with, we must download VirtualBox from `http://www.virtualbox.org/` and then follow the installation procedure once this has been downloaded. We will also need to download the CentOS 6.4 Server ISO image from `http://vault.centos.org/6.4/isos/`.

To set up our sandbox environment, we will create a minimum of three virtual machines; you can create even more machines for your Ceph cluster based on the hardware configuration of your host machine. We will first create a single VM and install OS on it; after this, we will clone this VM twice. This will save us a lot of time and increase our productivity. Let's begin by performing the following steps to create the first virtual machine:

The VirtualBox host machine used throughout in this demonstration is a Mac OS X which is a UNIX-type host. If you are performing these steps on a non-UNIX machine that is, on Windows-based host then keep in mind that `virtualbox hostonly` adapter name will be something like `VirtualBox Host-Only Ethernet Adapter #<adapter number>`. Please run these commands with the correct adapter names. On windows-based hosts, you can check VirtualBox networking options in Oracle VM VirtualBox Manager by navigating to File | **VirtualBox Settings** | **Network** | **Host-only Networks**.

1. After the installation of the VirtualBox software, a network adapter is created that you can use, or you can create a new adapter with a custom IP:

    For UNIX-based VirtualBox hosts

    ```
    # VBoxManage hostonlyif remove vboxnet1
    ```

    ```
    # VBoxManage hostonlyif create
    ```

    ```
    # VBoxManage hostonlyif ipconfig vboxnet1 --ip 192.168.57.1 --
    netmask 255.255.255.0
    ```

    For Windows-based VirtualBox hosts

    ```
    # VBoxManage.exe hostonlyif remove "VirtualBox Host-Only Ethernet
    Adapter"
    ```

    ```
    # VBoxManage.exe hostonlyif create
    ```

    ```
    # VBoxManage hostonlyif ipconfig "VirtualBox Host-Only Ethernet
    Adapter" --ip 192.168.57.1 --netmask 255.255.255.0
    ```

2. VirtualBox comes with a GUI manager. If your host is running Linux OS, it should have the X-desktop environment (Gnome or KDE) installed. Open Oracle VM VirtualBox Manager and create a new virtual machine with the

following specifications using GUI-based **New Virtual Machine Wizard,** or use the CLI commands mentioned at the end of every step:

- ° 1 CPU
- ° 1024 MB memory
- ° 10 GB X 4 hard disks (one drive for OS and three drives for Ceph OSD)
- ° 2 network adapters
- ° CentOS 6.4 ISO attached to VM

The following is the step-by-step process to create virtual machines using CLI commands:

1. Create your first virtual machine:

   ```
   # VBoxManage createvm --name ceph-node1 --ostype
   RedHat_64 --register
   ```

   ```
   # VBoxManage modifyvm ceph-node1 --memory 1024 --nic1 nat
   --nic2 hostonly --hostonlyadapter2 vboxnet1
   ```

   For Windows VirtualBox hosts:

   ```
   # VBoxManage.exe modifyvm ceph-node1 --memory 1024 --nic1
   nat --nic2 hostonly --hostonlyadapter2 "VirtualBox Host-
   Only Ethernet Adapter"
   ```

2. Create CD-Drive and attach CentOS ISO image to first virtual machine:

   ```
   # VBoxManage storagectl ceph-node1 --name "IDE
   Controller" --add ide --controller PIIX4 --hostiocache
   on --bootable on
   ```

   ```
   # VBoxManage storageattach ceph-node1 --storagectl "IDE
   Controller" --type dvddrive --port 0 --device 0 --medium
   CentOS-6.4-x86_64-bin-DVD1.iso
   ```

 Make sure you execute the preceding command from the same directory where you have saved CentOS ISO image or you can specify the location where you saved it.

3. Create SATA interface, OS hard drive and attach them to VM; make sure the VirtualBox host has enough free space for creating vm disks. If not, select the host drive which have free space:

   ```
   # VBoxManage storagectl ceph-node1 --name "SATA
   Controller" --add sata --controller IntelAHCI
   --hostiocache on --bootable on
   ```

```
# VBoxManage createhd --filename OS-ceph-node1.vdi --size
10240
```

```
# VBoxManage storageattach ceph-node1 --storagectl "SATA
Controller" --port 0 --device 0 --type hdd --medium OS-
ceph-node1.vdi
```

4. Create SATA interface, first ceph disk and attach them to VM:

```
# VBoxManage createhd --filename ceph-node1-osd1.vdi
--size 10240
```

```
# VBoxManage storageattach ceph-node1 --storagectl "SATA
Controller" --port 1 --device 0 --type hdd --medium ceph-
node1-osd1.vdi
```

5. Create SATA interface, second ceph disk and attach them to VM:

```
# VBoxManage createhd --filename ceph-node1-osd2.vdi
--size 10240
```

```
# VBoxManage storageattach ceph-node1 --storagectl "SATA
Controller" --port 2 --device 0 --type hdd --medium ceph-
node1-osd2.vdi
```

6. Create SATA interface, third ceph disk and attach them to VM:

```
# VBoxManage createhd --filename ceph-node1-osd3.vdi
--size 10240
```

```
# VBoxManage storageattach ceph-node1 --storagectl "SATA
Controller" --port 3 --device 0 --type hdd --medium ceph-
node1-osd3.vdi
```

3. Now, at this point, we are ready to power on our ceph-node1 VM. You can do this by selecting the **ceph-node1** VM from Oracle VM VirtualBox Manager, and then clicking on the **Start** button, or you can run the following command:

```
# VBoxManage startvm ceph-node1 --type gui
```

4. As soon as you start your VM, it should boot from the ISO image. After this, you should install CentOS on VM. If you are not already familiar with Linux OS installation, you can follow the documentation at https://access. redhat.com/site/documentation/en-US/Red_Hat_Enterprise_Linux/6/ html/Installation_Guide/index.html.

5. Once you have successfully installed the operating system, edit the network configuration of the machine:

    ◦ Edit `/etc/sysconfig/network` and change the hostname parameter `HOSTNAME=ceph-node1`

    ◦ Edit the `/etc/sysconfig/network-scripts/ifcfg-eth0` file and add:

        ```
        ONBOOT=yes
        BOOTPROTO=dhcp
        ```

    ◦ Edit the `/etc/sysconfig/network-scripts/ifcfg-eth1` file and add:

        ```
        ONBOOT=yes
        BOOTPROTO=static
        IPADDR=192.168.57.101
        NETMASK=255.255.255.0
        ```

    ◦ Edit the `/etc/hosts` file and add:

        ```
        192.168.57.101 ceph-node1
        192.168.57.102 ceph-node2
        192.168.57.103 ceph-node3
        ```

6. Once the network settings have been configured, restart VM and log in via SSH from your host machine. Also, test the Internet connectivity on this machine, which is required to download Ceph packages:

    ```
    # ssh root@192.168.57.101
    ```

7. Once the network setup has been configured correctly, you should shut down your first VM so that we can make two clones of your first VM. If you do not shut down your first VM, the cloning operation might fail.

    1. **Create clone of ceph-node1 as ceph-node2:**

        ```
        # VBoxManage clonevm --name ceph-node2 ceph-node1
        --register
        ```

    2. **Create clone of ceph-node1 as ceph-node3:**

        ```
        # VBoxManage clonevm --name ceph-node3 ceph-node1
        --register
        ```

8. After the cloning operation is complete, you can start all three VMs:

    ```
    # VBoxManage startvm ceph-node1
    ```

    ```
    # VBoxManage startvm ceph-node2
    ```

    ```
    # VBoxManage startvm ceph-node3
    ```

9. Set up VM ceph-node2 with the correct hostname and network configuration:

   ° Edit `/etc/sysconfig/network` and change the hostname parameter:
   ```
   HOSTNAME=ceph-node2
   ```

   ° Edit the `/etc/sysconfig/network-scripts/ifcfg-<first interface name>` file and add:
   ```
   DEVICE=<correct device name of your first network
   interface, check ifconfig -a>
   ONBOOT=yes
   BOOTPROTO=dhcp
   HWADDR= <correct MAC address of your first network
   interface, check ifconfig -a >
   ```

   ° Edit the `/etc/sysconfig/network-scripts/ifcfg-<second interface name>` file and add:
   ```
   DEVICE=<correct device name of your second network
   interface, check ifconfig -a>
   ONBOOT=yes
   BOOTPROTO=static
   IPADDR=192.168.57.102
   NETMASK=255.255.255.0
   HWADDR= <correct MAC address of your second network
   interface, check ifconfig -a >
   ```

   ° Edit the /etc/hosts file and add:
   ```
   192.168.57.101 ceph-node1
   192.168.57.102 ceph-node2
   192.168.57.103 ceph-node3
   ```

After performing these changes, you should restart your virtual machine to bring the new hostname into effect. The restart will also update your network configurations.

10. Set up VM ceph-node3 with the correct hostname and network configuration:

    ° Edit `/etc/sysconfig/network` and change the hostname parameter:
    ```
    HOSTNAME=ceph-node3
    ```

    ° Edit the `/etc/sysconfig/network-scripts/ifcfg-<first interface name>` file and add:
    ```
    DEVICE=<correct device name of your first network
    interface, check ifconfig -a>
    ONBOOT=yes
    BOOTPROTO=dhcp
    HWADDR= <correct MAC address of your first network
    interface, check ifconfig -a >
    ```

- ○ Edit the `/etc/sysconfig/network-scripts/ifcfg-<second interface name>` file and add:

  ```
  DEVICE=<correct device name of your second network
  interface, check ifconfig -a>
  ONBOOT=yes
  BOOTPROTO=static
  IPADDR=192.168.57.103
  NETMASK=255.255.255.0
  HWADDR= <correct MAC address of your second network
  interface, check ifconfig -a >
  ```

- ○ Edit the `/etc/hosts` file and add:

  ```
  192.168.57.101 ceph-node1
  192.168.57.102 ceph-node2
  192.168.57.103 ceph-node3
  ```

After performing these changes, you should restart your virtual machine to bring a new hostname into effect; the restart will also update your network configurations.

At this point, we prepare three virtual machines and make sure each VM communicates with each other. They should also have access to the Internet to install Ceph packages.

From zero to Ceph – deploying your first Ceph cluster

To deploy our first Ceph cluster, we will use the **ceph-deploy** tool to install and configure Ceph on all three virtual machines. The ceph-deploy tool is a part of the Ceph software-defined storage, which is used for easier deployment and management of your Ceph storage cluster.

Since we created three virtual machines that run CentOS 6.4 and have connectivity with the Internet as well as private network connections, we will configure these machines as Ceph storage clusters as mentioned in the following diagram:

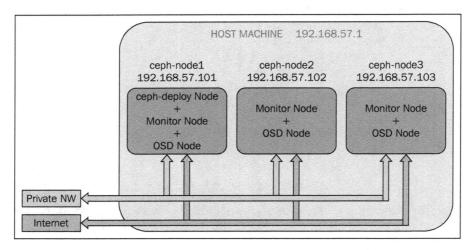

1. Configure ceph-node1 for an SSH passwordless login to other nodes. Execute the following commands from ceph-node1:

   ° While configuring SSH, leave the paraphrase empty and proceed with the default settings:

     ```
     # ssh-keygen
     ```

   ° Copy the SSH key IDs to ceph-node2 and ceph-node3 by providing their root passwords. After this, you should be able to log in on these nodes without a password:

     ```
     # ssh-copy-id ceph-node2
     ```

2. Installing and configuring EPEL on all Ceph nodes:

   1. Install EPEL which is the repository for installing extra packages for your Linux system by executing the following command on all Ceph nodes:

      ```
      # rpm -ivh http://dl.fedoraproject.org/pub/epel/6/x86_64/
      epel-release-6-8.noarch.rpm
      ```

   2. Make sure the `baserul` parameter is enabled under the `/etc/yum.repos.d/epel.repo` file. The `baseurl` parameter defines the URL for extra Linux packages. Also make sure the `mirrorlist` parameter must be disabled (commented) under this file. Problems been observed during installation if the `mirrorlist` parameter is enabled under `epel.repo` file. Perform this step on all the three nodes.

3. Install ceph-deploy on the ceph-node1 machine by executing the following command from ceph-node1:

```
# yum install ceph-deploy
```

4. Next, we will create a Ceph cluster using ceph-deploy by executing the following command from ceph-node1:

```
# ceph-deploy new ceph-node1
## Create a directory for ceph
# mkdir /etc/ceph
# cd /etc/ceph
```

The new subcommand of ceph-deploy deploys a new cluster with ceph as the cluster name, which is by default; it generates a cluster configuration and keying files. List the present working directory; you will find the ceph.conf and ceph.mon.keyring files.

 In this testing, we will intentionally install the Emperor release (v0.72) of Ceph software, which is not the latest release. Later in this book, we will demonstrate the upgradation of Emperor to Firefly release of Ceph.

5. To install Ceph software binaries on all the machines using ceph-deploy; execute the following command from ceph-node1:

```
ceph-deploy install --release emperor ceph-node1 ceph-node2 ceph-node3
```

The ceph-deploy tool will first install all the dependencies followed by the Ceph Emperor binaries. Once the command completes successfully, check the Ceph version and Ceph health on all the nodes, as follows:

```
# ceph -v
```

6. Create your first monitor on ceph-node1:

```
# ceph-deploy mon create-initial
```

Once monitor creation is successful, check your cluster status. Your cluster will not be healthy at this stage:

```
# ceph status
```

7. Create an **object storage device (OSD)** on the ceph-node1 machine, and add it to the Ceph cluster executing the following steps:

   1. List the disks on VM:

      ```
      # ceph-deploy disk list ceph-node1
      ```

      From the output, carefully identify the disks (other than OS-partition disks) on which we should create Ceph OSD. In our case, the disk names will ideally be sdb, sdc, and sdd.

   2. The `disk zap` subcommand will destroy the existing partition table and content from the disk. Before running the following command, make sure you use the correct disk device name.

      ```
      # ceph-deploy disk zap ceph-node1:sdb ceph-node1:sdc ceph-node1:sdd
      ```

   3. The `osd create` subcommand will first prepare the disk, that is, erase the disk with a filesystem, which is xfs by default. Then, it will activate the disk's first partition as data partition and second partition as journal:

      ```
      # ceph-deploy osd create ceph-node1:sdb ceph-node1:sdc ceph-node1:sdd
      ```

   4. Check the cluster status for new OSD entries:

      ```
      # ceph status
      ```

      At this stage, your cluster will not be healthy. We need to add a few more nodes to the Ceph cluster so that it can set up a distributed, replicated object storage, and hence become healthy.

Scaling up your Ceph cluster – monitor and OSD addition

Now we have a single-node Ceph cluster. We should scale it up to make it a distributed, reliable storage cluster. To scale up a cluster, we should add more monitor nodes and OSD. As per our plan, we will now configure ceph-node2 and ceph-node3 machines as monitor as well as OSD nodes.

Adding the Ceph monitor

A Ceph storage cluster requires at least one monitor to run. For high availability, a Ceph storage cluster relies on an odd number of monitors that's more than one, for example, 3 or 5, to form a quorum. It uses the Paxos algorithm to maintain quorum majority. Since we already have one monitor running on ceph-node1, let's create two more monitors for our Ceph cluster:

1. The firewall rules should not block communication between Ceph monitor nodes. If they do, you need to adjust the firewall rules in order to let monitors form a quorum. Since this is our test setup, let's disable firewall on all three nodes. We will run these commands from the ceph-node1 machine, unless otherwise specified:

    ```
    # service iptables stop
    # chkconfig iptables off
    # ssh ceph-node2 service iptables stop
    # ssh ceph-node2 chkconfig iptables off
    # ssh ceph-node3 service iptables stop
    # ssh ceph-node3 chkconfig iptables off
    ```

2. Deploy a monitor on ceph-node2 and ceph-node3:

    ```
    # ceph-deploy mon create ceph-node2
    # ceph-deploy mon create ceph-node3
    ```

3. The deploy operation should be successful; you can then check your newly added monitors in the Ceph status:

    ```
    [root@ceph-node1 ~]# ceph status
        cluster ffa7c0e4-6368-4032-88a4-5fb6a3fb383c
         health HEALTH_WARN 192 pgs degraded; 192 pgs stuck unclean
         monmap e9: 3 mons at {ceph-node1=192.168.57.101:6789/0,ceph-node2=192.168.57.102:6789/0,
    ceph-node3=192.168.57.103:6789/0}, election epoch 24, quorum 0,1,2 ceph-node1,ceph-node2,ceph
    -node3
         osdmap e20: 3 osds: 3 up, 3 in
          pgmap v37: 192 pgs, 3 pools, 0 bytes data, 0 objects
                106 MB used, 15220 MB / 15326 MB avail
                     192 active+degraded

    [root@ceph-node1 ~]# _
    ```

4. You might encounter warning messages related to *clock skew* on new monitor nodes. To resolve this, we need to set up **Network Time Protocol (NTP)** on new monitor nodes:

    ```
    # chkconfig ntpd on
    # ssh ceph-node2  chkconfig ntpd on
    # ssh ceph-node3  chkconfig ntpd on
    # ntpdate pool.ntp.org
    ```

```
# ssh ceph-node2 ntpdate pool.ntp.org
# ssh ceph-node3 ntpdate pool.ntp.org
# /etc/init.d/ntpd start
# ssh ceph-node2 /etc/init.d/ntpd start
# ssh ceph-node3 /etc/init.d/ntpd start
```

Adding the Ceph OSD

At this point, we have a running Ceph cluster with three monitors OSDs. Now we will scale our cluster and add more OSDs. To accomplish this, we will run the following commands from the ceph-node1 machine, unless otherwise specified.

We will follow the same method for OSD addition that we used earlier in this chapter:

```
# ceph-deploy disk list ceph-node2 ceph-node3
# ceph-deploy disk zap ceph-node2:sdb ceph-node2:sdc ceph-node2:sdd
# ceph-deploy disk zap ceph-node3:sdb ceph-node3:sdc ceph-node3:sdd

# ceph-deploy osd create ceph-node2:sdb ceph-node2:sdc ceph-node2:sdd
# ceph-deploy osd create ceph-node3:sdb ceph-node3:sdc ceph-node3:sdd
# ceph status
```

Check the cluster status for a new OSD. At this stage, your cluster will be healthy with nine OSDs in and up:

```
    cluster ffa7c0e4-6368-4032-88a4-5fb6a3fb383c
    health HEALTH_OK
    monmap e9: 3 mons at {ceph-node1=192.168.57.101:6789/0,ceph-node2=192.168.57.102:6789/0,
ceph-node3=192.168.57.103:6789/0}, election epoch 30, quorum 0,1,2 ceph-node1,ceph-node2,ceph
-node3
    osdmap e44: 9 osds: 9 up, 9 in
    pgmap v92: 192 pgs, 3 pools, 0 bytes data, 0 objects
        342 MB used, 45638 MB / 45980 MB avail
            192 active+clean
```

Summary

The software-defined nature of Ceph provides a great deal of flexibility to its adopters. Unlike other proprietary storage systems, which are hardware dependent, Ceph can be easily deployed and tested on almost any computer system available today. Moreover, if getting physical machines is a challenge, you can use virtual machines to install Ceph, as mentioned in this chapter, but keep in mind that such a setup should only be used for testing purposes.

In this chapter, we learned how to create a set of virtual machines using the VirtualBox software, followed by Ceph deployment as a three-node cluster using the ceph-deploy tool. We also added a couple of OSDs and monitor machines to our cluster in order to demonstrate its dynamic scalability. We recommend you deploy a Ceph cluster of your own using the instructions mentioned in this chapter. In the next chapter, we will discover Ceph's architecture, its core components, and how they interact with each other to form a cluster in detail.

3
Ceph Architecture and Components

In this chapter, we will cover the following topics:

- Ceph storage architecture
- Ceph RADOS
- Ceph Object Storage Device (OSD)
- Ceph monitors (MON)
- librados
- The Ceph block storage
- Ceph Object Gateway
- Ceph MDS and CephFS

Ceph storage architecture

A Ceph storage cluster is made up of several different software daemons. Each of these daemons takes care of unique Ceph functionalities and adds values to its corresponding components. Each of these daemons is separated from the others. This is one of the things that keeps Ceph cluster storage costs down when compared to an enterprise, proprietary black box storage system.

The following diagram briefly highlights the functions of each Ceph component:

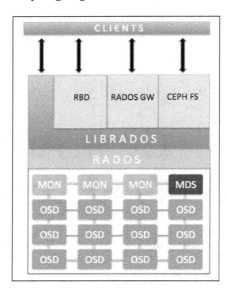

Reliable Autonomic Distributed Object Store (RADOS) is the foundation of the Ceph storage cluster. Everything in Ceph is stored in the form of objects, and the RADOS object store is responsible for storing these objects, irrespective of their data type. The RADOS layer makes sure that data always remains in a consistent state and is reliable. For data consistency, it performs data replication, failure detection, and recovery, as well as data migration and rebalancing across cluster nodes.

As soon as your application issues a write operation to your Ceph cluster, data gets stored in Ceph **Object Storage Device (OSD)** in the form of objects. This is the only component of a Ceph cluster where actual user data is stored and the same data is retrieved when a client issues a read operation. Usually, one OSD daemon is tied to one physical disk of your cluster. So, in general, the total number of physical disks in your Ceph cluster is the number of OSD daemons working underneath to store user data to each physical disk.

Ceph monitors (MONs) track the health of the entire cluster by keeping a map of the cluster state, which includes OSD, MON, PG, and CRUSH maps. All the cluster nodes report to monitor nodes and share information about every change in their state. A monitor maintains a separate map of information for each component. The monitor does not store actual data; this is the job of OSD.

The **librados** library is a convenient way to get access to RADOS with the support of the PHP, Ruby, Java, Python, C, and C++ programming languages. It provides a native interface to the Ceph storage cluster, RADOS, and a base for other services such as RBD, RGW, as well as the POSIX interface for CephFS. The librados API supports direct access to RADOS and enables you to create your own interface to the Ceph storage cluster.

Ceph Block Device, formerly known as **RADOS block device (RBD)**, provides block storage, which can be mapped, formatted, and mounted just like any other disk to the server. A Ceph block device is equipped with enterprise storage features such as thin provisioning and snapshots.

Ceph Object Gateway, also known as **RADOS gateway (RGW)**, provides a RESTful API interface, which is compatible with Amazon **S3 (Simple Storage Service)** and OpenStack Object Storage API (Swift). RGW also supports the multitenancy and OpenStack Keystone authentication services.

Ceph **Metadata Server (MDS)** keeps track of file hierarchy and stores metadata only for CephFS. A Ceph block device and RADOS gateway do not require metadata, hence they do not need a Ceph MDS daemon. MDS does not serve data directly to clients, thus removing a single point of failure from the system.

Ceph File System (CephFS) offers a POSIX-compliant, distributed filesystem of any size. CephFS relies on Ceph MDS to keep track of file hierarchy, that is, metadata. CephFS is not production ready at the moment, but it's an idle candidate for POC tests. Its development is going at a very fast pace, and we can expect it to be in production ready very soon.

Ceph RADOS

RADOS (Reliable Autonomic Distributed Object Store) is the heart of the Ceph storage system, which is also referred to as the Ceph storage cluster. RADOS provides all the precious features to Ceph, including distributed object store, high availability, reliablity, no single point of failure, self-healing, self-managing, and so on. As a result, the RADOS layer holds a special importance in the Ceph storage architecture. The data access methods of Ceph, such as RBD, CephFS, RADOSGW, and librados, all operate on top of the RADOS layer.

When the Ceph cluster receives a write request from clients, the CRUSH algorithm calculates the location and decides where the data should be written. This information is then passed to the RADOS layer for further processing. Based on the CRUSH ruleset, RADOS distributes the data to all the cluster nodes in the form of small objects. Finally, these objects are stored on OSDs.

RADOS, when configured with a replication factor of more than one, takes care of data reliability. At the same time, it replicates objects, creates copies, and stores them to a different failure zone, that is, the same object replicas should not reside on the same failure zone. However, for a more customization and higher reliability, you should tune your CRUSH ruleset as per your needs and infrastructure requirements. RADOS guarantees that there will always be more than one copy of an object in a RADOS cluster, provided that you have a sufficient level of replication set.

In addition to storing and replicating objects across the cluster, RADOS also makes sure that the object state is consistent. In case of object inconsistency, recoveries are performed with the remaining object copies. This operation is performed automagically and is user transparent, thus providing self-managing and self-healing capabilities to Ceph. If you do an analysis on Ceph's architectural diagram, you will find that it has two parts, RADOS as the lower part that is totally internal to the Ceph cluster with no direct client interface, and the upper part that has all the client interfaces.

RADOS stores data in the form of objects inside a pool. Take a look at RADOS pools, as follows:

```
# rados lspools
```

You will get an output similar to what is shown in the following screenshot:

```
[root@ceph-node1 /]# rados lspools
data
metadata
rbd
[root@ceph-node1 /]#
```

Check the list of objects in a pool using the following command:

```
# rados -p metadata ls
```

Check the cluster utilization with the following command:

```
# rados df
```

The output may or may not be similar to what is shown in the following screenshot:

```
[root@ceph-node1 ~]# rados df
pool name       category              KB      objects       clones      degraded      unfound           rd
data            -                      0            0            0            0            0            0
metadata        -                      0            0            0            0            0            0
rbd             -                      0            0            0            0            0            0
  total used             328196
  total avail          46756168
  total space          47084364
[root@ceph-node1 ~]#
```

RADOS consists of two core components, OSD and monitors. We will now discuss these components in detail.

Ceph Object Storage Device

Ceph's OSD is one of the most important building blocks of the Ceph storage cluster. It stores the actual data on the physical disk drives of each cluster node in the form of objects. The majority of the work inside a Ceph cluster is done by Ceph OSD daemons. These are the real workhorses which store user data. We will now discuss the roles and responsibilities of a Ceph OSD daemon.

Ceph OSD stores all the client data in the form of objects and serves the same data to clients when they request for it. A Ceph cluster consists of multiple OSDs. For any read or write operation, the client requests for cluster maps from monitors, and after this, they can directly interact with OSDs for I/O operations, without the intervention of a monitor. This makes the data transaction process fast as clients who generate data can directly write to OSD that stores data without any additional layer of data handling. This type of data-storage-and-retrieval mechanism is relatively unique in Ceph as compared to other storage solutions.

The core features of Ceph, including reliability, rebalancing, recovery, and consistency, come with OSD. Based on the configured replication size, Ceph provides reliability by replicating each object several times across cluster nodes, making them highly available and fault tolerant. Each object in OSD has one primary copy and several secondary copies, which are scattered across all other OSDs. Since Ceph is a distributed system and objects are distributed across multiple OSDs, each OSD plays the role of primary OSD for some objects, and at the same time, it becomes the secondary OSD for other objects. The secondary OSD remains under the control of the primary OSD; however, they are capable of becoming the primary OSD. Starting with the Ceph Firefly release (0.80), a new mechanism of data protection known as erasure coding has been added. We will learn erasure coding in detail in the upcoming chapters.

In the event of a disk failure, the Ceph OSD daemon intelligently peers with other OSDs to perform recovery operations. During this time, the secondary OSD holding replica copies of failed objects is promoted to the primary, and at the same time, new secondary object copies are generated during the OSD recovery operation, which is totally transparent to clients. This makes the Ceph cluster reliable and consistent. A typical Ceph cluster deployment creates one OSD daemon for each physical disk in a cluster node, which is a recommended practice. However, OSD supports the flexible deployment of one OSD daemon per disk, per host, or per RAID volume. Majority of the Ceph cluster deployment in a JBOD environment uses one OSD daemon per physical disk.

The Ceph OSD filesystem

Ceph OSD consists of a physical disk drive, the Linux filesystem on top of it, and the Ceph OSD service. The Linux filesystem is significant to the Ceph OSD daemon as it supports **extended attributes** (**XATTRs**). These filesystems' extended attributes provide internal information about the object state, snapshot, metadata, and ACL to the Ceph OSD daemon, which helps in data management. Have a look at the following diagram:

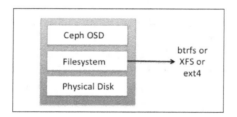

Ceph OSD operates on top of a physical disk drive having a valid Linux partition. The Linux partition can be either Btrfs (B-tree file system), XFS, or ext4. The filesystem selection is one of the major criteria for performance benchmarking of your Ceph cluster. With respect to Ceph, these filesystems differ from each other in various ways:

- **Btrfs**: The OSD, with the Btrfs filesystem underneath, delivers the best performance as compared to XFS and ext4 filesystem-based OSDs. One of the major advantages of using Btrfs is its support to copy-on-write and writable snapshots, which are very advantageous when it comes to VM provisioning and cloning. It also supports transparent compression and pervasive checksums, and incorporates multidevice management in a filesystem. Btrfs also supports efficient XATTRs and inline data for small files, provides integrated volume management that is SSD aware, and has the demanding feature of online fsck. However, despite these new features, Btrfs is currently not production ready, but it's a good candidate for test deployment.

- **XFS**: It is a reliable, mature, and very stable filesystem, and hence, it is recommended for production usage in Ceph clusters. As Btrfs is not production ready, XFS is the most-used filesystem in Ceph storage and is recommended for OSDs. However, XFS stands at a lower side as compared to Btrfs. XFS has performance issues in metadata scaling. Also, XFS is a journaling filesystem, that is, each time a client sends data to write to a Ceph cluster, it is first written to a journaling space and then to an XFS filesystem. This increases the overhead of writing the same data twice, and thus makes XFS perform slower as compared to Btrfs, which does not uses journals.

- **Ext4**: The fourth extended filesystem is also a journaling filesystem that is a production-ready filesystem for Ceph OSD; however, it's not as popular as XFS. From a performance point of view, the ext4 filesystem is not at par with Btrfs.

  Ceph OSD makes use of the extended attributes of the underlying filesystem for various forms of internal object states and metadata. XATTRs allow storing additional information related to objects in the form of `xattr_name` and `xattr_value`, and thus provide a way of tagging objects with more metadata information. The ext4 filesystem does not provide sufficient capacity for XATTRs due to limits on the number of bytes stored as XATTRs, thus making it less popular among filesystem choices. On the other hand, Btrfs and XFS have a relatively large limit for XATTRs.

The Ceph OSD journal

Ceph uses journaling filesystems such as Btrfs and XFS for OSD. Before committing data to a backing store, Ceph first writes the data to a separate storage area called journal, which is a small buffer-sized partition either on the same or a separate spinning disk as OSD, on a separate SSD disk or partition, or even as a file on a filesystem. In this mechanism, Ceph writes everything first to journal, and then to the backing storage as shown in following diagram:

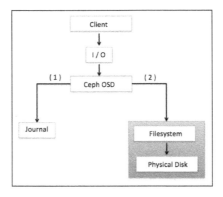

A journal lasts through backing store syncs, running every five seconds, by default. 10 GB is the common size of the journal, but the bigger the partition, the better it is. Ceph uses journals for speed and consistency. The journal allows Ceph OSD to do small writes quickly; a random write is first written in a sequential pattern on journals, and then flushed to a filesystem. This gives filesystems enough time to merge writes to disk. Relatively high performance improvements have been seen when journals are created on SSD disk partition. In such a scenario, all the client writes are written to superfast SSD journals, and then flushed to spinning disks.

Using SSDs as journals for OSD absorb spikes in your workload. However, if journals are slower than your backing store, it will be a limiting factor on your cluster performance. As per the recommendation, you should not exceed OSD to journal ratio of 4 to 5 OSDs per journal disk when using external SSDs for journals. Exceeding the OSD count per journal disk might create performance bottlenecks for your cluster. Also, if your journal disk that hosts multiple OSDs running on XFS or ext4 filesystems fails, you will lose your OSD and its data.

This is where Btrfs takes the advantage; in case of journal failure in a Btrfs-based filesystem, it will go back in time, causing minimal or no data loss. Btrfs is a copy-on-write filesystem, that is, if the content of a block is changed, the changed block is written separately, thus preserving the old block. In case of journal disasters, data remains available since the old content is still available. For more information on Btrfs, visit `https://btrfs.wiki.kernel.org`.

Till now, we discussed using physical disk drives for Ceph OSD; however, Ceph cluster deployments also use RAID underneath for OSD. We do not recommend you to use RAID underneath your Ceph storage cluster due to several reasons, which are listed as follows:

- *Doing RAID and then replication on top of it is a pain*. Ceph, by default, performs internal replication for data protection; doing RAID on the same replicated data will not provide any benefit. It will eventually add an additional layer of data protection and increase complexity. In a RAID group, if you lose a disk, the recovery operation will require an additional spare disk of the same type before it can even start. Next, we have to wait for a whole drive worth of data to be written on a new disk. Resilvering a RAID volume takes a huge amount of time as well as degrades performance as compared to a distributed replication method. So, you should not do RAID with replication. However, if your system has a RAID controller, you should use each disk drive as RAID 0.

- For data protection, Ceph relies on replication instead of RAID. The benefit is that replication does not require a free disk or the same capacity of disk drive in the event of disk failure of the storage system. It uses a cluster network for recovery of failed data from the other nodes. During the recovery operation, based on your replication level and placement groups, almost all the cluster nodes participate in data recovery, which makes the recovery operation complete faster as there are a higher number of disks participating in the recovery process.

- There can be a performance impact on a Ceph cluster with RAID as random I/O operations on RAID 5 and 6 are pretty slow.

There are scenarios where RAID can be useful. For example, if you have a lot more physical disks per host and have to run a daemon for each, you can think of creating a RAID volume by collecting some disks and then running an OSD on top of the RAID volume. This will decrease your OSD count as compared to a physical disk count.

For example, if you have a fat node of 64 physical disks with a low system memory of 24 GB, a recommended OSD configuration will require 128 GB of system memory (2 GB per physical disk) for 64 physical disk machines. Since you do not have enough system resources for OSD, you can consider creating RAID groups for your physical disks (six RAID groups with 10 physical disks per RAID group and four spare), and then running OSD for these six RAID groups. In this way, you will require 12 GB of memory approximately, which is available.

The downside of this kind of setup is that if any OSD fails, you will lose all the 10 disks of data (the entire RAID group), which will be a big risk. Hence, if possible, try to avoid using RAID groups underneath OSD.

OSD commands

The following is the command to check the OSD status for a single node:

```
# service ceph status osd
```

```
[root@ceph-node1 ~]# service ceph status osd
=== osd.2 ===
osd.2: running {"version":"0.72.2"}
=== osd.1 ===
osd.1: running {"version":"0.72.2"}
=== osd.0 ===
osd.0: running {"version":"0.72.2"}
[root@ceph-node1 ~]#
```

The following is the command to check the OSD status for an entire cluster. Keep in mind that in order to monitor entire cluster OSDs from a single node, the `ceph.conf` file must have information of all the OSDs with their host name. You would need to update the `ceph.conf` file to achieve this. This concept has been explained in later chapters.

```
# service ceph -a status osd
```

```
[root@ceph-node1 ~]# service ceph -a status osd
=== osd.2 ===
osd.2: running {"version":"0.72.2"}
=== osd.1 ===
osd.1: running {"version":"0.72.2"}
=== osd.0 ===
osd.0: running {"version":"0.72.2"}
=== osd.3 ===
osd.3: running {"version":"0.72.2"}
=== osd.4 ===
osd.4: running {"version":"0.72.2"}
=== osd.5 ===
osd.5: running {"version":"0.72.2"}
=== osd.6 ===
osd.6: running {"version":"0.72.2"}
=== osd.7 ===
osd.7: running {"version":"0.72.2"}
=== osd.8 ===
osd.8: running {"version":"0.72.2"}
[root@ceph-node1 ~]# █
```

The following is the command to check OSD ID:

```
# ceph osd ls
```

The following is the command to check an OSD map and state:

```
# ceph osd stat
```

The following is the command to check an OSD tree:

```
# ceph osd tree
```

Ceph monitors

As the name suggests, Ceph monitors are responsible for monitoring the health of the entire cluster. These are daemons that maintain the cluster membership state by storing critical cluster information, the state of peer nodes, and cluster configuration information. The Ceph monitor performs its tasks by maintaining a master copy of a cluster. The cluster map includes the monitor, OSD, PG, CRUSH, and MDS maps. All these maps are collectively known as a cluster map. Let's have a quick look at the functionality of each map:

- **Monitor map**: This holds end-to-end information about a monitor node, which includes the Ceph cluster ID, monitor hostname, and IP address with port number. It also stores the current epoch for map creation and the last-changed information. You can check your cluster's monitor map by executing:

```
# ceph mon dump
```

- **OSD map**: This stores some common fields such as the cluster ID; epoch for OSD map creation and last-changed information; and information related to pools such as pool names, pool ID, type, replication level, and placement groups. It also stores OSD information such as count, state, weight, last clean interval, and OSD host information. You can check your cluster's OSD maps by executing:

```
# ceph osd dump
```

- **PG map**: This holds the in-placement group version, time stamp, last OSD map epoch, full ratio, and near full ratio information. It also keeps track of each placement group ID, object count, state, state stamp, up and acting OSD sets, and finally, the scrub details. To check your cluster PG map, execute:

```
# ceph pg dump
```

- **CRUSH map**: This holds information of your cluster's storage devices, failure domain hierarchy, and the rules defined for the failure domain when storing data. To check your cluster CRUSH map, execute the following command:

```
# ceph osd crush dump
```

- **MDS map**: This stores information of the current MDS map epoch, map creation and modification time, data and metadata pool ID, cluster MDS count, and MDS state. To check your cluster MDS map, execute:

```
# ceph mds dump
```

Ceph monitor does not store and serve data to clients, rather, it serves updated cluster maps to clients as well as other cluster nodes. Clients and other cluster nodes periodically check with monitors for the most recent copies of cluster maps.

Monitors are lightweight daemons that usually do not require a huge amount of system resources. A low-cost, entry-level server with a fair amount of CPU, memory, and a gigabit Ethernet is enough for most of the scenarios. A monitor node should have enough disk space to store cluster logs, including OSD, MDS, and monitor logs. A regular healthy cluster generates logs under few MB to some GB; however, storage requirements for logs increase when the verbosity/debugging level is increased for a cluster. Several GB of disk space might be required to store logs.

It is important to make sure that a system disk should not be filled up, otherwise clusters might run into problems. A scheduled log rotation policy as well as regular filesystem utilization monitoring is recommended, especially for the nodes hosting monitors as increasing the debugging verbosity might lead to generate huge logs with an average rate of 1 GB per hour.

A typical Ceph cluster consists of more than one monitor node. A multimonitored Ceph architecture develops quorum and provides consensus for distributed decision-making in clusters by using the Paxos algorithm. The monitor count in your cluster should be an odd number; the bare minimum requirement is one monitor node, and the recommended count is three. Since a monitor operates in quorum, more than half of the total monitor nodes should always be available to prevent split-brain problems that are seen by other systems. This is why odd numbers of monitors are recommended. Out of all the cluster monitors, one of them operates as the leader. The other monitor nodes are entitled to become leaders if the leader monitor is unavailable. A production cluster must have at least three monitor nodes to provide high availability.

```
[root@ceph-node1 ceph]# ceph daemon mon.ceph-node1 mon_status
{ "name": "ceph-node1",
  "rank": 0,
  "state": "leader",
  "election_epoch": 34,
  "quorum": [
        0,
        1,
        2],
  "outside_quorum": [],
  "extra_probe_peers": [
        "192.168.57.102:6789\/0",
        "192.168.57.103:6789\/0"],
  "sync_provider": [],
  "monmap": { "epoch": 9,
      "fsid": "ffa7c0e4-6368-4032-88a4-5fb6a3fb383c",
      "modified": "2014-04-15 23:16:08.649712",
      "created": "0.000000",
      "mons": [
            { "rank": 0,
              "name": "ceph-node1",
              "addr": "192.168.57.101:6789\/0"},
            { "rank": 1,
              "name": "ceph-node2",
              "addr": "192.168.57.102:6789\/0"},
            { "rank": 2,
              "name": "ceph-node3",
              "addr": "192.168.57.103:6789\/0"}]}}

[root@ceph-node1 ceph]#
```

The preceding output demonstrates ceph-node1 as our initial monitor and cluster leader. The output also explains the quorum status and other monitor details.

If you have budget constraints or are hosting a small Ceph cluster, the monitor daemons can run on the same nodes as OSD. However, the recommendation for such a scenario is to use more CPU, memory, and a larger system disk to store monitor logs if you plan to serve monitor and OSD services from a single common node.

For enterprise production environments, the recommendation is to use dedicated monitor nodes. If you lose the OSD node, you can still be able to connect to your Ceph cluster if enough monitors run on separate machines. The physical racking layout should also be considered during your cluster-planning phase. You should scatter your monitor nodes throughout all the failure domains you have, for example, different switches, power supplies, and physical racks. If you have multiple data centers in a single high-speed network, your monitor nodes should belong to different data centers.

Monitor commands

To check the monitor service status, run the following command:

```
# service ceph status mon
```

There are multiple ways to check the monitor status, such as:

```
# ceph mon stat
# ceph mon_status
# ceph mon dump
```

Have a look at the following screenshot:

```
[root@ceph-node1 ~]# ceph mon stat
e9: 3 mons at {ceph-node1=192.168.57.101:6789/0,ceph-node2=192.168.5
7.102:6789/0,ceph-node3=192.168.57.103:6789/0}, election epoch 152,
quorum 0,1,2 ceph-node1,ceph-node2,ceph-node3
[root@ceph-node1 ~]#
[root@ceph-node1 ~]# ceph mon_status
{"name":"ceph-node1","rank":0,"state":"leader","election_epoch":152,
"quorum":[0,1,2],"outside_quorum":[],"extra_probe_peers":[],"sync_pr
ovider":[],"monmap":{"epoch":9,"fsid":"ffa7c0e4-6368-4032-88a4-5fb6a
3fb383c","modified":"2014-04-15 23:16:08.649712","created":"0.000000
","mons":[{"rank":0,"name":"ceph-node1","addr":"192.168.57.101:6789\
/0"},{"rank":1,"name":"ceph-node2","addr":"192.168.57.102:6789\/0"},
{"rank":2,"name":"ceph-node3","addr":"192.168.57.103:6789\/0"}]}}
[root@ceph-node1 ~]#
[root@ceph-node1 ~]# ceph mon dump
dumped monmap epoch 9
epoch 9
fsid ffa7c0e4-6368-4032-88a4-5fb6a3fb383c
last_changed 2014-04-15 23:16:08.649712
created 0.000000
0: 192.168.57.101:6789/0 mon.ceph-node1
1: 192.168.57.102:6789/0 mon.ceph-node2
2: 192.168.57.103:6789/0 mon.ceph-node3

[root@ceph-node1 ~]#
```

librados

librados is a native C library that allows applications to work directly with RADOS, bypassing other interface layers to interact with the Ceph cluster. librados is a library for RADOS, which offers rich API support, granting applications to do direct and parallel access to clusters, with no HTTP overhead. Applications can extend their native protocols to get access to RADOS by linking with librados. Similar libraries are available to extend support to C++, Java, Python, Ruby, and PHP. librados serves as the base for other service interfaces that are built on top of the librados native interface, which includes the Ceph block device, Ceph filesystem, and Ceph RADOS gateway. librados provides rich API subsets, efficiently storing key/value inside an object. API supports atomic-single-object transaction by updating data, key, and attributes together. Interclient communication is supported via objects.

Direct interaction with RADOS clusters via the librados library drastically improves application performance, reliability, and efficiency. librados offers a very powerful library set, which can provide added advantages to Platform-as-a-Service and Software-as-a-Service cloud solutions.

The Ceph block storage

Block storage is one of the most common formats to store data in an enterprise environment. The Ceph block device is also known as RADOS block device (RBD); it provides block storage solutions to physical hypervisors as well as virtual machines. The Ceph RBD driver has been integrated with the Linux mainline kernel (2.6.39 and higher) and supported by QEMU/KVM, allowing access to a Ceph block device seamlessly.

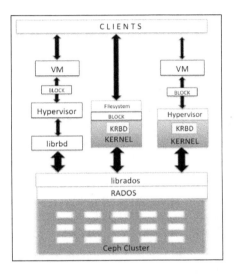

Linux hosts extended full support to **Kernel RBD (KRBD)** and maps Ceph block devices using librados. RADOS then stores Ceph block device objects across clusters in a distributed pattern. Once a Ceph block device is mapped to a Linux host, it can either be used as a RAW partition or can be labelled with a filesystem followed by mounting.

From the roots, Ceph has been tightly integrated with cloud platforms such as OpenStack. For Cinder and Glance, which are volume and image programs for OpenStack, Ceph provides its block device backend to store virtual machine volumes and OS images. These images and volumes are thin provisioned. Only the changed objects needed to be stored; this helps in a significant amount of storage space, saving for OpenStack.

The copy-on-write and instant cloning features of Ceph help OpenStack to spin hundreds of virtual machine instances in less time. RBD also supports snapshots, thus quickly saving the state of virtual machine, which can be further cloned to produce the same type of virtual machines and used for point-in-time restores. Ceph acts as a common backend for virtual machines, and thus helps in virtual machine migration since all the machines can access a Ceph storage cluster. Virtualization containers such as QEMU, KVM, and XEN can be configured to boot virtual machines from volumes stored in a Ceph cluster.

RBD makes use of librbd libraries to leverage the benefits of RADOS and provides reliable, fully distributed, and object-based block storage. When a client writes data to RBD, librbd libraries map data blocks into objects to store them in Ceph clusters, strip these data objects, and replicate them across the cluster, thus providing improved performance and reliability. RBD on top of the RADOS layer supports efficient updates to objects. Clients can perform write, append, or truncate operations on existing objects. This makes RBD the optimal solution for virtual machine volumes and supports frequent writes to their virtual disks.

Ceph RBD is stealing the show and replacing expensive SAN storage solutions by providing enterprise class features such as thin provisioning, copy-on-write snapshots and clones, revertible read-only snapshots, and support to cloud platforms such as OpenStack and CloudStack. In the upcoming chapters, we will learn more about the Ceph block device.

Ceph Object Gateway

Ceph Object Gateway, also known as RADOS gateway, is a proxy that converts HTTP requests to RADOS requests and vice versa, providing RESTful object storage, which is S3 and Swift compatible. Ceph Object Storage uses the Ceph Object Gateway daemon (radosgw) to interact with librgw and the Ceph cluster, librados. It is implemented as a FastCGI module using libfcgi, and can be used with any FastCGI-capable web server. Ceph Object Store supports three interfaces:

- **S3 compatible**: This provides an Amazon S3 RESTful API-compatible interface to Ceph storage clusters.

- **Swift compatible**: This provides an OpenStack Swift API-compatible interface to Ceph storage clusters. Ceph Object Gateway can be used as a replacement for Swift in an OpenStack cluster.

- **Admin API**: This supports the administration of your Ceph cluster over HTTP RESTful API.

The following diagram shows different access methods that uses RADOS gateway and librados for object storage.

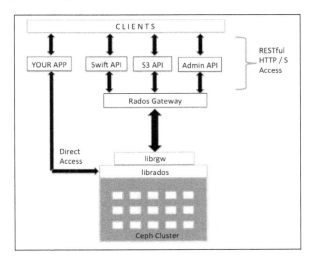

Ceph Object Gateway has its own user management. Both S3 and Swift API share a common namespace inside a Ceph cluster, so you can write data from one API and retrieve it from another. For quick processing, it can use memory to effectively cache metadata. You can also use more than one gateway and keep them under a load balancer to efficiently manage the load on your object storage. Performance improvements are taken care of by striping large REST objects over smaller RADOS objects. Apart from S3 and Swift API, your application can be made to bypass the RADOS gateway and get direct parallel access to librados, that is, to the Ceph cluster. This can be used effectively in custom enterprise applications that require extreme performances from a storage point of view by removing additional layers. Ceph allows direct access to its cluster; this makes it superior to other storage solutions that are rigid and have limited interfaces.

Ceph MDS

Ceph MDS stands for Metadata Server and is required only for a Ceph filesystem (CephFS) and other storage method blocks; object-based storage does not require MDS services. Ceph MDS operates as a daemon, which allows a client to mount a POSIX filesystem of any size. MDS does not serve any data directly to a client; data serving is done by OSD. MDS provides a shared coherent filesystem with a smart caching layer; hence, drastically reducing reads and writes. MDS extends its benefits towards dynamic subtree partitioning and single MDS for a piece of metadata. It is dynamic in nature; daemons can join and leave, and takeover of failed nodes is quick.

MDS is the only component of Ceph that is not production ready; current metadata servers are not currently scale only, and one MDS is supported as of now. A lot of Q&A work is going on to make it production ready; we can expect some news very soon.

MDS does not store local data, which is quite useful in some scenarios. If an MDS daemon dies, we can start it up again on any system that has cluster access. A metadata server's daemons are configured as active and passive. The primary MDS node becomes active, and the rest will go into standby. In the event of a primary MDS failure, the second node takes charge and is promoted to active. For even faster recovery, you can specify that a standby node should follow one of your active nodes, which will keep the same data in memory to prepopulate the cache.

Deploying MDS for your Ceph cluster

To configure Ceph MDS for a Ceph filesystem, you should have a running Ceph cluster. In the previous chapter, we deployed a Ceph cluster. We will use the same cluster for MDS deployment. MDS configuration is relatively simple to configure:

1. Use `ceph-deploy` from the ceph-node1 machine to configure MDS:

    ```
    # ceph-deploy mds create  ceph-node2
    ```

2. Check the status of your Ceph cluster and look for an `mdsmap` entry. You will see your newly configured MDS node:

```
[root@ceph-node1 ceph]# ceph -s
    cluster ffa7c0e4-6368-4032-88a4-5fb6a3fb383c
    health HEALTH_OK
    monmap e9: 3 mons at {ceph-node1=192.168.57.101:6789/0,ceph-node2=192.168.57.102:6789/0,
ceph-node3=192.168.57.103:6789/0}, election epoch 76, quorum 0,1,2 ceph-node1,ceph-node2,ceph
-node3
    mdsmap e25: 1/1/1 up {0=ceph-node2=up:active}
    osdmap e281: 9 osds: 9 up, 9 in
    pgmap v603: 192 pgs, 3 pools, 9470 bytes data, 21 objects
        345 MB used, 45635 MB / 45980 MB avail
            192 active+clean
```

The Ceph filesystem

CephFS provides a POSIX-compliant filesystem on top of RADOS. It uses the MDS daemon, which manages its metadata and keeps it separated from the data, which helps in reduced complexity and improves reliability. CephFS inherits features from RADOS and provides dynamic rebalancing for data.

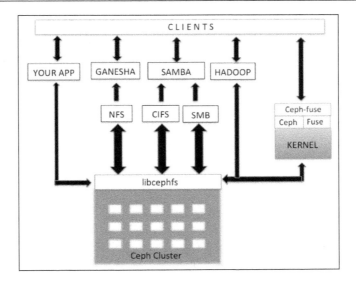

libcephfs libraries play an important role in supporting its multiple client implementations. It has native Linux kernel driver support, thus clients can use native filesystem mounting using the `mount` command. It has a tight integration with SAMBA and support for CIFS and SMB. CephFS extends its support to filesystems in userspace (FUSE) using the `cephfuse` modules. It also allows direct application interaction, with the RADOS cluster using libcephfs libraries.

CephFS is getting popular as a replacement for Hadoop HDFS. HDFS has a single name node, which impacts its scalability and creates a single point of failure. Unlike HDFS, CephFS can be implemented over multiple MDSes in an active-active state, thus making it highly scalable and high performing with no single point of failure. In the upcoming chapters, we will focus on implementing CephFS.

Summary

From the ground, Ceph has been designed to behave as a powerful unified storage solution featuring Ceph Block Device, Ceph Object Storage, and a Ceph filesystem from a single Ceph cluster. During the cluster formation, Ceph makes use of components such as monitors, OSD, and MDS, which are fault tolerant, highly scalable, and high performing. Ceph uses a unique approach to store data on to physical disks. Any type of data, whether it's from Ceph Block Device, an object store, or a filesystem, is chopped in the form of small objects, and then stored to a dynamically calculated data storage location. Monitor maps maintain the information and keep cluster nodes and clients updated with it. This mechanism makes Ceph stand out from the crowd and deliver highly scalable, reliable, and high-performing storage solutions.

4
Ceph Internals

In this chapter, we will cover the following points:

- Ceph objects
- The CRUSH algorithm
- Placement groups
- Ceph pools
- Ceph data management

Ceph under the hood

You are now very well versed in the architecture of Ceph and its core components; next, we will focus on how Ceph does its magic in the background. There are a few elements that work undercover and form the basis of a Ceph cluster. Let's get to know about these in detail.

Object

An object typically comprises data and metadata components that are bundled together and provided with a globally unique identifier. The unique identifier makes sure that there is no other object with the same object ID in the entire storage cluster, and thus guarantees object uniqueness.

Unlike file-based storage, where files are limited by size, objects can be of enormous size along with variable-sized metadata. In an object, data is stored with rich metadata, storing information about context and content of data. The metadata of object storage allows users to properly manage and access unstructured data. Consider the following example of storing a patient record as an object:

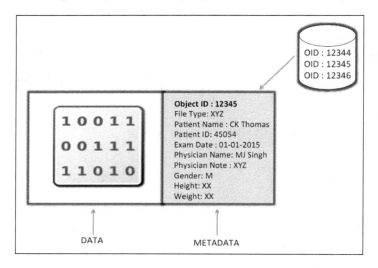

An object is not limited to any type or amount of metadata; it gives you the flexibility to add a custom type in metadata, and thus gives you full ownership of your data. It does not use a directory hierarchy or a tree structure for storage; rather, it is stored in a flat address space containing billions of objects without any complexity. Objects can be stored locally, or they can be geographically separated in a flat-address space, that is, in a contiguous storage space. This storing mechanism helps objects to uniquely represent themselves in the entire cluster. Any application can retrieve data from an object based on its object ID through the use of RESTful API calls. In the same way that URLs work on the Internet, an object ID serves as a unique pointer to its object. These objects are stored in **Object-based Storage Device (OSDs)** in a replicated fashion, which provide high availability. When the Ceph storage cluster receives data-write requests from clients, it stores the data as objects. The OSD daemon then writes the data to a file in the OSD filesystem.

Locating objects

Every unit of data in Ceph is stored in the form of objects inside a pool. A Ceph pool is a logical partition to store objects that provides an organized way of storage. We will learn about pools in detail later in this chapter. Now, let's discover objects, which are the smallest unit of data storage in Ceph. Once a Ceph cluster is deployed, it creates some default storage pools as data, metadata, and RBD pools. After MDS deployment on one of the Ceph nodes, it creates objects inside the metadata pool, which are required by CephFS to function properly. Since we deployed a Ceph cluster earlier in this book, let's examine these objects:

 Starting from the Ceph Giant release, which is the next release after Firefly, metadata and data pools will not be created by default until you configure MDS for your Ceph cluster. The only default pool is the RBD pool.

1. Check the status of your Ceph cluster using the following command in `pgmap`. You will find three pools and some objects:

    ```
    # ceph -s
    ```

```
[root@ceph-node1 ceph]# ceph -s
    cluster ffa7c0e4-6368-4032-88a4-5fb6a3fb383c
    health HEALTH_OK
    monmap e9: 3 mons at {ceph-node1=192.168.57.101:6789/0,ceph-node2=192.168.57.102:6789/0,
ceph-node3=192.168.57.103:6789/0}, election epoch 76, quorum 0,1,2 ceph-node1,ceph-node2,ceph
-node3
    mdsmap e25: 1/1/1 up {0=ceph-node2=up:active}
    osdmap e281: 9 osds: 9 up, 9 in
    pgmap v603: 192 pgs, 3 pools, 9470 bytes data, 21 objects
        345 MB used, 45635 MB / 45980 MB avail
            192 active+clean
```

2. List the pool names of your Ceph cluster using the following command. It will show you the default pools, since we did not create any pool. Three pools will be listed here.

    ```
    # rados lspools
    ```

    ```
    [root@ceph-node1 /]# rados lspools
    data
    metadata
    rbd
    [root@ceph-node1 /]#
    ```

3. Finally, list the object names from the metadata pool. You will find system-generated objects in this pool:

```
# rados -p metadata ls
```

```
[root@ceph-node1 /]# rados -p metadata ls
1.00000000.inode
100.00000000
100.00000000.inode
1.00000000
2.00000000
200.00000000
200.00000001
600.00000000
601.00000000
602.00000000
603.00000000
604.00000000
605.00000000
606.00000000
607.00000000
608.00000000
609.00000000
mds0_inotable
mds0_sessionmap
mds_anchortable
mds_snaptable
[root@ceph-node1 /]#
```

CRUSH

For the last three decades, storage mechanisms have involved storing data and its metadata. The metadata, which is the data about data, stores information such as where the data is actually stored in a series of storage nodes and disk arrays. Each time new data is added to the storage system, its metadata is first updated with the physical location where the data will be stored, after which the actual data is stored. This process has been proven to work well when we have a low storage size on the scale of gigabytes to a few terabytes of data, but what about storing petabyte- or exabyte-level data? This mechanism will definitely not be suitable for storage in the future. Moreover, it creates a single point of failure for your storage system. Unfortunately, if you lose your storage metadata, you lose all your data. So, it's of utmost importance to keep central metadata safe from disasters by any means, either by keeping multiple copies on a single node or replicating the entire data and metadata for a higher degree of fault tolerance. Such complex management of metadata is a bottleneck in a storage system's scalability, high availability, and performance.

Ceph is revolutionary when it comes to data storage and management. It uses the **Controlled Replication Under Scalable Hashing (CRUSH)** algorithm, the intelligent data distribution mechanism of Ceph. The CRUSH algorithm is one of the jewels in Ceph's crown; it is the core of the entire data storage mechanism of Ceph. Unlike traditional systems that rely on storing and managing a central metadata / index table, Ceph uses the CRUSH algorithm to deterministically compute where the data should be written to or read from. Instead of storing metadata, CRUSH computes metadata on demand, thus removing all the limitations encountered in storing metadata in a traditional way.

The CRUSH lookup

The CRUSH mechanism works in such a way that the metadata computation workload is distributed and performed only when needed. The metadata computation process is also known as a CRUSH lookup, and today's computer hardware is powerful enough to perform CRUSH lookup operations quickly and efficiently. The unique thing about a CRUSH lookup is that it's not system dependent. Ceph provides enough flexibility to clients to perform on-demand metadata computation, that is, perform a CRUSH lookup with their own system resources, thus eliminating central lookups.

For a read-and-write operation to Ceph clusters, clients first contact a Ceph monitor and retrieve a copy of the cluster map. The cluster map helps clients know the state and configuration of the Ceph cluster. The data is converted to objects with object and pool names/IDs. The object is then hashed with the number of placement groups to generate a final placement group within the required Ceph pool. The calculated placement group then goes through a CRUSH lookup to determine the primary OSD location to store or retrieve data. After computing the exact OSD ID, the client contacts this OSD directly and stores the data. All these compute operations are performed by the clients, hence it does not impact cluster performance. Once the data is written to the primary OSD, the same node performs a CRUSH lookup operation and computes the location for secondary placement groups and OSDs so that the data is replicated across clusters for high availability. Consider the following example for a CRUSH lookup and object placement to OSD.

First of all, the object name and cluster placement group number are applied with the hash function and based on pool IDs; a placement group ID, PGID, is generated. Next, a CRUSH lookup is performed on this PGID to find out the primary and secondary OSD to write data.

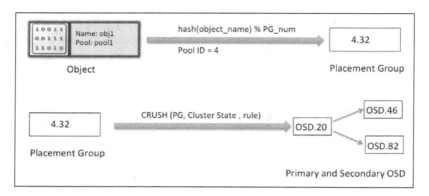

The CRUSH hierarchy

CRUSH is fully infrastructure aware and absolutely user configurable; it maintains a nested hierarchy for all components of your infrastructure. The CRUSH device list usually includes disk, node, rack, row, switch, power circuit, room, data center, and so on. These components are known as failure zones or CRUSH buckets. The CRUSH map contains a list of available buckets to aggregate devices into physical locations. It also includes a list of rules that tells CRUSH how to replicate data for different Ceph pools. The following diagram will give you an overview of how CRUSH looks at your physical infrastructure:

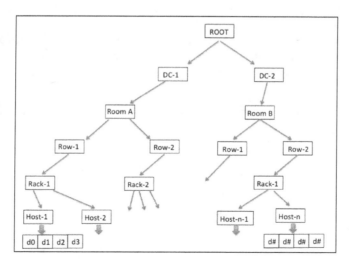

Depending on your infrastructure, CRUSH spreads data and its replica across these failure zones such that it should be safe and available even if some components fail. This is how CRUSH removes single points of failure problems from your storage infrastructure, which is made up of commodity hardware, and yet guarantees high availability. CRUSH writes data evenly across the cluster disks, which improves performance and reliability, and forces all the disks to participate in the cluster. It makes sure that all cluster disks are equally utilized, irrespective of their capacity. To do so, CRUSH allocates weights to each OSD. The higher the weight of an OSD, the more physical storage capacity it will have, and CRUSH will write more data to such OSDs. Hence, on average, OSDs with a lower weight are equally filled as compared to OSDs with a higher weight.

Recovery and rebalancing

In an event of failure of any component from the failure zone, Ceph waits for 300 seconds, by default, before it marks the OSD down and out and initiates the recovery operation. This setting can be controlled using the `mon osd down out interval` parameter under a Ceph cluster configuration file. During the recovery operation, Ceph starts regenerating the affected data that was hosted on the node that failed.

Since CRUSH replicates data to several disks, these replicated copies of data are used at the time of recovery. CRUSH tries to move a minimum amount of data during recovery operations and develops a new cluster layout, making Ceph fault tolerant even after the failure of some components.

When a new host or disk is added to a Ceph cluster, CRUSH starts a rebalancing operation, under which it moves the data from existing hosts/disks to a new host/disk. Rebalancing is performed to keep all disks equally utilized, which improves the cluster performance and keeps it healthy. For example, if a Ceph cluster contains 2000 OSDs, and a new system is added with 20 new OSDs, only 1 percent of data will be moved during the rebalancing operation, and all the existing OSDs will work in parallel to move the data, helping the operation to complete quickly. However, for Ceph clusters that are highly utilized, it is recommended to add new OSDs with weight 0 and gradually increase their weight to a higher number based on their size. In this way, the new OSD will exert less rebalancing load on Ceph clusters and avoid performance degradation.

Editing a CRUSH map

When we deploy Ceph with `ceph-deploy`, it generates a default CRUSH map for our configuration. The default CRUSH map is idle in the testing and sandbox environment, but if you plan to deploy a Ceph cluster in a large production environment, you should consider developing a custom CRUSH map for your environment. The following process will help you to compile a new CRUSH map:

1. Extract your existing CRUSH map. With `-o`, Ceph will output a compiled CRUSH map to the file you specify:

   ```
   # ceph osd getcrushmap -o crushmap.txt
   ```

2. Decompile your CRUSH map. With `-d`, Ceph will decompile the CRUSH map to the file specified by `-o`:

   ```
   # crushtool -d crushmap.txt -o crushmap-decompile
   ```

3. Edit the CRUSH map with any editor:

   ```
   # vi crushmap-decompile
   ```

4. Recompile the new CRUSH map:

   ```
   #  crushtool -c crushmap-decompile -o crushmap-compiled
   ```

5. Set the new CRUSH map into the Ceph cluster:

   ```
   #  ceph osd setcrushmap -i crushmap-compiled
   ```

Customizing a cluster layout

Customizing a cluster layout is one of the most important steps towards building a robust and reliable Ceph storage cluster. It's equally important to install cluster hardware in a fault tolerant zone and include it in a high-available layout from the Ceph software perspective. The default Ceph deployment is not aware of noninteractive components such as rack, row, and data center. After initial deployment, we need to customize the layout as per our requirements. For example, if you execute the `ceph osd tree` command, you will notice that it will only have hosts and OSDs listed under `root`, which is the default. Let's try to allocate these hosts to racks:

1. Execute `ceph osd tree` to get the current cluster layout:

```
[root@ceph-node1 ~]# ceph osd tree
# id    weight  type name        up/down reweight
-1      0       root default
-2      0               host ceph-node1
0       0                       osd.0   up      1
1       0                       osd.1   up      1
2       0                       osd.2   up      1
-3      0               host ceph-node2
3       0                       osd.3   up      1
4       0                       osd.4   up      1
5       0                       osd.5   up      1
-4      0               host ceph-node3
6       0                       osd.6   up      1
7       0                       osd.7   up      1
8       0                       osd.8   up      1
```

2. Add a few racks in your Ceph cluster layout:

   ```
   # ceph osd crush add-bucket rack01 rack
   # ceph osd crush add-bucket rack02 rack
   # ceph osd crush add-bucket rack03 rack
   ```

3. Move each host under specific racks:

   ```
   # ceph osd crush move ceph-node1 rack=rack01
   # ceph osd crush move ceph-node2 rack=rack02
   # ceph osd crush move ceph-node3 rack=rack03
   ```

4. Now, move each rack under the default root:

   ```
   # ceph osd crush move rack03 root=default
   # ceph osd crush move rack02 root=default
   # ceph osd crush move rack01 root=default
   ```

5. Check your new layout. You will notice that all your hosts have now been moved under specific racks. In this way, you can customize your CRUSH layouts to complement your physically installed layout:

```
[root@ceph-node1 ~]# ceph osd tree
# id    weight  type name        up/down reweight
-1      0       root default
-7      0               rack rack03
-4      0                       host ceph-node3
6       0                               osd.6   up      1
7       0                               osd.7   up      1
8       0                               osd.8   up      1
-6      0               rack rack02
-3      0                       host ceph-node2
3       0                               osd.3   up      1
4       0                               osd.4   up      1
5       0                               osd.5   up      1
-5      0               rack rack01
-2      0                       host ceph-node1
0       0                               osd.0   up      1
1       0                               osd.1   up      1
2       0                               osd.2   up      1
```

Placement groups

When a Ceph cluster receives requests for data storage, it splits into sections known as **placement groups** (**PG**). However, CRUSH data is first broken down into a set of objects, and based on the hash operation on object names, replication levels and total number of placement groups in the system, placement group IDs are generated. A placement group is a logical collection of objects that are replicated on OSDs to provide reliability in a storage system. Depending on the replication level of your Ceph pool, each placement group is replicated and distributed on more than one OSD of a Ceph cluster. You can consider a placement group as a logical container holding multiple objects such that this logical container is mapped to multiple OSDs. The placement groups are essential for the scalability and performance of a Ceph storage system.

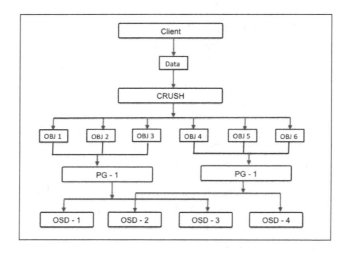

Without placement groups, it will be difficult to manage and track tens of millions of objects that are replicated and spread over hundreds of OSDs. The management of these objects without a placement group will also result in a computational penalty. Instead of managing every object individually, a system has to manage placement groups with numerous objects. This makes Ceph a more manageable and less complex function. Each placement group requires some amount of system resources, CPU, and memory since every placement group has to manage multiple objects. The number of placement groups in a cluster should be meticulously calculated. Usually, increasing the number of placement groups in your cluster reduces the per OSD load, but the increment should always be done in a regulated way. 50 to 100 placement groups per OSD is recommended. This is to avoid high resource utilization from an OSD node. As your data needs to increase, you will need to scale your cluster up by adjusting placement group counts. When devices are added or removed from a cluster, most of the placement groups remain in position; CRUSH manages the relocation of placement groups across clusters.

PGP is the total number of placement groups for placement purposes. This should be equal to the total number of placement groups.

Calculating PG numbers

Deciding the correct number of placement groups is an essential step in building enterprise class Ceph storage clusters. Placement groups can improve or affect storage performance to a certain extent.

The formula to calculate the total number of placement groups for a Ceph cluster is:

```
Total PGs = (Total_number_of_OSD * 100) / max_replication_count
```

This result must be rounded up to the nearest power of 2. For example, if a Ceph cluster has 160 OSDs and the replication count is 3, the total number of placement groups will come as 5333.3, and rounding up this value to the nearest power of 2 will give the final value as 8192 PGs.

We should also make a calculation to find out the total number of PGs per pool in the Ceph cluster. The formula for this is as follows:

```
Total PGs = ((Total_number_of_OSD * 100) / max_replication_count)
/ pool count
```

We will consider the same example that we used earlier. The total number of OSDs is 160, the replication level is 3, and the total number of pools is three. Based on this assumption, the formula will generate 1777.7. Finally, rounding it up to the power of 2 will give 2048 PGs per pool.

It's important to balance the number of PGs per pool with the number of PGs per OSD in order to reduce the variance per OSD and avoid the recovery process, which is slow.

Modifying PG and PGP

If you manage a Ceph storage cluster, you might need to change the PG and PGP count for your pool at some point. Before proceeding towards PG and PGP modification, let's understand what PGP is.

PGP is Placement Group for Placement purpose, which should be kept equal to the total number of placement groups (pg_num). For a Ceph pool, if you increase the number of placement groups, that is, pg_num, you should also increase pgp_num to the same integer value as pg_num so that the cluster can start rebalancing. The undercover rebalancing mechanism can be understood in the following way.

The pg_num value defines the number of placement groups, which are mapped to OSDs. When pg_num is increased for any pool, every PG of this pool splits into half, but they all remain mapped to their parent OSD. Until this time, Ceph does not start rebalancing. Now, when you increase the pgp_num value for the same pool, PGs start to migrate from the parent to some other OSD, and cluster rebalancing starts. In this way, PGP plays an important role in cluster rebalancing. Now, let's learn how to change pg_num and pgp_num:

1. Check the existing PG and PGP numbers:

   ```
   # ceph osd pool get data pg_num
   # ceph osd pool get data pgp_num
   ```

   ```
   [root@ceph-node1 /]#
   [root@ceph-node1 /]# ceph osd pool get data pg_num
   pg_num: 64
   [root@ceph-node1 /]# ceph osd pool get data pgp_num
   pgp_num: 64
   [root@ceph-node1 /]#
   ```

2. Check the pool replication level by executing the following command, and look for the rep size value:

   ```
   # ceph osd dump | grep size
   ```

   ```
   [root@ceph-node1 /]# ceph osd dump | grep -i size
   pool 3 'rbd' rep size 2 min_size 1 crush_ruleset 0 object_hash rjenkins pg_num 64 pgp_num 64 last_change 452 owner 0
   pool 4 'data' rep size 2 min_size 1 crush_ruleset 0 object_hash rjenkins pg_num 64 pgp_num 64 last_change 454 owner 0
   pool 5 'metadata' rep size 2 min_size 1 crush_ruleset 0 object_hash rjenkins pg_num 64 pgp_num 64 last_change 456 owner 0
   [root@ceph-node1 /]#
   ```

3. Calculate the new placement group count for our setup using the following formula:

   ```
   Total OSD = 9, Replication pool level (rep size) = 2, pool
   count = 3
   ```

   Based on the preceding formula, the placement group count for each pool comes to 150, rounding it up to the next power of 2 gives us 256.

4. Modify the PG and PGP for the pool:

```
# ceph osd pool set data pg_num 256

# ceph osd pool set data pgp_num 256
```

```
[root@ceph-node1 /]# ceph osd pool set data pg_num 256
set pool 6 pg_num to 256
[root@ceph-node1 /]#
[root@ceph-node1 /]# ceph osd pool set data pgp_num 256
set pool 6 pgp_num to 256
[root@ceph-node1 /]#
```

5. Similarly, modify the PG and PGP numbers for metadata and RBD pools:

```
[root@ceph-node1 /]# ceph osd pool get data pg_num
pg_num: 256
[root@ceph-node1 /]# ceph osd pool get data pgp_num
pgp_num: 256
[root@ceph-node1 /]# ceph osd pool get metadata pg_num
pg_num: 256
[root@ceph-node1 /]# ceph osd pool get metadata pgp_num
pgp_num: 256
[root@ceph-node1 /]# ceph osd pool get rbd pg_num
pg_num: 256
[root@ceph-node1 /]# ceph osd pool get rbd pgp_num
pgp_num: 256
[root@ceph-node1 /]#
```

PG peering, up and acting sets

A Ceph OSD daemon performs the peering operation for the state of all objects and their metadata for particular PGs, which involves the agreement between OSDs storing a placement group. A Ceph storage cluster stores multiple copies of any object on multiple PGs, which are then stored on multiple OSDs. These OSDs are referred to as primary, secondary, tertiary, and so on. An acting set refers to a group of OSDs responsible for PGs. The primary OSD is known as the first OSD from the acting set and is responsible for the peering operation for each PG with its secondary/tertiary OSD. The primary OSD is the only OSD that entertains write operations from clients. The OSD, which is up, remains in the acting set. Once the primary OSD is down, it is first removed from the up set; the secondary OSD is then promoted to the primary OSD. Ceph recovers PGs of the failed OSD on to the new OSD and adds it to the up and acting sets to ensure high availability.

In a Ceph cluster, an OSD can be the primary OSD for some PGs, while at the same time, it's the secondary or tertiary OSD for other PGs.

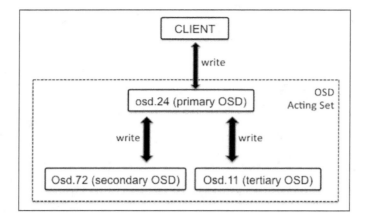

In the preceding example, the acting set contains three OSDs (**osd.24**, **osd.72**, and **osd.11**). Out of these, **osd.24** is the primary OSD, and **osd.72** and **osd.11** are the secondary and tertiary OSDs, respectively. Since **osd.24** is the primary OSD, it takes care of the peering operation for all the PGs that are on these three OSDs. In this way, Ceph makes sure PGs are always available and consistent.

Ceph pools

The concept of a pool is not new in storage systems. Enterprise storage systems are managed by creating several pools; Ceph also provides easy storage management by means of storage pools. A Ceph pool is a logical partition to store objects. Each pool in Ceph holds a number of placement groups, which in turn holds a number of objects that are mapped to OSDs across clusters. Hence, every single pool is distributed across cluster nodes, and thus this provides resilience. The initial Ceph deployment creates a default pool based on your requirement; it is recommended that you should create pools other than the default one.

A pool ensures data availability by creating the desired number of object copies, that is, replicas or erasure codes. The **erasure coding** (**EC**) feature has been recently added to Ceph, starting with the Ceph Firefly release. Erasure coding is a method of data protection in which data is broken into fragments, encoded, and then stored in a distributed manner. Ceph, being distributed in nature, makes use of EC amazingly well.

At the time of pool creation, we can define the replica size; the default replica size is 2. The pool replication level is very flexible; at any point in time, we can change it. We can also define the erasure code ruleset at the time of pool creation, which provides the same level of reliability but less amount of space as compared to the replication method.

 A pool can be created with either replication or erasure coding, but not both at the same time.

A Ceph pool is mapped with a CRUSH ruleset when data is written to a pool; it is identified by the CRUSH ruleset for the placement of objects and its replica inside the cluster. The CRUSH ruleset provides new capabilities to Ceph pools. For example, we can create a faster pool, also known as cache pool, out of SSD disk drives, or a hybrid pool out of SSD and SAS or SATA disk drivers.

A Ceph pool also supports snapshot features. We can use the `ceph osd pool mksnap` command to take snapshots of a particular pool, and we can restore these when necessary. In addition to this, a Ceph pool allows us to set ownership and access to objects. A user ID can be assigned as the owner of a pool. This is very useful in several scenarios where we need to provide restrictive access to a pool.

Pool operations

Performing Ceph pool operations is one of the day-to-day jobs for a Ceph admin. Ceph provides the rich `cli` tools for pool creation and management. We will learn about Ceph pool operation in the following section.

Creating and listing pools

Creating a Ceph pool requires a pool name, PG and PGP numbers, and a pool type which is either replicated or erasure. The default is replicated. Let's start creating a pool:

1. Create a pool, `web-services`, with `128` PG and PGP numbers. This will create a replicated pool as it's the default option.

   ```
   # ceph osd pool create web-services 128 128
   ```

2. The listing of pools can be done in two ways. However, the output of the third command will provide us more information such as the pool ID, replication size, CRUSH ruleset, and PG and PGP numbers:

```
# ceph osd lspools
```

```
# rados lspools
```

```
# ceph osd dump | grep -i pool
```

```
[root@ceph-node1 /]# ceph osd dump | grep -i pool
pool 3 'rbd' rep size 2 min_size 1 crush_ruleset 0 object_hash rjenkins pg_num 256 pgp_num 256 last_change 478 owner 0
pool 5 'metadata' rep size 2 min_size 1 crush_ruleset 0 object_hash rjenkins pg_num 256 pgp_num 256 last_change 476 owner 0
pool 6 'data' rep size 2 min_size 1 crush_ruleset 0 object_hash rjenkins pg_num 256 pgp_num 256 last_change 470 owner 0
pool 8 'web-services' rep size 2 min_size 1 crush_ruleset 0 object_hash rjenkins pg_num 128 pgp_num 128 last_change 503 owner 0
[root@ceph-node1 /]#
```

3. The default replication size for a Ceph pool created with Ceph Emperor or an earlier release is 2; we can change the replication size using the following command:

```
# ceph osd pool set web-services size 3
```

```
# ceph osd dump | grep -i pool
```

```
[root@ceph-node1 /]# ceph osd pool set web-services size 3
set pool 8 size to 3
[root@ceph-node1 /]#
[root@ceph-node1 /]# ceph osd dump | grep -i pool
pool 3 'rbd' rep size 2 min_size 1 crush_ruleset 0 object_hash rjenkins pg_num 256 pgp_num 256 last_change 478 owner 0
pool 5 'metadata' rep size 2 min_size 1 crush_ruleset 0 object_hash rjenkins pg_num 256 pgp_num 256 last_change 476 owner 0
pool 6 'data' rep size 2 min_size 1 crush_ruleset 0 object_hash rjenkins pg_num 256 pgp_num 256 last_change 470 owner 0
pool 8 'web-services' rep size 3 min_size 1 crush_ruleset 0 object_hash rjenkins pg_num 128 pgp_num 128 last_change 505 owner 0
```

> For Ceph Emperor and earlier releases, the default replication size for a pool was 2; this default replication size has been changed to 3 starting from Ceph Firefly.

4. Rename a pool, as follows:

```
# ceph osd pool rename web-services frontend-services
```

```
# ceph osd lspools
```

5. Ceph pools support snapshots; we can restore objects from a snapshot in the event of a failure. In the following example, we will create an object in a pool and then take pool snapshots. After this, we will intentionally remove the object from the pool and try to restore the object from its snapshot:

```
# rados -p frontend-services put object1 /etc/hosts
```

```
# rados -p frontend-services ls
```

```
# rados mksnap snapshot01 -p frontend-services
```

```
# rados lssnap -p frontend-services
```

```
# rados -p frontend-services rm object1
```

```
# rados -p frontend-services listsnaps object1
# rados rollback -p frontend-services object1 snapshot01
# rados -p frontend-services ls
```

```
[root@ceph-node1 /]#
[root@ceph-node1 /]#
[root@ceph-node1 /]# rados -p frontend-services put object1 /etc/hosts
[root@ceph-node1 /]# rados -p frontend-services ls
object1
[root@ceph-node1 /]# rados mksnap snapshot01 -p frontend-services
created pool frontend-services snap snapshot01
[root@ceph-node1 /]# rados lssnap -p frontend-services
5       snapshot01      2014.05.12 13:20:58
1 snaps
[root@ceph-node1 /]# rados -p frontend-services rm object1
[root@ceph-node1 /]#
[root@ceph-node1 /]# rados -p frontend-services listsnaps object1
object1:
cloneid snaps   size    overlap
5       5       237     []

[root@ceph-node1 /]# rados rollback -p frontend-services object1 snapshot01
rolled back pool frontend-services to snapshot snapshot01
[root@ceph-node1 /]# rados -p frontend-services ls
object1
[root@ceph-node1 /]#
[root@ceph-node1 /]# ▌
```

6. Removing a pool will also remove all its snapshots. After removing a pool, you should delete CRUSH rulesets if you created them manually. If you created users with permissions strictly for a pool that no longer exists, you should consider deleting these users too:

```
# ceph osd pool delete frontend-services frontend-services --
yes-i-really-really-mean-it
```

Ceph data management

The data management inside a Ceph cluster involves all the components that we have discussed so far. The coordination between these components gives power to Ceph to provide a reliable and robust storage system. Data management starts as soon as a client writes data to a Ceph pool. Once the client writes data to a Ceph pool, data is first written to a primary OSD based on the pool replication size. The primary OSD replicates the same data to its secondary and tertiary OSDs and waits for their acknowledgement. As soon as the secondary and tertiary OSDs complete data writing, they send an acknowledgement signal to the primary OSD, and finally, the primary OSD returns an acknowledgement to the client confirming the write operation completion.

In this way, Ceph consistently stores each client write operation and provides data availability from its replicas in the event of failures. Let's now see how data is stored in a Ceph cluster:

1. We will first create a test file, a Ceph pool, and set the pool replication to 3 copies:

   ```
   # echo "Hello Ceph, You are Awesome like MJ" > /tmp/helloceph
   # ceph osd pool create HPC_Pool 128 128
   # ceph osd pool set HPC_Pool size 3
   ```

2. Put some data in this pool and verify its contents:

   ```
   # rados -p HPC_Pool put object1 /tmp/helloceph
   # rados -p HPC_Pool ls
   ```

3. The file has now been stored in a Ceph pool. As you know, everything in Ceph gets stored in the form of objects, which belong to a placement group, and these placement groups belong to multiple OSDs. Now, let's see this concept practically:

   ```
   # ceph osd map HPC_Pool object1
   ```

   This command will show you OSD maps for object1, which is inside HPC_Pool:

   ```
   [root@ceph-node1 /]# ceph osd map HPC_Pool object1
   osdmap e566 pool 'HPC_Pool' (10) object 'object1' -> pg 10.bac5debc (10.3c) -> up [0,6,3] acting [0,6,3]
   [root@ceph-node1 /]#
   ```

   Let's discuss the output of this command:

   - osdmap e566: This is the OSD map version ID or OSD epoch 556.
   - pool 'HPC_Pool' (10): This is a Ceph pool name and pool ID.
   - object 'object1': This is an object name.
   - pg 10.bac5debc (10.3c): This is the placement group number, that is, object1, which belongs to PG 10.3c.
   - up [0,6,3]: This is the OSD up set that contains osd.0, osd.6, and osd.3. Since the pool has a replication level set to 3, each PG will be stored in three OSDs. This also means that all the OSDs holding PG 10.3c are up. It is the ordered list of OSDs that is responsible for a particular OSD at a particular epoch as per the CRUSH map. This is usually the same as the acting set.

○ `acting [0,6,3]`: `osd.0`, `osd.6`, and `osd.3` are in the acting set where `osd.0` is the primary OSD, `osd.6` is the secondary OSD, and `osd.3` is the tertiary OSD. The acting set is the ordered list of OSD, which is responsible for a particular OSD.

4. Check the physical location of each of these OSDs. You will find OSDs 0, 6, and 3 are physically separated on `ceph-node1`, `ceph-node3`, and `ceph-node2` hosts, respectively.

```
[root@ceph-node1 ~]# ceph osd tree
# id    weight  type name          up/down reweight
-1      0           root default
-7      0               rack rack03
-4      0                   host ceph-node3
6       0                       osd.6   up      1
7       0                       osd.7   up      1
8       0                       osd.8   up      1
-6      0               rack rack02
-3      0                   host ceph-node2
3       0                       osd.3   up      1
4       0                       osd.4   up      1
5       0                       osd.5   up      1
-5      0               rack rack01
-2      0                   host ceph-node1
0       0                       osd.0   up      1
1       0                       osd.1   up      1
2       0                       osd.2   up      1
```

5. Now, log in to any of these nodes to check where the real data resides on OSD. You will observe that `object1` is stored at PG 10.3c of ceph-node2 , on partition sdb1 which is osd.3; note that these PG ID and OSD ID might differ with your setup:

```
# ssh ceph-node2
# df -h | grep -i ceph-3
# cd /var/lib/ceph/osd/ceph-3/current
# ls -l | grep -i 10.3c
# cd 10.3c_head/
# ls -l
```

```
[root@ceph-node1 /]# ssh ceph-node2
Last login: Wed May 14 12:45:59 2014 from ceph-node1
[root@ceph-node2 ~]# df -h | grep -i ceph-3
/dev/sdb1            5.0G    54M  5.0G    2% /var/lib/ceph/osd/ceph-3
[root@ceph-node2 ~]# cd /var/lib/ceph/osd/ceph-3/current
[root@ceph-node2 current]# ls -l | grep -i 10.3c
drwxr-xr-x. 2 root root    38 May 14 12:06 10.3c_head
[root@ceph-node2 current]# cd 10.3c_head/
[root@ceph-node2 10.3c_head]# ls -l
total 64
-rw-r--r--. 1 root root 35 May 14 12:06 object1__head_BAC5DEBC__a
[root@ceph-node2 10.3c_head]#
```

In this way, Ceph stores each data object in a replicated manner over different failure domains. This intelligence mechanism is the core of Ceph's data management.

Summary

In this chapter, we learned about Ceph's internal components, including objects, the CRUSH algorithm, placement groups, and pools, and how they interact with each other to provide a highly reliable and scalable storage cluster. This chapter is based on the practical approach for these components so that you can understand each bit of it. We also demonstrated how data is stored in the cluster, right from the point when it enters as a write request to a Ceph pool until it reaches the correct OSD filesystem and is stored in the form of an object. We recommend you repeat these practical examples on your test cluster; this will give you a broader view of how Ceph stores your data in a highly replicated, readily available form. If you are a system admin, you should focus more on discovering Ceph pools and CRUSH maps as mentioned in this chapter. This is something that is expected from a system admin both before and after cluster provisioning. In the next chapter, we will learn about Ceph cluster hardware planning and its various installation methods, followed by upgrading the Ceph cluster version and scaling it up.

5
Deploying Ceph – the Way You Should Know

By this time, you must have learned enough about Ceph, including some hands-on practice. In this chapter, we will learn the following interesting stuff around Ceph:

- Ceph cluster hardware planning
- Preparing your Ceph installation
- Ceph cluster manual deployment
- Scaling up your cluster
- Ceph cluster deployment using the ceph-deploy tool
- Upgrading your Ceph cluster

Hardware planning for a Ceph cluster

Ceph is a software-based storage system that is designed to run on generally available commodity hardware. This ability of Ceph makes it an economic, scalable, and vendor-free storage solution.

Cluster hardware configuration requires planning based on your storage needs. The type of hardware as well as the cluster design are the factors that should be considered during the initial phase of project. Meticulous planning at an early stage can go a long way to avoid performance bottlenecks and helps in better cluster reliability. Hardware selection depends on various factors such as budget, whether the system needs to focus on performance or capacity or both, fault tolerance level, and the final use case. In this chapter, we will discuss general considerations with respect to hardware and cluster design.

For more information on hardware recommendation, you can refer to Ceph's official documentation at `http://ceph.com/docs/master/start/hardware-recommendations/`.

Monitor requirements

A Ceph monitor takes care of the health of an entire cluster by maintaining cluster maps. They do not participate in storing cluster data. Hence they are not CPU and memory intensive and have fairly low system resource requirements. A low-cost, entry-level server with a single core CPU with a few gigabytes of memory is good enough in most cases for being a monitor node.

If you have an existing server with a fair amount of available system resources, you can choose that node to handle the additional responsibility of running Ceph monitors. In this case, you should make sure that the other services running on that node leave sufficient resources for Ceph monitor daemons. In a nonproduction environment where you have budget or hardware constraints, you can think of running Ceph monitors on physically separated virtual machines. However, the production practice is to run Ceph monitor on low-cost, low-configuration physical machines.

If you have configured your cluster to store logs on local monitor node, make sure you have a sufficient amount of local disk space on the monitor node to store the logs. For a healthy cluster, logs can grow as much as few gigabytes, but for an unhealthy cluster, when the debugging level is more, it could easily reach to several gigabytes. Please make sure that the cluster does not remain unhealthy for a long time with any space for logs. For a production environment, you should allocate a large enough partition for logs and develop a log rotation policy to keep up the free space.

The network for a monitor node should be redundant, since the monitor does not participate in cluster recovery. A redundant NIC with 1 Gbps is sufficient. Redundancy at the network level is important as the monitor forms quorum with other monitors, and failure of more than 50 percent of the monitor nodes would create a problem while connecting to a cluster. For a nonproduction environment, you can manage with a single NIC monitor node, but for a production setup, redundancy at the network level is a big factor.

OSD requirements

A typical Ceph cluster deployment creates one OSD for each physical disk in a cluster node, which is a recommended practice. However, OSD supports flexible deployment of one OSD per disk or one OSD per RAID volume. The majority of Ceph cluster deployment in a JBOD environment uses one OSD per physical disk. A Ceph OSD needs:

- CPU and memory
- An OSD journal (block device or a file)
- An underlying filesystem (XFS, ext4, and Btrfs)
- A separate OSD or cluster redundant network (recommended)

The recommended CPU and memory configuration that you should have is 1 GHz of CPU and 2 GB of RAM per OSD. This should be suitable for most of the cluster environments; however, it is crucial to note that in the event of a disaster, the recovery process requires more system resource than usual.

 It is usually cost-effective to overallocate CPU and memory at an earlier stage of your cluster planning as we can anytime add more physical disks in a JBOD style to the same host if it has enough system resources, rather than purchasing an entirely new node, which is a bit costly.

The OSD is the main storage unit in Ceph; you should have plenty of hard disks as per your need for storage capacity. For a disk drive, it's usually the higher the capacity, the lower the price in terms of *cost per gigabyte*. You should take the cost-per-gigabyte advantage and use fairly large-sized OSDs. However, it's worth keeping in mind that the higher the size of a disk, the more memory it needs to operate.

From a performance point of view, you should consider separate journal disks for an OSD. Performance improvements have been seen when OSD journals are created on SSD disk partition and OSD data on a separate spinning disk. When SSD disks are used as journals, it improves cluster performance and manages workload quickly and efficiently. However, the downside of an SSD is that it increases storage cost per gigabyte for your cluster. The efficient way to invest in an SSD is to designate a single SSD disk as journals for more than one OSDs. The trade-off here is that if you lose the SSD journal disk, which is common for multiple OSDs, you will lose your data on those OSD disks, so try to avoid overloading the SSD with journals. A decent journal count should be two to four journals per SSD.

Network requirements

With respect to networking configuration, it's recommended that your cluster should have at least two separate networks, one for front-side data network or public networks and the other for the backside data network or clustered network. Two different physical networks are recommended so as to keep client data and Ceph cluster traffic separate. Most of the time, Ceph cluster traffic is more as compared to client data traffic as Ceph uses a cluster network to perform replication of each object as well as recovery in case of failure. If you keep both the networks physically the same, you might encounter some performance problems. Again, it is recommended to have two separate networks but you can always run your Ceph cluster with one physical network. These separate networks should have a bandwidth of a minimum of 1 Gbps. However, it's always good to have a 10 Gbps network based on your workload or performance needs. If you are designing a Ceph cluster that is going to scale up in the near future and might be responsible for a good amount of workload, starting with 10 Gbps physically separated networks for both data and cluster will be a wise choice as long as ROI and performance are concerned.

It is also advisable to have redundancy at each layer of your network configuration such as network controllers, ports, switches, and routers. The front-side data network or the public network provides interconnection between clients and the Ceph cluster. Every I/O operation between clients and the Ceph cluster will traverse from this interconnect. You should make sure that you have enough bandwidth per client. The second interconnect, which is your backend cluster network, is used internally by the Ceph OSD nodes. Since Ceph possesses distributed architecture, for every client write operation, data is replicated N times and stored across cluster. So for a single write operation, the Ceph cluster has to write $N*$ *the amount of one operation*. All of this replicated data travels to peer nodes through cluster interconnect network. In addition to initial write replication, cluster network is also used for data rebalancing and recovery. Hence it plays a vital role for deciding your cluster performance.

Considering your business needs, workload, and overall performance, you should always rethink your network configuration and can opt for a 40 Gbps separate interconnect for both public as well as cluster network. This can make significant improvements for extra large Ceph clusters of hundreds of terabytes in size. Most of the cluster deployment relies on Ethernet networks; however, InfiniBand is also gaining popularity as high-speed Ceph frontend and backend networks. As an optional case, based on your budget, you can even consider a separate network for management as well as an emergency network to provide additional layer of network redundancy to your production cluster.

MDS requirements

As compared to the Ceph monitor (MON) and OSD, Ceph MDS is a bit more resource hungry. They require significantly high CPU processing powers with quad core or more. Ceph MDS depends a lot on data caching; as they need to serve data quickly, they would require plenty of RAM. The higher the RAM for Ceph MDS, the better the performance of CephFS will be. If you have a high amount of workload with CephFS, you should keep Ceph MDS on dedicated physical machines with relatively more physical CPU cores and memory. A redundant network interface with 1 GB or more speed will work for most cases for Ceph MDS.

It is recommended that you use separate disks for operating system configured under RAID for MON, OSDs, and MDS. You should not use an operating system disk/partition for cluster data.

Setting up your VirtualBox environment – again

In *Chapter 2*, *Ceph Instant Deployment*, we created three VirtualBox virtual machines, which we used for deploying your first instant Ceph cluster. You should now destroy that Ceph cluster and uninstall Ceph packages or destroy those virtual machines. In this chapter, we will be installing Ceph again but in a different way. You should follow the *Creating a sandbox environment with VirtualBox* section in *Chapter 2*, *Ceph Instant Deployment* to recreate virtual machines that we will be using throughout this chapter.

Preparing your Ceph installation

Earlier in this chapter, we discussed some traits of selecting the right hardware depending on your needs and use case. You should make the necessary arrangements for your cluster hardware including networking components. The cluster hardware should be mounted, cabled, powered on, and should have valid networking between its nodes. Once you are ready with the hardware, the next task is to perform software arrangements for your cluster.

Ceph is a software-defined storage system, which runs on top of a Linux-based operating system. All the cluster nodes should be installed with Ceph-supported operating system. As of now, the valid operating system choice for running a Ceph cluster is RHEL, CentOS, Fedora, Ubuntu, Debian, and OpenSuse. You can check out more information for supported platforms on `http://ceph.com/docs/master/start/os-recommendations/`.

 It is recommended that you use the same OS distribution, release, and kernel version across all Ceph cluster nodes.

Getting the software

Ceph is an open source project; there are several ways to get its software from the Internet.

Getting packages

Getting packages over the Internet is one of the most used options for getting Ceph. There are again two different ways to get these packages:

- The first method is manually downloading Ceph and its related packages in the desired format. This would be a feasible option for you if due to security reasons, you do not have Internet access to your Ceph nodes. You can download Ceph and its dependencies on any of the machines in your network and copy them to each node and proceed with the Ceph installation.

  You can visit `http://ceph.com/rpm-<ceph-release-name>` for RPM-based packages and `http://ceph.com/debian-<ceph-release-name>` for Debian-based packages. The valid Ceph release names are Argonaut, Bobtail, Cuttlefish, Dumpling, Emperor, Firefly, and Giant.

  In addition to this, you will also require third-party libraries, which needs to be installed before Ceph packages. You can check out the list of additional binaries on Ceph documentation at `http://ceph.com/docs/master/install/get-packages/#download-packages`.

- The second method is using package management tools by adding Ceph package repositories to either **Advanced Package Tool (APT)** for Debian-based Linux distributions or **Yellowdog Updater Modifier (YUM)** for RHEL-based Linux distributions. For RPM packages, you should create a new repository file as /etc/yum.repos.d/ceph.repo. Add the following code in this file; replace {ceph-release} with valid Ceph release names and {distro} with Linux distribution such as el6 and rhel6. For more information on getting Ceph packages, check out http://ceph.com/docs/master/install/get-packages/.

```
[ceph]
name=Ceph packages for $basearch
baseurl=http://ceph.com/rpm-{ceph-
release}/{distro}/$basearch
enabled=1
gpgcheck=1
type=rpm-md
gpgkey=https://ceph.com/git/?p=ceph.git;a=blob_plain;f=keys
/release.asc

[ceph-noarch]
name=Ceph noarch packages
baseurl=http://ceph.com/rpm-{ceph-release}/{distro}/noarch
enabled=1
gpgcheck=1
type=rpm-md
gpgkey=https://ceph.com/git/?p=ceph.git;a=blob_plain;f=keys
/release.asc
[ceph-source]
name=Ceph source packages
baseurl=http://ceph.com/rpm-{ceph-release}/{distro}/SRPMS
enabled=0
gpgcheck=1
type=rpm-md
gpgkey=https://ceph.com/git/?p=ceph.git;a=blob_plain;f=keys
/release.asc
```

Getting Ceph tarballs

You can download Ceph source code from http://ceph.com/download/ and can compile and build a Ceph version from source.

Getting Ceph from GitHub

You can clone Ceph master branch source code from the online GitHub Ceph repository. To do this, you will require Git toolkit installed on your local machine. If you are a developer, this will be quite helpful for you to build Ceph and contribute to the open source project. If you need the latest development version of Ceph or a bug fix for a stable release, you can clone and build specific bug fixes before they are released officially.

Ceph cluster manual deployment

We can install Ceph either by using the ceph-deploy tool or manual deployment method. In this section, we will learn about the manual process of deploying Ceph.

Installing perquisites

Ceph requires additional third-party libraries. For RHEL-based Linux distributions, you can get additional packages from the EPEL repository. Perform the following steps to install Ceph:

1. Install the EPEL repository. Make sure the `baserul` parameter is enabled under the `/etc/yum.repos.d/epel.repo` file. The `baseurl` parameter defines the URL for extra Linux packages. Also make sure the `mirrorlist` parameter must be disabled (commented) under this file. Problems been observed during installation if the `mirrorlist` parameter is enabled under `epel.repo` file. Perform this step on all the three nodes.

   ```
   # rpm -Uvh http://dl.fedoraproject.org/pub/epel/6/x86_64/epel-
   release-6-8.noarch.rpm
   ```

2. Install third-party binaries required by Ceph:

   ```
   # yum install -y snappy leveldb gdisk python-argparse gperftools-
   libs
   ```

3. Create a Ceph repository file for Emperor release as shown in the following screenshot:

```
[root@ceph-node1 ~]# cat /etc/yum.repos.d/ceph.repo
[ceph]
name=Ceph packages for $basearch
baseurl=http://ceph.com/rpm-emperor/el6/$basearch
enabled=1
gpgcheck=1
type=rpm-md
gpgkey=https://ceph.com/git/?p=ceph.git;a=blob_plain;f=keys/release.asc

[ceph-noarch]
name=Ceph noarch packages
baseurl=http://ceph.com/rpm-emperor/el6/noarch
enabled=1
gpgcheck=1
type=rpm-md
gpgkey=https://ceph.com/git/?p=ceph.git;a=blob_plain;f=keys/release.asc

[ceph-source]
name=Ceph source packages
baseurl=http://ceph.com/rpm-emperor/el6/SRPMS
enabled=0
gpgcheck=1
type=rpm-md
gpgkey=https://ceph.com/git/?p=ceph.git;a=blob_plain;f=keys/release.asc
[root@ceph-node1 ~]#
```

4. Install Ceph packages:

   ```
   yum install ceph -y --disablerepo=epel
   ```

   In this command, we are adding an option --disablerepo=epel, because
   we do not want to install Ceph packages provided by EPEL as EPEL installs
   the latest version of Ceph, which is Firefly. We want to install Emperor,
   hence we will disable epel repo so that Ceph should be installed using ceph.
   repo file.

5. Once the packages are installed, verify whether they installed or not (optional):

   ```
   # rpm -qa | egrep -i "ceph|rados|rbd"
   ```

   The preceding command will give you an output similar to the one shown in
   the following screenshot:

   ```
   [root@ceph-node1 ~]# rpm -qa | egrep -i "ceph|rados|rbd"
   ceph-0.72.2-0.el6.x86_64
   libcephfs1-0.72.2-0.el6.x86_64
   python-ceph-0.72.2-0.el6.x86_64
   librbd1-0.72.2-0.el6.x86_64
   librados2-0.72.2-0.el6.x86_64
   [root@ceph-node1 ~]#
   ```

6. Repeat steps 1 to 5 for other two Ceph nodes, that is, ceph-node2 and
   ceph-node3.

Deploying the Ceph cluster

We have now installed Ceph packages on all the nodes and are good to go with Ceph manual deployment. The manual deployment process is mainly for developers who are involved in developing Ceph deployment scripts for configuration management tools such as Ansible, Chef, and Puppet to know the deployment flow. As an administrator, you might hardly use manual deployment process, but it's an add-on to your Ceph expertise. Most of the production deployment of Ceph is based on ceph-deploy tool. Our current deployment setup looks like this:

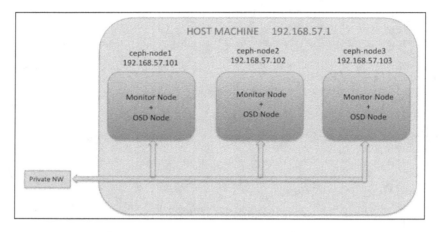

Deploying monitors

A Ceph storage cluster requires at least one monitor node to operate. However, it's always recommended that you have an odd number of monitor nodes more than one. In this section, we will learn to deploy Ceph monitor nodes:

1. Create a directory for Ceph and create your Ceph cluster configuration file:

   ```
   # mkdir /etc/ceph
   ```

   ```
   # touch /etc/ceph/ceph.conf
   ```

2. Generate a FSID for your Ceph cluster:

   ```
   # uuidgen
   ```

3. Create your cluster configuration file; by default the cluster name will be ceph. The configuration file name will be /etc/ceph/ceph.conf. You should use the output of the uuidgen command from the preceding step as an fsid parameter in the configuration file.

```
[root@ceph-node1 ceph]# cat /etc/ceph/ceph.conf
[global]
fsid = 07a92ca3-347e-43db-87ee-e0a0a9f89e97
public network = 192.168.57.0/24

osd pool default min size = 1
osd pool default pg num = 128
osd pool default pgp num = 128
osd journal size = 1024

[mon]
mon initial members = ceph-node1
mon host = ceph-node1,ceph-node2,ceph-node3
mon addr = 192.168.57.101,192.158.57.102,192.168.57.103

[mon.ceph-node1]
host = ceph-node1
mon addr = 192.168.57.101

[root@ceph-node1 ceph]#
```

4. Create a keyring for your cluster and generate a monitor secret key as follows:

   ```
   # ceph-authtool --create-keyring /tmp/ceph.mon.keyring --gen-key -n mon. --cap mon 'allow *'
   ```

5. Create a client.admin user and add the user to the keyring:

   ```
   # ceph-authtool --create-keyring /etc/ceph/ceph.client.admin.keyring --gen-key -n client.admin --set-uid=0 --cap mon 'allow *' --cap osd 'allow *' --cap mds 'allow'
   ```

6. Add the client.admin key to ceph.mon.keyring:

   ```
   # ceph-authtool /tmp/ceph.mon.keyring --import-keyring /etc/ceph/ceph.client.admin.keyring
   ```

   The following screenshot shows these preceding commands in action:

```
[root@ceph-node1 ceph]# ceph-authtool --create-keyring /tmp/ceph.mon.keyring --gen-key -n mon. --cap mon 'allow *'
creating /tmp/ceph.mon.keyring
[root@ceph-node1 ceph]#
[root@ceph-node1 ceph]# ceph-authtool --create-keyring /etc/ceph/ceph.client.admin.keyring --gen-key -n client.admi
n --set-uid=0 --cap mon 'allow *' --cap osd 'allow *' --cap mds 'allow'
creating /etc/ceph/ceph.client.admin.keyring
[root@ceph-node1 ceph]#
[root@ceph-node1 ceph]# ceph-authtool /tmp/ceph.mon.keyring --import-keyring /etc/ceph/ceph.client.admin.keyring
importing contents of /etc/ceph/ceph.client.admin.keyring into /tmp/ceph.mon.keyring
[root@ceph-node1 ceph]#
```

7. Generate a monitor map for your first monitor with the following syntax:

```
monmaptool --create --add {hostname} {ip-address} --fsid
{uuid} /tmp/monmap
```

Have a look at the following example:

```
# monmaptool --create --add ceph-node1 192.168.57.101 --fsid
07a92ca3-347e-43db-87ee-e0a0a9f89e97 /tmp/monmap
```

```
[root@ceph-node1 ceph]# monmaptool --create --add ceph-node1 192.168.57.101 --fsid 07a92ca3-347e-43db-87ee-e0a0a9f89e97 /tmp/monmap
monmaptool: monmap file /tmp/monmap
monmaptool: set fsid to 07a92ca3-347e-43db-87ee-e0a0a9f89e97
monmaptool: writing epoch 0 to /tmp/monmap (1 monitors)
[root@ceph-node1 ceph]#
```

8. Create directories for the monitor as /path/cluster_name-monitor_node:

```
# mkdir /var/lib/ceph/mon/ceph-ceph-node1
```

9. Populate the first monitor daemon:

```
# ceph-mon --mkfs -i ceph-node1 --monmap /tmp/monmap --keyring
/tmp/ceph.mon.keyring
```

10. Start monitor service as shown in the following screenshot:

```
[root@ceph-node1 ceph]# ceph-mon --mkfs -i ceph-node1 --monmap /tmp/monmap --keyring /tmp/ceph.mon.keyring
ceph-mon: set fsid to 07a92ca3-347e-43db-87ee-e0a0a9f89e97
ceph-mon: created monfs at /var/lib/ceph/mon/ceph-ceph-node1 for mon.ceph-node1
[root@ceph-node1 ceph]#
[root@ceph-node1 ceph]# service ceph start
=== mon.ceph-node1 ===
Starting Ceph mon.ceph-node1 on ceph-node1...
Starting ceph-create-keys on ceph-node1...
[root@ceph-node1 ceph]#
```

11. Check your cluster status and check for default pools:

```
[root@ceph-node1 ceph]#
[root@ceph-node1 ceph]# ceph status
    cluster 07a92ca3-347e-43db-87ee-e0a0a9f89e97
     health HEALTH_ERR 192 pgs stuck inactive; 192 pgs stuck unclean; no osds
     monmap e1: 1 mons at {ceph-node1=192.168.57.101:6789/0}, election epoch 1, quorum 0 ceph-node1
     osdmap e1: 0 osds: 0 up, 0 in
      pgmap v2: 192 pgs, 3 pools, 0 bytes data, 0 objects
            0 kB used, 0 kB / 0 kB avail
                 192 creating

[root@ceph-node1 ceph]#
[root@ceph-node1 ceph]# ceph osd lspools
0 data,1 metadata,2 rbd,
[root@ceph-node1 ceph]#
```

You should check for monitor map. You will find that your first node is configured correctly as a monitor node. Do not worry about cluster health at this time. We will need to add a few OSDs to make your cluster healthy.

Creating OSDs

Once you have set up your initial monitor, you should add some OSDs to your cluster. The following are the steps to do so:

1. Check available disks for your system. In our test setup, each virtual machine has three disks (ideally, sdb, sdc, and sdd):

   ```
   # ceph-disk list
   ```

2. Ceph OSD works on **GUID Partition Table (GPT)**. If the OSD is not already labeled with GPT, you should change the partition label from any other type to GPT:

   ```
   # parted /dev/sdb mklabel GPT
   ```

```
[root@ceph-node1 ~]# parted /dev/sdb mklabel GPT
Warning: The existing disk label on /dev/sdb will be destroyed and all data on this disk will be lost. Do you want to continue?
Yes/No? yes
Information: You may need to update /etc/fstab.

[root@ceph-node1 ~]#
```

3. Perform GPT type partition labeling for other disks as well:

   ```
   # parted /dev/sdc mklabel GPT
   ```

   ```
   # parted /dev/sdd mklabel GPT
   ```

4. Prepare the OSD disk by providing cluster and filesystem information; use the following syntax:

   ```
   ceph-disk prepare --cluster {cluster-name} --cluster-uuid
   {fsid} --fs-type {ext4|xfs|btrfs} {data-path} [{journal-
   path}]
   ```

   Have a look at the following example:

   ```
   # ceph-disk prepare --cluster ceph --cluster-uuid 07a92ca3-
   347e-43db-87ee-e0a0a9f89e97 --fs-type xfs /dev/sdb
   ```

The following screenshot shows the output of the previous command:

```
[root@ceph-node1 ~]# ceph-disk prepare --cluster ceph --cluster-uuid 07a92ca3-347e-43db-87ee-e0a0a9f89e97 --fs-type xfs /dev/sdb
INFO:ceph-disk:Will colocate journal with data on /dev/sdb
Setting name!
partNum is 1
REALLY setting name!
The operation has completed successfully.
Setting name!
partNum is 0
REALLY setting name!
The operation has completed successfully.
meta-data=/dev/sdb1              isize=2048   agcount=4, agsize=589759 blks
         =                       sectsz=512   attr=2, projid32bit=0
data     =                       bsize=4096   blocks=2359035, imaxpct=25
         =                       sunit=0      swidth=0 blks
naming   =version 2              bsize=4096   ascii-ci=0
log      =internal log           bsize=4096   blocks=2560, version=2
         =                       sectsz=512   sunit=0 blks, lazy-count=1
realtime =none                   extsz=4096   blocks=0, rtextents=0
The operation has completed successfully.
[root@ceph-node1 ~]#
```

5. Prepare the rest of the disks as follows:

   ```
   # ceph-disk prepare --cluster ceph --cluster-uuid 07a92ca3-
   347e-43db-87ee-e0a0a9f89e97 --fs-type xfs /dev/sdc
   ```

   ```
   # ceph-disk prepare --cluster ceph --cluster-uuid 07a92ca3-
   347e-43db-87ee-e0a0a9f89e97 --fs-type xfs /dev/sdd
   ```

6. Finally, activate the OSD:

   ```
   # ceph-disk activate /dev/sdb1
   ```

   Have look at the following screenshot:

   ```
   [root@ceph-node1 ~]# ceph-disk activate /dev/sdb1
   INFO:ceph-disk:ceph osd.0 already mounted in position; unmounting ours.
   === osd.0 ===
   Starting Ceph osd.0 on ceph-node1...already running
   [root@ceph-node1 ~]#
   [root@ceph-node1 ~]#
   [root@ceph-node1 ~]#
   [root@ceph-node1 ~]# service ceph status osd
   === osd.0 ===
   osd.0: running {"version":"0.72.2"}
   [root@ceph-node1 ~]#
   ```

7. Activate the rest of the disks:

   ```
   # ceph-disk activate /dev/sdc1
   ```

   ```
   # ceph-disk activate /dev/sdd1
   ```

8. Check the status of your cluster. You will see three OSDs in UP and IN states:

```
[root@ceph-node1 ~]# ceph -s
    cluster 07a92ca3-347e-43db-87ee-e0a0a9f89e97
    health HEALTH_WARN 63 pgs degraded; 192 pgs stuck unclean
    monmap e1: 1 mons at {ceph-node1=192.168.57.101:6789/0}, election epoch 1, quorum 0 ceph-node1
    osdmap e16: 3 osds: 3 up, 3 in
     pgmap v26: 192 pgs, 3 pools, 0 bytes data, 0 objects
           106 MB used, 27508 MB / 27614 MB avail
                52 active
                77 active+remapped
                63 active+degraded

[root@ceph-node1 ~]#
```

9. Copy the `ceph.conf` and `ceph.client.admin.keyring` files from ceph-node1 to ceph-node2 and ceph node3 using the following commands; this will allow ceph-node2 and ceph-node3 to issue cluster commands:

    ```
    # scp /etc/ceph/ceph.* ceph-node2:/etc/ceph
    ```

    ```
    # scp /etc/ceph/ceph.* ceph-node3:/etc/ceph
    ```

10. Even after copying `ceph.conf` and `ceph.client.admin.keyring` to ceph-node2 and ceph-node3, if you are not able to issue cluster commands from ceph-node2 and ceph-node3 and are getting an error such as `Error connecting to cluster`, you should adjust the firewall rules for the `ceph-monitor` daemons on all three nodes or disable the firewall on all three nodes.

Scaling up your cluster

Scaling up the Ceph cluster is one of the important tasks for the Ceph administrator. This includes adding more monitor and OSD nodes to your cluster. We recommend that you use an odd number of monitor nodes for high availability and quorum maintenance; however, this is not mandatory. Scaling up and scaling down operation for monitor and OSD nodes are absolute online operations and does not cost downtime. In our test deployment, we have a single node, ceph-node1, which acts as monitor and OSD nodes. Let's now add two more monitors to our Ceph cluster.

Adding monitors

Proceed with the following steps:

1. Log in to ceph-node2 and create directories:

    ```
    # mkdir -p /var/lib/ceph/mon/ceph-ceph-node2 /tmp/ceph-node2
    ```

2. Edit the /etc/ceph/ceph.conf file and add the new monitor information under [mon] section:

    ```
    [mon.ceph-node2]
    mon_addr = 192.168.57.102:6789
    host = ceph-node2
    ```

3. Extract keyring information from the Ceph cluster:

    ```
    # ceph auth get mon. -o /tmp/ceph-node2/monkeyring
    ```

    ```
    [root@ceph-node2 ceph]# mkdir -p /var/lib/ceph/mon/ceph-ceph-node2 /tmp/ceph-node2
    [root@ceph-node2 ceph]#
    [root@ceph-node2 ceph]#
    [root@ceph-node2 ceph]#
    [root@ceph-node2 ceph]# ceph auth get mon. -o /tmp/ceph-node2/monkeyring
    exported keyring for mon.
    [root@ceph-node2 ceph]#
    ```

4. Retrieve the monitor map from the Ceph cluster:

    ```
    # ceph mon getmap -o /tmp/ceph-node2/monmap
    ```

5. Build a fresh monitor, fs, using key and existing monmap:

    ```
    # ceph-mon -i ceph-node2 --mkfs --monmap /tmp/ceph-node2/monmap --keyring /tmp/ceph-node2/monkeyring
    ```

6. Add the new monitor to the cluster:

    ```
    # ceph mon add ceph-node2 192.168.57.102:6789
    ```

    ```
    [root@ceph-node2 ceph]# ceph mon getmap -o /tmp/ceph-node2/monmap
    got latest monmap
    [root@ceph-node2 ceph]#
    [root@ceph-node2 ceph]# ceph-mon -i ceph-node2 --mkfs --monmap /tmp/ceph-node2/monmap --keyring /tmp/ceph-node2/monkeyring
    ceph-mon: set fsid to 07a92ca3-347e-43db-87ee-e0a0a9f89e97
    ceph-mon: created monfs at /var/lib/ceph/mon/ceph-ceph-node2 for mon.ceph-node2
    [root@ceph-node2 ceph]#
    [root@ceph-node2 ceph]#
    [root@ceph-node2 ceph]#
    [root@ceph-node2 ceph]#
    [root@ceph-node2 ceph]# ceph mon add ceph-node2 192.168.57.102:6789

    added mon.ceph-node2 at 192.168.57.102:6789/0
    [root@ceph-node2 ceph]#
    ```

7. Once the monitor is added, check the cluster status. You will notice that we now have two monitors in our Ceph cluster. You can ignore the *clock skew* warning as of now, or you can configure NTP on all your nodes so that they can be synced. We have already discussed NTP configuration in the *Scaling up your Ceph cluster – monitor and OSD addition* section of *Chapter 2, Ceph Instant Deployment*.

```
[root@ceph-node2 ceph]# ceph -s
    cluster 07a92ca3-347e-43db-87ee-e0a0a9f89e97
    health HEALTH_WARN 63 pgs degraded; 192 pgs stuck unclean; clock skew detected on mon.ceph-node2
    monmap e2: 2 mons at {ceph-node1=192.168.57.101:6789/0,ceph-node2=192.168.57.102:6789/0}, election epoch 2, quorum 0,1 ceph-node1,ceph-nod
e2
    osdmap e27: 3 osds: 3 up, 3 in
    pgmap v43: 192 pgs, 3 pools, 0 bytes data, 0 objects
            104 MB used, 27510 MB / 27614 MB avail
                87 active+remapped
                41 active+degraded
                42 active+replay+remapped
                22 active+replay+degraded
```

8. Repeat the same steps for adding ceph-node3 as your third monitor. Once you add your third monitor, check your cluster status and you will notice the third monitor in the Ceph cluster:

```
[root@ceph-node3 ceph]# ceph -s
    cluster 07a92ca3-347e-43db-87ee-e0a0a9f89e97
    health HEALTH_WARN 63 pgs degraded; 192 pgs stuck unclean; 1 mons down, quorum 0,1 ceph-node1,ceph-node2; clock skew detected on mon.ceph-
node2
    monmap e3: 3 mons at {ceph-node1=192.168.57.101:6789/0,ceph-node2=192.168.57.102:6789/0,ceph-node3=192.168.57.103:6789/0}, election epoch
4, quorum 0,1 ceph-node1,ceph-node2
    osdmap e27: 3 osds: 3 up, 3 in
    pgmap v43: 192 pgs, 3 pools, 0 bytes data, 0 objects
            104 MB used, 27510 MB / 27614 MB avail
                87 active+remapped
                41 active+degraded
                42 active+replay+remapped
                22 active+replay+degraded

[root@ceph-node3 ceph]#
```

Adding OSDs

It is easy to scale up your cluster by adding OSDs on the fly. Earlier in this chapter, we learned to create OSD; this process is similar to scaling up your cluster for adding more OSDs. Log in to the node, which needs its disks to be added to cluster and perform the following operations:

1. List the available disks:

   ```
   # ceph-disk list
   ```

2. Label the disk with GPT:

   ```
   # parted /dev/sdb mklabel GPT
   # parted /dev/sdc mklabel GPT
   # parted /dev/sdd mklabel GPT
   ```

3. Prepare the disk with the required filesystem and instruct it to connect to the cluster by providing the cluster uuid:

   ```
   # ceph-disk prepare --cluster ceph --cluster-uuid 07a92ca3-
   347e-43db-87ee-e0a0a9f89e97 --fs-type xfs /dev/sdb

   # ceph-disk prepare --cluster ceph --cluster-uuid 07a92ca3-
   347e-43db-87ee-e0a0a9f89e97 --fs-type xfs /dev/sdc

   # ceph-disk prepare --cluster ceph --cluster-uuid 07a92ca3-
   347e-43db-87ee-e0a0a9f89e97 --fs-type xfs /dev/sdd
   ```

4. Activate the disk so that Ceph can start OSD services and help OSD to join the cluster:

```
# ceph-disk activate /dev/sdb1
# ceph-disk activate /dev/sdc1
# ceph-disk activate /dev/sdd1
```

5. Repeat these steps for all other nodes for which you want to add their disk to cluster. Finally, check your cluster status; you will notice the disks will be in UP and IN states:

```
[root@ceph-node1 ceph]# ceph -s
    cluster 07a92ca3-347e-43db-87ee-e0a0a9f89e97
     health HEALTH_OK
     monmap e3: 3 mons at {ceph-node1=192.168.57.101:6789/0,ceph-node2=192.168.57.102:6789/0,ceph-node3=192.168.57.103:6789/0}, election epoch
668, quorum 0,1,2 ceph-node1,ceph-node2,ceph-node3
     osdmap e62: 9 osds: 9 up, 9 in
      pgmap v112: 192 pgs, 3 pools, 0 bytes data, 0 objects
            338 MB used, 78409 MB / 78748 MB avail
                 192 active+clean

[root@ceph-node1 ceph]#
```

6. Check your cluster OSD tree; this will give you information about OSD and its physical node:

```
[root@ceph-node1 ceph]# ceph osd tree
# id    weight  type name           up/down reweight
-1      0.08995 root default
-2      0.02998         host ceph-node1
0       0.009995                        osd.0   up      1
1       0.009995                        osd.1   up      1
2       0.009995                        osd.2   up      1
-3      0.02998         host ceph-node2
3       0.009995                        osd.3   up      1
5       0.009995                        osd.5   up      1
4       0.009995                        osd.4   up      1
-4      0.02998         host ceph-node3
6       0.009995                        osd.6   up      1
7       0.009995                        osd.7   up      1
8       0.009995                        osd.8   up      1

[root@ceph-node1 ceph]#
```

Ceph cluster deployment using the ceph-deploy tool

Ceph comes with a vey powerful deployment tool known as **ceph-deploy**. The ceph-deploy tool relies on SSH for deploying Ceph software on cluster nodes, so it has the basic requirement that node should be installed with OS and it should be reachable on the network. The ceph-deploy tool does not demand additional system resources and it can perform well on a regular workstation machine that should have access to cluster nodes.

You can also consider using any of your monitor nodes as a ceph-deploy node. The ceph-deploy tool makes Ceph deployment easy with initial default configuration that can be modified later based on your use case. The ceph-deploy tool provides features such as installing Ceph packages, cluster creation, monitor and OSD addition, Ceph key management, MDS creation, configuring admin hosts, and tearing down the Ceph cluster.

Earlier in this book, in *Chapter 2, Ceph Instant Deployment*, we have seen how to deploy a Ceph cluster using the ceph-deploy tool. We will now briefly go through steps for deploying the Ceph cluster using ceph-deploy:

1. Set up an SSH-based login to all your ceph nodes. If possible, make them passwordless logins. You should always follow security practices of your environments while setting up passwordless SSH logins.

2. Set up the Ceph software repository file for your Linux package manager. This repository file should be present on all nodes in the cluster.

3. Install ceph-deploy on any one-cluster node. This is typically an admin node that you should use for Ceph management.

4. Create a new cluster, the default cluster name would be ceph:

   ```
   # ceph-deploy new ceph-node1
   ```

5. Install Ceph software on cluster nodes:

   ```
   # ceph-deploy install ceph-node1 ceph-node2 ceph-node3
   ```

    By default, ceph-deploy will install the latest release of Ceph, if you want to install any specific release of Ceph, use the --release {Ceph-release-name} option with ceph-deploy.

6. Create initial monitors and gather the keys:

   ```
   # ceph-deploy mon create ceph-node1
   ```
   ```
   # ceph-deploy gatherkeys ceph-node1
   ```

   Starting from ceph-deploy Version 1.1.3, you no longer require multiple commands for creating initial monitors and gathering keys. This can be achieved in one step using the following command. Before running this command, initial monitors should be configured in your ceph.conf file.

   ```
   # ceph-deploy mon create-initial
   ```

7. For a high availability, set up more monitor machines. An odd number of monitors are recommended. Make sure you add firewall rules for monitor ports 6789 so that they can connect to each other. If you are performing this just for testing, you can consider disabling firewall.

```
# ceph-deploy mon create ceph-node2

# ceph-deploy mon create ceph-node3
```

8. If you are using disks that have old filesystem, clear the partitions so that it can be used with Ceph. This operation will destroy all the data on disk.

```
# ceph-deploy disk zap ceph-node1:sdb ceph-node1:sdc ceph-node1:sdd
```

Create OSDs for your Ceph cluster. Repeat the step to add more OSDs. To achieve a clean state for your Ceph cluster, you should add OSDs on machines that are physically separated.

```
# ceph-deploy osd create ceph-node1:sdb ceph-node1:sdc ceph-node1:sdd
```

9. Finally, check the status of your Ceph cluster. It should be healthy.

The ceph-deploy tool is a stable and amazing tool for easy Ceph cluster deployment. It is rapidly getting developed with new features and bug fixes. Now, most of the Ceph clusters are getting deployments using the ceph-deploy tool.

Upgrading your Ceph cluster

Upgrading your Ceph cluster software version is relatively simple. You just need to update the Ceph package followed by a service restart and you are done. The upgradation process is sequential and usually does not require any downtime for your storage services if you have configured your cluster in high availability, that is, with multiple OSDs, monitors, MDS, and RADOSGW. As a general practice, you should plan your cluster upgradation during nonpeak hours. The upgradation process upgrades each Ceph daemon one by one. The recommended upgradation sequence for a Ceph cluster is as follows:

1. Monitor
2. OSD
3. Metadata Server (MDS)
4. RADOS gateway

You should upgrade all daemons of a specific type and then proceed for upgradation of the next type. For example, if your cluster contains three monitor nodes, 100 OSDS, 2 MDS, and a RADOSGW. You should first upgrade all your monitor nodes one by one, followed by upgrading all OSD nodes one by one, then MDS, and then RADOSGW. This is to keep all specific types of daemons on the same release level.

Before proceeding with upgradation of Ceph daemons, please read the release notes and any other upgradation-related information on Ceph official documentation. Once you upgrade a daemon, you cannot downgrade it.

Warning

Before upgradation, you should always check the Ceph client requirements such as the kernel version or any other relevant components.

Upgrading a monitor

Proceed with the following steps to upgrade a monitor:

1. Check the current version of your Ceph daemons:

```
[root@ceph-node1 ~]# service ceph status
=== osd.1 ===
osd.1: running {"version":"0.72.2"}
=== osd.0 ===
osd.0: running {"version":"0.72.2"}
=== osd.2 ===
osd.2: running {"version":"0.72.2"}
=== mon.ceph-node1 ===
mon.ceph-node1: running {"version":"0.72.2"}
[root@ceph-node1 ~]#
```

Since our test cluster setup has MON and OSD daemons running on the same machine, upgrading Ceph software binaries to the Firefly release (0.80) will result in upgrading MON and OSD daemons in one step. However, in the production deployment of Ceph, upgradation should take place one by one. Otherwise, you might face problems.

2. Upgrade your Ceph repositories to the targeted Firefly repositories. Usually, you just need to update your new Ceph release name in the /etc/yum. repos.d/ceph.repo file that is already present:

```
[root@ceph-node1 ~]# cat /etc/yum.repos.d/ceph.repo
[ceph]
name=Ceph packages for $basearch
baseurl=http://ceph.com/rpm-firefly/el6/$basearch
enabled=1
gpgcheck=1
type=rpm-md
gpgkey=https://ceph.com/git/?p=ceph.git;a=blob_plain;f=keys/release.asc

[ceph-noarch]
name=Ceph noarch packages
baseurl=http://ceph.com/rpm-firefly/el6/noarch
enabled=1
gpgcheck=1
type=rpm-md
gpgkey=https://ceph.com/git/?p=ceph.git;a=blob_plain;f=keys/release.asc

[ceph-source]
name=Ceph source packages
baseurl=http://ceph.com/rpm-firefly/el6/SRPMS
enabled=0
gpgcheck=1
type=rpm-md
gpgkey=https://ceph.com/git/?p=ceph.git;a=blob_plain;f=keys/release.asc
[root@ceph-node1 ~]#
```

3. Update your Ceph software:

```
# yum update ceph
```

4. Once the Ceph software binaries are updated, you should restart the Ceph monitor daemons to have the changes take effect:

```
# service ceph restart mon
```

5. Check the monitor daemon version; it should be updated:

```
# service ceph status mon
```

```
[root@ceph-node1 ceph]# service ceph restart mon
=== mon.ceph-node1 ===
=== mon.ceph-node1 ===
Stopping Ceph mon.ceph-node1 on ceph-node1...kill 2106...done
=== mon.ceph-node1 ===
Starting Ceph mon.ceph-node1 on ceph-node1...
Starting ceph-create-keys on ceph-node1...
[root@ceph-node1 ceph]#
[root@ceph-node1 ceph]# service ceph status mon
=== mon.ceph-node1 ===
mon.ceph-node1: running {"version":"0.80.1"}
[root@ceph-node1 ceph]#
```

6. Check the monitor stats:

```
# ceph mon stat
```

7. Repeat these steps for other monitor nodes in your cluster. Make sure all the monitor nodes are on the same Ceph release before proceeding to OSD, MDS, or RGW upgradation.

Upgrading OSDs

Proceed with the following steps to upgrade OSDs:

1. Similar to the monitor upgradation process, upgrade your Ceph repositories to the targeted Firefly repositories.

2. Perform the Ceph software upgradation:

```
# yum update ceph
```

3. Once the Ceph software is successfully updated, restart the OSD daemons:

```
# service ceph restart osd
```

4. Check the OSD status; you should discover the updated OSD version:

```
# service ceph status osd
```

```
[root@ceph-node1 ceph]# service ceph status osd
=== osd.1 ===
osd.1: running {"version":"0.80.1"}
=== osd.0 ===
osd.0: running {"version":"0.80.1"}
=== osd.2 ===
osd.2: running {"version":"0.80.1"}
[root@ceph-node1 ceph]#
```

5. Repeat these steps for other OSD nodes in your cluster. Make sure all OSDs of your cluster are on the same Ceph release.

Summary

Planning your storage needs is extremely important for your Ceph cluster. The planning phase is something that defines your Ceph clusters capacity, performance, and fault tolerance level. You know your requirements, storage needs, and workload better than anyone else does; so, you should decide your own Ceph hardware and software configuration, keeping your needs in mind. From the deployment context, Ceph provides both the manual and automated ways of deployment. The manual deployment procedure is mostly used by configuration management tools such as Puppet, Ansible, and Chef.

The manual deployment process helps these tools to implement a number of checks during deployment, thus improving flexibility. The automated deployment method is to use ceph-deploy tool, which is relatively simple and provides easy-to-use command sets for various cluster-related activities. The Ceph storage cluster can scale up on the fly; also, upgradation from one release to another is extremely simple with no services getting impacted.

6
Storage Provisioning with Ceph

In this chapter, we will cover the following topics:

- Setting up a Ceph block device
- Setting up the Ceph filesystem
- Setting up Ceph object storage using a RADOS gateway
- Configuring S3 and Swift with a Ceph RADOS gateway

Storage provisioning is the primary and most important task of a storage system administrator. It is the process of assigning storage space or capacity to both physical and virtual servers in the form of blocks, files, or objects. A typical computer system and servers come with a limited local storage capacity that is not enough for your data storage needs. Storage solutions such as Ceph provide virtually unlimited storage capacity to these servers, making them capable to store all your data and making sure you do not run out of space.

In addition to providing extra storage, there are numerous benefits of having a centralized storage system.

Ceph can provision storage capacity in a unified way, which includes block storage, filesystem, and object storage. Depending on your use case, you can select one or more storage solutions as shown in the following diagram. Now, let's discuss these storage types in detail and implement them on our test cluster.

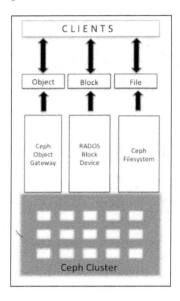

The RADOS block device

The **RADOS block device (RBD)**—formerly known as the Ceph block device—provides block-based persistent storage to Ceph clients, which they use as an additional disk. The client has the flexibility to use the disk as they require, either as a raw device or by formatting it with a filesystem followed by mounting it. A RADOS block device makes use of the librbd library and stores blocks of data in a sequential form striped over multiple OSDs in a Ceph cluster. RBD is backed by the RADOS layer of Ceph, and thus, every block device is spread over multiple Ceph nodes, delivering high performance and excellent reliability. RBD is rich with enterprise features such as thin provisioning, dynamically resizable, snapshots, copy-on-write, and caching, among others. The RBD protocol is fully supported with Linux as a mainline kernel driver; it also supports various virtualization platforms such as KVM, Qemu, and libvirt, allowing virtual machines to take advantage of a Ceph block device. All these features make RBD an ideal candidate for cloud platforms such as OpenStack and CloudStack. We will now learn how to create a Ceph block device and make use of it:

1. To create a Ceph block device, log in to any of the Ceph monitor nodes, or to an admin host that has admin access to a Ceph cluster. You can also create Ceph RBD from any client node that is configured as a Ceph client. For security reasons, you should not store Ceph admin keys on multiple nodes other than Ceph nodes and admin hosts.

2. The following command will create a RADOS block device named `ceph-client1-rbd1` of size 10240 MB:

   ```
   # rbd create ceph-client1-rbd1 --size 10240
   ```

3. To list rbd images, issue the following command:

   ```
   # rbd ls
   ```

4. To check details of an rbd image, use the following command:

   ```
   # rbd --image ceph-client1-rbd1 info
   ```

   Have a look at the following screenshot to see the preceding command in action:

   ```
   [root@ceph-node1 ~]# rbd --image ceph-client1-rbd1 info
   rbd image 'ceph-client1-rbd1':
           size 10240 MB in 2560 objects
           order 22 (4096 kB objects)
           block_name_prefix: rb.0.1d63.2ae8944a
           format: 1
   [root@ceph-node1 ~]#
   ```

5. By default, RBD images are created under the `rbd` pool of the Ceph cluster. You can specify other pools by using the `-p` parameter with the `rbd` command. The following command will give you the same output as the last command, but we manually specify the pool name using the `-p` parameter here. Similarly, you can create RBD images on other pools using the `-p` parameter:

   ```
   # rbd --image ceph-client1-rbd1 info -p rbd
   ```

Setting up your first Ceph client

Ceph is a storage system; to store your data on a Ceph cluster, you will require a client machine. Once storage space is provisioned from the Ceph cluster, the client maps or mounts a Ceph block or filesystem and allows us to store data on to the Ceph cluster. For object storage, clients have HTTP access to Ceph clusters to store data. A typical production-class Ceph cluster consists of two different networks, frontend network and backend network, also known as public network and cluster network, respectively.

The frontend network is the client network by which Ceph serves data to its clients. All Ceph clients interact with clusters using the frontend network. Clients do not have access to the backend network, and Ceph mainly uses the backend network for its replication and recovery .We will now set up our first Ceph client virtual machine that we will use throughout this book. During the setup process, we will create a new client virtual machine as we did in *Chapter 2, Ceph Instant Deployment*:

1. Create a new VirtualBox virtual machine for the Ceph client:

   ```
   # VboxManage createvm --name ceph-client1 --ostype RedHat_64 -
   -register
   ```

   ```
   # VBoxManage modifyvm ceph-client1 --memory 1024 --nic1 nat  -
   -nic2 hostonly --hostonlyadapter2 vboxnet1
   ```

   ```
   # VBoxManage storagectl ceph-client1 --name "IDE Controller" -
   -add ide --controller PIIX4 --hostiocache on --bootable on
   ```

   ```
   # VBoxManage storageattach ceph-client1 --storagectl "IDE
   Controller" --type dvddrive --port 0 --device 0 --medium
   /downloads/CentOS-6.4-x86_64-bin-DVD1.iso
   ```

   ```
   # VBoxManage storagectl ceph-client1 --name "SATA Controller"
   --add sata --controller IntelAHCI --hostiocache on --bootable
   on
   ```

   ```
   # VBoxManage createhd --filename OS-ceph-client1.vdi --size 10240
   ```

   ```
   # VBoxManage storageattach ceph-client1 --storagectl "SATA
   Controller" --port 0 --device 0 --type hdd --medium OS-ceph-
   client1.vdi
   ```

   ```
   # VBoxManage startvm ceph-client1 --type gui
   ```

2. Once the virtual machine is created and started, install the CentOS operating system by following the OS installation documentation at https://access.redhat.com/site/documentation/en-US/Red_Hat_Enterprise_Linux/6/html/Installation_Guide/index.html. During the installation process, provide the hostname as ceph-client1.

3. Once you have successfully installed the operating system, edit the network configuration of the machine as stated in the following steps and restart network services:

   ° Edit the /etc/sysconfig/network-scripts/ifcfg-eth0 file and add the following:

   ```
   ONBOOT=yes
   BOOTPROTO=dhcp
   ```

     °   Edit the `/etc/sysconfig/network-scripts/ifcfg-eth1` file and add the following:

```
ONBOOT=yes
BOOTPROTO=static
IPADDR=192.168.57.200
NETMASK=255.255.255.0
```

     °   Edit the `/etc/hosts` file and add the following:

```
192.168.57.101 ceph-node1
192.168.57.102 ceph-node2
192.168.57.103 ceph-node3
192.168.57.200 ceph-client1
```

Mapping the RADOS block device

Earlier in this chapter, we created an RBD image on a Ceph cluster; in order to use this block device image, we need to map it to the client machine. Let's see how the mapping operation works.

Ceph support has been added to Linux kernel from Version 2.6.32. For client machines that need native access to Ceph block devices and filesystems, it is recommended that they use Linux kernel release 2.6.34 and later.

Check the Linux kernel version and RBD support using the `modprobe` command. Since this client runs on an older release of Linux kernel, it does not support Ceph natively.

 # uname -r

 # modprobe rbd

Have a look at the following screenshot:

```
[root@ceph-client1 ~]# uname -r
2.6.32-358.el6.x86_64
[root@ceph-client1 ~]#
[root@ceph-client1 ~]# modprobe rbd
FATAL: Module rbd not found.
[root@ceph-client1 ~]#
```

In order to add support for Ceph, we need to upgrade the Linux kernel version.

Note that this kernel's upgradation is just for demonstration purpose required only for this chapter. In your production environment, you should plan prior to the kernel upgrade. Please take the decision wisely before performing these steps to your production environment.

1. Install ELRepo rpm as follows:

   ```
   # rpm -Uvh http://www.elrepo.org/elrepo-release-6-
   6.el6.elrepo.noarch.rpm
   ```

2. Install a new kernel using the following command:

   ```
   # yum --enablerepo=elrepo-kernel install kernel-ml
   ```

3. Edit /etc/grub.conf, update default = 0, and then gracefully reboot the machine.

Once the machine is rebooted, check the Linux kernel version and its RBD support, as we did earlier:

```
[root@ceph-client1 ~]# uname -r
3.15.0-1.el6.elrepo.x86_64
[root@ceph-client1 ~]#
[root@ceph-client1 ~]# modprobe rbd
[root@ceph-client1 ~]#
```

To grant clients' permission to access the Ceph cluster, we need to add the keyring and Ceph configuration file to them. Client and Ceph cluster authentication will be based on the keyring. The admin user of Ceph has full access to the Ceph cluster, so for security reasons, you should not unnecessarily distribute the admin keyrings to other hosts if they do not need it. As per best practice, you should create separate users with limited capabilities to access the Ceph cluster, and use these keyrings to access RBD. In the upcoming chapters, we will discuss more on Ceph users and keyrings. As of now, we will make use of the admin user keyring.

Install Ceph binaries on ceph-node1 and push ceph.conf and ceph.admin.keyring to it:

```
# ceph-deploy install ceph-client1
# ceph-deploy admin ceph-client1
```

Once the Ceph configuration file and admin keyring are placed in ceph-client1 node, you can query the Ceph cluster for RBD images:

```
[root@ceph-client1 ceph]# pwd
/etc/ceph
[root@ceph-client1 ceph]# ls -l
total 8
-rw-r--r--. 1 root root 137 Jun 12 21:16 ceph.client.admin.keyring
-rw-r--r--. 1 root root 573 Jun 12 21:16 ceph.conf
[root@ceph-client1 ceph]# rbd ls
ceph-client1-rbd1
[root@ceph-client1 ceph]#
[root@ceph-client1 ceph]# rbd info --image ceph-client1-rbd1
rbd image 'ceph-client1-rbd1':
        size 10240 MB in 2560 objects
        order 22 (4096 kB objects)
        block_name_prefix: rb.0.1d63.2ae8944a
        format: 1
[root@ceph-client1 ceph]#
```

Map the RBD image `ceph-client1-rbd1` to a ceph-client1 machine. Since RBD is now natively supported by Linux kernel, you can execute the following command from the ceph-client1 machine to map RBD:

```
# rbd map --image ceph-client1-rbd1
```

Alternatively, you can use the following command to specify the pool name of the RBD image and can achieve the same results. In our case, the pool name is `rbd`, as explained earlier in this chapter:

```
# rbd map rbd/ceph-client1-rbd1
```

You can find out the operating system device name used for this mapping, as follows:

```
# rbd showmapped
```

The following screenshot shows this command in action:

```
[root@ceph-client1 ceph]# rbd map --image ceph-client1-rbd1
[root@ceph-client1 ceph]# rbd showmapped
id pool image              snap device
0  rbd  ceph-client1-rbd1  -    /dev/rbd0
[root@ceph-client1 ceph]#
```

Once RBD is mapped to OS, we should develop a filesystem on it to make it usable. It will now be used as an additional disk or as a block device:

```
# fdisk -l /dev/rbd0
# mkfs.xfs /dev/rbd0
# mkdir /mnt/ceph-vol1
# mount /dev/rbd0 /mnt/ceph-vol1
```

Have a look at the following screenshot:

```
[root@ceph-client1 ceph]# mkfs.xfs /dev/rbd0
log stripe unit (4194304 bytes) is too large (maximum is 256KiB)
log stripe unit adjusted to 32KiB
meta-data=/dev/rbd0              isize=256    agcount=17, agsize=162816 blks
         =                       sectsz=512   attr=2, projid32bit=0
data     =                       bsize=4096   blocks=2621440, imaxpct=25
         =                       sunit=1024   swidth=1024 blks
naming   =version 2              bsize=4096   ascii-ci=0
log      =internal log           bsize=4096   blocks=2560, version=2
         =                       sectsz=512   sunit=8 blks, lazy-count=1
realtime =none                   extsz=4096   blocks=0, rtextents=0
[root@ceph-client1 ceph]#
[root@ceph-client1 ceph]# mkdir /mnt/ceph-vol1
[root@ceph-client1 ceph]# mount /dev/rbd0 /mnt/ceph-vol1
[root@ceph-client1 ceph]# df -h
Filesystem                  Size  Used Avail Use% Mounted on
/dev/mapper/vg_cephnode1-lv_root
                            7.3G  2.4G  4.6G  35% /
tmpfs                       499M   72K  499M   1% /dev/shm
/dev/sda1                   477M   52M  396M  12% /boot
/dev/rbd0                    10G   33M   10G   1% /mnt/ceph-vol1
[root@ceph-client1 ceph]#
```

Put some data on Ceph RBD:

```
# dd if=/dev/zero of=/mnt/ceph-vol1/file1 count=100 bs=1M
```

```
[root@ceph-client1 ceph-vol1]# dd if=/dev/zero of=/mnt/ceph-vol1/file1 count=100 bs=1M
100+0 records in
100+0 records out
104857600 bytes (105 MB) copied, 0.286933 s, 365 MB/s
[root@ceph-client1 ceph-vol1]#
[root@ceph-client1 ceph-vol1]#
[root@ceph-client1 ceph-vol1]#
[root@ceph-client1 ceph-vol1]# ls -la
total 102404
drwxr-xr-x. 2 root root        18 Jun 14 21:13 .
drwxr-xr-x. 3 root root      4096 Jun 12 21:28 ..
-rw-r--r--. 1 root root 104857600 Jun 14 21:13 file1
[root@ceph-client1 ceph-vol1]#
```

Resizing Ceph RBD

Ceph supports thin-provisioned block devices, that is, the physical storage space will not get occupied until you really begin storing data to the block device. Ceph RADOS block devices are very flexible; you can increase or decrease the size of RBD on the fly from the Ceph storage end. However, the underlying filesystem should support resizing. Advance filesystems such as XFS, Btrfs, EXT, and ZFS support filesystem resizing to a certain extent. Follow filesystem-specific documentation to know more on resizing.

To increase or decrease the Ceph RBD image size, use the `--size <New_Size_in_MB>` parameter with the `rbd resize` command; this will set the new size for an RBD image. The original size of the RBD image `ceph-client1-rbd1` was 10 GB; the following command will increase its size to 20 GB:

```
# rbd resize rbd/ceph-client1-rbd1 --size 20480
```

```
[root@ceph-node1 ~]# rbd resize --image ceph-client1-rbd1 --size 20480
Resizing image: 100% complete...done.
[root@ceph-node1 ~]#
[root@ceph-node1 ~]# rbd info --image ceph-client1-rbd1
rbd image 'ceph-client1-rbd1':
        size 20480 MB in 5120 objects
        order 22 (4096 kB objects)
        block_name_prefix: rb.0.1d63.2ae8944a
        format: 1
[root@ceph-node1 ~]#
```

Now that the Ceph RBD image has been resized, you should check if the new size is being accepted by the kernel as well by executing the following command:

```
# xfs_growfs -d /mnt/ceph-vol1
```

```
[root@ceph-client1 /]# xfs_growfs -d /mnt/ceph-vol1
meta-data=/dev/rbd0              isize=256    agcount=17, agsize=162816 blks
         =                       sectsz=512   attr=2, projid32bit=0
data     =                       bsize=4096   blocks=2621440, imaxpct=25
         =                       sunit=1024   swidth=1024 blks
naming   =version 2              bsize=4096   ascii-ci=0
log      =internal               bsize=4096   blocks=2560, version=2
         =                       sectsz=512   sunit=8 blks, lazy-count=1
realtime =none                   extsz=4096   blocks=0, rtextents=0
data blocks changed from 2621440 to 5242880
[root@ceph-client1 /]#
[root@ceph-client1 /]#
[root@ceph-client1 /]# df -h
Filesystem            Size  Used Avail Use% Mounted on
/dev/mapper/vg_cephnode1-lv_root
                      7.3G  2.2G  4.8G  31% /
tmpfs                 499M  112K  499M   1% /dev/shm
/dev/sda1             477M   52M  396M  12% /boot
/dev/rbd0              20G  134M   20G   1% /mnt/ceph-vol1
[root@ceph-client1 /]#
```

From the client machine, grow the filesystem so that it can make use of increased storage space. From the client perspective, capacity resize is a feature of an OS filesystem; you should read the filesystem documentation before resizing any partition. An XFS filesystem supports online resizing.

Ceph RBD snapshots

Ceph extends full support to snapshots, which are point-in-time, read-only copies of an RBD image. You can preserve the state of a Ceph RBD image by creating snapshots and restoring them to get the original data.

To test the snapshot functionality of Ceph RBD, let's create a file on RBD:

```
# echo "Hello Ceph This is snapshot test" > /mnt/ceph-
vol1/snaptest_file
```

```
[root@ceph-client1 ceph-vol1]# echo "Hello Ceph This is snapshot test" > /mnt/ceph-vol1/snaptest_file
[root@ceph-client1 ceph-vol1]# ls -l
total 102404
-rw-r--r--. 1 root root 104857600 Jun 14 21:13 file1
-rw-r--r--. 1 root root        33 Jun 15 03:04 snaptest_file
[root@ceph-client1 ceph-vol1]#
```

Now our filesystem has two files. Let's create a snapshot of Ceph RBD using the `rbd snap create <pool-name>/<image-name>@<snap-name>`syntax, as follows:

```
# rbd snap create rbd/ceph-client1-rbd1@snap1
```

To list a snapshot of an image, use the `rbd snap ls <pool-name>/<image-name>` syntax, as follows:

```
# rbd snap ls rbd/ceph-client1-rbd1
```

```
[root@ceph-client1 /]# rbd snap create rbd/ceph-client1-rbd1@snap1
[root@ceph-client1 /]#
[root@ceph-client1 /]# rbd snap ls rbd/ceph-client1-rbd1
SNAPID NAME      SIZE
     2 snap1 20480 MB
[root@ceph-client1 /]#
```

To test the snapshot restore functionality of Ceph RBD, let's delete files from the filesystem:

```
# cd /mnt/ceph-vol1
```

```
# rm -f file1 snaptest_file
```

```
[root@ceph-client1 ceph-vol1]# rm -f file1 snaptest_file
[root@ceph-client1 ceph-vol1]# ls -l
total 0
[root@ceph-client1 ceph-vol1]#
```

We will now restore Ceph RBD snapshots to get the files that we deleted in the last step back.

 The rollback operation will overwrite the current version of an RBD image and its data with the snapshot version. You should perform this operation carefully.

The syntax for this is `rbd snap rollback <pool-name>/<image-name>@<snap-name>`. The following is the command:

```
# rbd snap rollback rbd/ceph-client1-rbd1@snap1
```

Once the snapshot rollback operation is completed, remount the Ceph RBD filesystem to refresh the state of the filesystem. You should able to get your deleted files back.

```
# umount /mnt/ceph-vol1
```

```
# mount /dev/rbd0 /mnt/ceph-vol1
```

```
[root@ceph-client1 ceph-vol1]# rbd snap rollback rbd/ceph-client1-rbd1@snap1
Rolling back to snapshot: 100% complete...done.
[root@ceph-client1 ceph-vol1]#
[root@ceph-client1 ceph-vol1]# ls -l
total 0
[root@ceph-client1 ceph-vol1]#
[root@ceph-client1 ceph-vol1]# cd /
[root@ceph-client1 /]#
[root@ceph-client1 /]# umount /mnt/ceph-vol1
[root@ceph-client1 /]#
[root@ceph-client1 /]# mount /dev/rbd0 /mnt/ceph-vol1
[root@ceph-client1 /]# cd /mnt/ceph-vol1/
[root@ceph-client1 ceph-vol1]# ls -l
total 102404
-rw-r--r--. 1 root root 104857600 Jun 14 21:13 file1
-rw-r--r--. 1 root root        33 Jun 15 03:04 snaptest_file
[root@ceph-client1 ceph-vol1]#
```

When you no longer need snapshots, you can remove a specific snapshot using the `rbd snap rm <pool-name>/<image-name>@<snap-name>` syntax. Deleting the snapshot will not delete your current data on the Ceph RBD image:

```
# rbd snap rm rbd/ceph-client1-rbd1@snap1
```

If you have multiple snapshots of an RBD image and you wish to delete all the snapshots in a single command, you can make use of the `purge` subcommand.

The syntax for it is `rbd snap purge <pool-name>/<image-name>`. The following is the command to delete all snapshots with a single command:

```
# rbd snap purge rbd/ceph-client1-rbd1
```

The `rbd rm <RBD_image_name> -p <Image_pool_name>` syntax is used to remove an RBD image, as follows:

```
# rbd rm ceph-client1-rbd1 -p rbd
```

Ceph RBD clones

The Ceph storage cluster is capable of creating **Copy-on-write (COW)** clones from RBD snapshots. This is also known as snapshot layering in Ceph. This layering feature of Ceph allows clients to create multiple instant clones of Ceph RBD. This feature is extremely useful for Cloud and virtualization platforms such as OpenStack, CloudStack, and Qemu/KVM. These platforms usually protect Ceph RBD images containing OS/VM images in the form of a snapshot. Later, this snapshot is cloned multiple times to spin new virtual machines/instances. Snapshots are read only, but COW clones are fully writable; this feature of Ceph provides a greater flexibility and is extremely useful for cloud platforms. The following diagram shows relationship between RADOS block device, RBD snapshot, and COW snapshot clone. In the upcoming chapters of this book, we will discover more on COW clones to spawn OpenStack instances.

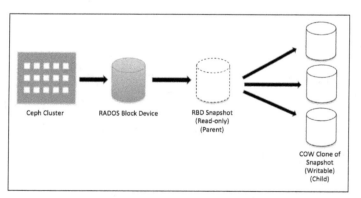

Every cloned image (child image) stores references of its parent snapshot to read image data. Hence, the parent snapshot should be protected before it can be used for cloning. At the time of data writing on COW-cloned images, it stores new data references to itself. COW-cloned images are as good as RBD.

They are quite flexible, similar to RBD, that is, they are writable, resizable, can create new snapshots, and can be cloned further.

The type of the RBD image defines the feature it supports. In Ceph, an RBD image is of two types: format-1 and format-2. The RBD snapshot feature is available on both format-1 and format-2 RBD images. However, the layering feature, that is, the COW cloning feature is available only for RBD images with format-2. Format-1 is the default RBD image format.

For demonstration purposes, we will first create a format-2 RBD image, create its snapshot, protect its snapshot, and finally, create COW clones out of it:

1. Create a format-2 RBD image:

    ```
    # rbd create ceph-client1-rbd2 --size 10240 --image-format 2
    ```

    ```
    [root@ceph-node1 ~]# rbd create ceph-client1-rbd2 --size 10240 --image-format 2
    [root@ceph-node1 ~]#
    [root@ceph-node1 ~]# rbd --image ceph-client1-rbd2 info
    rbd image 'ceph-client1-rbd2':
            size 10240 MB in 2560 objects
            order 22 (4096 kB objects)
            block_name_prefix: rbd_data.20bd2ae8944a
            format: 2
            features: layering
    [root@ceph-node1 ~]#
    ```

2. Create a snapshot of this RBD image:

    ```
    # rbd snap create rbd/ceph-client1-rbd2@snapshot_for_clone
    ```

3. To create a COW clone, protect the snapshot. This is an important step; we should protect the snapshot because if the snapshot gets deleted, all the attached COW clones will be destroyed:

    ```
    # rbd snap protect rbd/ceph-client1-rbd2@snapshot_for_clone
    ```

4. Cloning the snapshot requires the parent pool, RBD image, and snapshot names. For a child, it requires the pool and RBD image names.

    The syntax for this is `rbd clone <pool-name>/<parent-image>@<snap-name> <pool-name>/<child-image-name>`. The command to be used is as follows:

    ```
    # rbd clone rbd/ceph-client1-rbd2@snapshot_for_clone rbd/ceph-client1-rbd3
    ```

5. Creating a clone is a quick process. Once it's completed, check the new image information. You will notice that its parent pool, image, and snapshot information are displayed.

```
# rbd --pool rbd --image ceph-client1-rbd3 info
```

```
[root@ceph-node1 ~]# rbd clone rbd/ceph-client1-rbd2@snapshot_for_clone rbd/ceph-client1-rbd3
[root@ceph-node1 ~]#
[root@ceph-node1 ~]#
[root@ceph-node1 ~]# rbd --pool rbd --image ceph-client1-rbd3 info
rbd image 'ceph-client1-rbd3':
        size 10240 MB in 2560 objects
        order 22 (4096 kB objects)
        block_name_prefix: rbd_data.20c32eb141f2
        format: 2
        features: layering
        parent: rbd/ceph-client1-rbd2@snapshot_for_clone
        overlap: 10240 MB
[root@ceph-node1 ~]#
```

At this point, you have a cloned RBD image, which is dependent upon its parent image snapshot. To make the cloned RBD image independent of its parent, we need to flatten the image, which involves copying the data from a parent snapshot to a child image. The time it takes to complete the flattening process depends upon the size of data present in the parent snapshot. Once the flattening process is completed, there is no dependency between the cloned RBD image and its parent snapshot. Let's perform this flattening process practically:

1. To initiate the flattening process, use the following command:

```
# rbd flatten rbd/ceph-client1-rbd3
```

After the completion of the flattening process, if you check the image information, you will notice that the parent image/snapshot name is released, which makes the clone image independent.

```
[root@ceph-node1 ~]# rbd flatten rbd/ceph-client1-rbd3
Image flatten: 100% complete...done.
[root@ceph-node1 ~]#
[root@ceph-node1 ~]# rbd --pool rbd --image ceph-client1-rbd3 info
rbd image 'ceph-client1-rbd3':
        size 10240 MB in 2560 objects
        order 22 (4096 kB objects)
        block_name_prefix: rbd_data.20c32eb141f2
        format: 2
        features: layering
[root@ceph-node1 ~]#
```

2. You can also remove the parent image snapshot if you no longer require it. Before removing the snapshot, you first have to unprotect it using the following command:

```
# rbd snap unprotect rbd/ceph-client1-rbd2@snapshot_for_clone
```

3. Once the snapshot is unprotected, you can remove it using the following command:

```
# rbd snap rm rbd/ceph-client1-rbd2@snapshot_for_clone
```

The Ceph filesystem

The Ceph filesystem is also known as CephFS; it is a POSIX-compliant distributed filesystem that uses Ceph RADOS to store its data. To implement the Ceph filesystem, you need a running Ceph storage cluster and at least one **Ceph Metadata Server (MDS)**. For demonstration purposes, we will use the same metadata server that we deployed in *Chapter 3, Ceph Architecture and Components*. We can use the Ceph filesystem in two ways: by mounting CephFS using a native kernel driver and by using Ceph FUSE. We will see both these methods one by one.

Mounting CephFS with a kernel driver

Linux kernel 2.6.34 and later natively support Ceph. To use CephFS with kernel level support, clients should use Linux kernel 2.6.34 and above. The following steps will guide you through mounting CephFS with a kernel driver:

1. Check your client's Linux kernel version:

```
# uname -r
```

2. Create a mount point directory:

```
# mkdir /mnt/kernel_cephfs
```

3. Make a note of the admin secret key:

```
# cat /etc/ceph/ceph.client.admin.keyring
```

4. Mount CephFS using a native Linux mount call. The syntax for this is `mount -t ceph <Monitor_IP>:<Monitor_port>:/ <mount_point_name> -o name=admin,secret=<admin_secret_key>`.

   # mount -t ceph 192.168.57.101:6789:/ /mnt/kernel_cephfs -o name=admin,secret=AQAinItT8Ip9AhAAS93FrXLrrnVp8/sQhjvTIg==

```
[root@ceph-client1 ceph]# cat ceph.client.admin.keyring
[client.admin]
        key = AQAinItT8Ip9AhAAS93FrXLrrnVp8/sQhjvTIg==
        auid = 0
        caps mds = "allow"
        caps mon = "allow *"
        caps osd = "allow *"
[root@ceph-client1 ceph]#
[root@ceph-client1 ceph]#
[root@ceph-client1 ceph]# mount -t ceph 192.168.57.101:6789:/ /mnt/kernel_cephfs -o name=admin,secret=AQAinItT8Ip9AhAAS93FrXLrrnVp8/sQhjvTIg==
[root@ceph-client1 ceph]#
[root@ceph-client1 ceph]#
[root@ceph-client1 ceph]# df -h
Filesystem               Size  Used Avail Use% Mounted on
/dev/mapper/vg_cephnode1-lv_root
                         7.3G  2.2G  4.8G  31% /
tmpfs                    499M  112K  499M   1% /dev/shm
/dev/sda1                477M   52M  396M  12% /boot
/dev/rbd0                 20G  134M   20G   1% /mnt/ceph-vol1
192.168.57.101:6789:/
                          81G  424M   81G   1% /mnt/kernel_cephfs
[root@ceph-client1 ceph]#
```

5. To mount CephFS more securely, avoid the admin secret key to be visible in the bash history. Store the admin keyring as a plain text in a separate file and use this new file as a mount option for the secret key. Use the following command:

   # echo AQAinItT8Ip9AhAAS93FrXLrrnVp8/sQhjvTIg== > /etc/ceph/adminkey

   # mount -t ceph 192.168.57.101:6789:/ /mnt/kernel_cephfs -o name=admin,secretfile=/etc/ceph/adminkey

```
[root@ceph-client1 /]# umount /mnt/kernel_cephfs/
[root@ceph-client1 /]#
[root@ceph-client1 /]#
[root@ceph-client1 /]# echo AQAinItT8Ip9AhAAS93FrXLrrnVp8/sQhjvTIg== > /etc/ceph/adminkey
[root@ceph-client1 /]#
[root@ceph-client1 /]# mount -t ceph 192.168.57.101:6789:/ /mnt/kernel_cephfs -o name=admin,secretfile=/etc/ceph/adminkey
[root@ceph-client1 /]# df -h /mnt/kernel_cephfs
Filesystem               Size  Used Avail Use% Mounted on
192.168.57.101:6789:/
                          81G  424M   81G   1% /mnt/kernel_cephfs
[root@ceph-client1 /]#
```

6. To mount CephFS in your filesystem table, add the following lines in the `/etc/fstab` file on the client. The syntax for this is `<Mon_ipaddress>:<monitor_port>:/ <mount_point> <filesystem-name> [name=username,secret=secretkey|secretfile=/path/to/secretfile], [{mount.options}]`. The following is the command:

   192.168.57.101:6789:/ /mnt/kernel_ceph ceph name=admin,secretfile=/etc/ceph/adminkey,noatime 0 2

7. Unmount and mount CephFS again:

```
# umount /mnt/kernel_cephfs
```

```
# mount /mnt/kernel_cephfs
```

```
[root@ceph-client1 /]# cat /etc/fstab | grep -i cephfs
# CephFS Entry
192.168.57.101:6789:/  /mnt/kernel_cephfs    ceph    name=admin,secretfile=/etc/ceph/adminkey,noatime    0    2
[root@ceph-client1 /]#
[root@ceph-client1 /]# mount mnt/kernel_cephfs
[root@ceph-client1 /]# df -h mnt/kernel_cephfs
Filesystem          Size  Used Avail Use% Mounted on
192.168.57.101:6789:/
                     81G  424M   81G   1% /mnt/kernel_cephfs
[root@ceph-client1 /]#
```

Mounting CephFS as FUSE

The Ceph filesystem is natively supported by Linux kernel starting from Version 2.6.34 and above. If your host is running on a lower kernel version, you can use the **FUSE (Filesystem in User Space)** client for Ceph to mount the Ceph filesystem:

1. Since we have already added Ceph yum repositories earlier in this chapter, let's install Ceph FUSE on the client machine:

```
# yum install ceph-fuse
```

2. Ensure that the client has the Ceph configuration and keyring file before performing mounting. Create a directory for mounting:

```
# mkdir /mnt/cephfs
```

3. Mount CephFS using the Ceph FUSE client. The syntax for this is `ceph-fuse -m <Monitor_IP:Monitor_Port_Number> <mount_point_name>`. Use the following command:

```
# ceph-fuse -m 192.168.57.101:6789 /mnt/cephfs
```

```
[root@ceph-client1 ~]# ceph-fuse -m 192.168.57.101:6789 /mnt/cephfs
ceph-fuse[2506]: starting ceph client
ceph-fuse[2506]: starting fuse
[root@ceph-client1 ~]#
[root@ceph-client1 ~]# df -h /mnt/cephfs
Filesystem          Size  Used Avail Use% Mounted on
ceph-fuse            81G  428M   81G   1% /mnt/cephfs
[root@ceph-client1 ~]#
```

4. To mount CephFS in your filesystem table so that CephFS will automatically mount at startup, add the following lines in the `/etc/fstab` file on client:

```
#Ceph ID     #mountpoint     #Type      #Options
id=admin        /mnt/cephfs  fuse.ceph  defaults  0  0
```

5. Unmount and mount CephFS again:

```
# umount /mnt/cephfs
# mount /mnt/cephfs
```

Object storage using the Ceph RADOS gateway

Object storage, as the name suggests, manages data in the form of objects. Each object stores data, metadata, and a unique identifier. Object storage cannot be directly accessed by operating systems as a local or remote filesystem. It can only be accessed via API at application level. Ceph provides an object storage interface known as the RADOS gateway, which has been built on top of the Ceph RADOS layer. The RADOS gateway provides applications with RESTful S3- or Swift-compatible API interfaces to store data in the form of objects into a Ceph cluster.

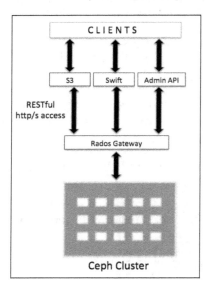

In a production environment, if you have a huge workload for Ceph object storage, you should configure the RADOS gateway on a physical dedicated machine, else you can consider using any of the monitor nodes as the RADOS gateway. We will now perform a basic RADOS gateway configuration to use Ceph storage cluster as object storage.

Setting up a virtual machine

In a usual Ceph-based setup, the RADOS gateway is configured on a machine other than MON and OSD. However, if you have limited hardware, you can use MON machines to configure RGW. In this demonstration, we will create a separate virtual machine for Ceph RGW:

1. Create a new VirtualBox virtual machine for the RADOS gateway:

    ```
    # VboxManage createvm --name ceph-rgw --ostype RedHat_64 --
    register

    # VBoxManage modifyvm ceph-rgw --memory 1024 --nic1 nat  --
    nic2 hostonly --hostonlyadapter2 vboxnet1


    # VBoxManage storagectl ceph-rgw --name "IDE Controller" --add
    ide --controller PIIX4 --hostiocache on --bootable on

    # VBoxManage storageattach ceph-rgw --storagectl "IDE
    Controller" --type dvddrive --port 0 --device 0 --medium
    /downloads/CentOS-6.4-x86_64-bin-DVD1.iso

    # VBoxManage storagectl ceph-rgw --name "SATA Controller" --
    add sata --controller IntelAHCI --hostiocache on --bootable on

    # VBoxManage createhd --filename OS-ceph-rgw.vdi --size 10240

    # VBoxManage storageattach ceph-rgw --storagectl "SATA
    Controller" --port 0 --device 0 --type hdd --medium OS-ceph-
    rgw.vdi

    # VBoxManage startvm ceph-rgw --type gui
    ```

2. Once the virtual machine is created and started, install the CentOS operating system by following the OS installation documentation available at https:// access.redhat.com/site/documentation/en-US/Red_Hat_Enterprise_ Linux/6/html/Installation_Guide/index.html. During the installation process, provide the hostname as ceph-client1.

3. Once you have successfully installed the operating system, edit the network configuration of the machine and restart network services:

    °   Edit the /etc/sysconfig/network-scripts/ifcfg-eth0 file and add:

        ```
        ONBOOT=yes
        BOOTPROTO=dhcp
        ```

    °   Edit the /etc/sysconfig/network-scripts/ifcfg-eth1 file and add:

        ```
        ONBOOT=yes
        BOOTPROTO=static
        ```

```
IPADDR=192.168.57.110
NETMASK=255.255.255.0
```

○ Edit the /etc/hosts file and add:

```
192.168.57.101 ceph-node1
192.168.57.102 ceph-node2
192.168.57.103 ceph-node3
192.168.57.200 ceph-client1
192.168.57.110 ceph-rgw
```

Installing the RADOS gateway

The last section was about setting up a virtual machine for RGW. In this section, we will learn to install and configure RGW:

1. Ceph object storage requires Apache and FastCGI; it is recommended to install 100-continue optimized versions for Apache and FastCGI provided by the Ceph community.

    Execute the following commands on the RADOS gateway node ceph-rgw, unless otherwise specified. Create a ceph-apache repository file, ceph-apache.repo, for YUM under the /etc/yum.repos.d directory:

    ```
    # vim /etc/yum.repos.d/ceph-apache.repo

    ## replace {distro} with OS distribution type , ex centos6 ,
    rhel6 etc. You can grab this code at publishers website.
                     [apache2-ceph-noarch]
    name=Apache noarch packages for Ceph
    baseurl=http://gitbuilder.ceph.com/apache2-rpm-{distro}-
    x86_64-basic/ref/master
    enabled=1
    priority=2
    gpgcheck=1
    type=rpm-md
    gpgkey=https://ceph.com/git/?p=ceph.git;a=blob_plain;f=keys/au
    tobuild.asc


    [apache2-ceph-source]
    name=Apache source packages for Ceph
    baseurl=http://gitbuilder.ceph.com/apache2-rpm-{distro}-
    x86_64-basic/ref/master
    enabled=0
    ```

```
priority=2
gpgcheck=1
type=rpm-md
gpgkey=https://ceph.com/git/?p=ceph.git;a=blob_plain;f=keys/au
tobuild.asc
```

```
[root@ceph-rgw ~]# cat /etc/yum.repos.d/ceph-apache.repo
[apache2-ceph-noarch]
name=Apache noarch packages for Ceph
baseurl=http://gitbuilder.ceph.com/apache2-rpm-centos6-x86_64-basic/ref/master
enabled=1
priority=2
gpgcheck=1
type=rpm-md
gpgkey=https://ceph.com/git/?p=ceph.git;a=blob_plain;f=keys/autobuild.asc

[apache2-ceph-source]
name=Apache source packages for Ceph
baseurl=http://gitbuilder.ceph.com/apache2-rpm-centos6-x86_64-basic/ref/master
enabled=0
priority=2
gpgcheck=1
type=rpm-md
gpgkey=https://ceph.com/git/?p=ceph.git;a=blob_plain;f=keys/autobuild.asc
[root@ceph-rgw ~]#
```

2. Create the `ceph-fastcgi.repo` file under the `/etc/yum.repos.d` directory:

   ```
   # vim /etc/yum.repos.d/ceph-fastcgi.repo
   ```

   ```
   ## replace {distro}with OS distribution type , ex centos6 , rhel6
   etc. You can grab this code at publishers website.
   ```

   ```
   [fastcgi-ceph-basearch]
   name=FastCGI basearch packages for Ceph
   baseurl=http://gitbuilder.ceph.com/mod_fastcgi-rpm-{distro}-
   x86_64-basic/ref/master
   enabled=1
   priority=2
   gpgcheck=1
   type=rpm-md
   gpgkey=https://ceph.com/git/?p=ceph.git;a=blob_plain;f=keys/au
   tobuild.asc
   ```

   ```
   [fastcgi-ceph-noarch]
   name=FastCGI noarch packages for Ceph
   ```

```
baseurl=http://gitbuilder.ceph.com/mod_fastcgi-rpm-{distro}-
x86_64-basic/ref/master
```

enabled=1

priority=2

gpgcheck=1

type=rpm-md

```
gpgkey=https://ceph.com/git/?p=ceph.git;a=blob_plain;f=keys/au
tobuild.asc
```

[fastcgi-ceph-source]

name=FastCGI source packages for Ceph

```
baseurl=http://gitbuilder.ceph.com/mod_fastcgi-rpm-{distro}-
x86_64-basic/ref/master
```

enabled=0

priority=2

gpgcheck=1

type=rpm-md

```
gpgkey=https://ceph.com/git/?p=ceph.git;a=blob_plain;f=keys/au
tobuild.asc
```

```
[root@ceph-rgw ~]# cat /etc/yum.repos.d/ceph-fastcgi.repo
[fastcgi-ceph-basearch]
name=FastCGI basearch packages for Ceph
baseurl=http://gitbuilder.ceph.com/mod_fastcgi-rpm-centos6-x86_64-basic/ref/master
enabled=1
priority=2
gpgcheck=1
type=rpm-md
gpgkey=https://ceph.com/git/?p=ceph.git;a=blob_plain;f=keys/autobuild.asc

[fastcgi-ceph-noarch]
name=FastCGI noarch packages for Ceph
baseurl=http://gitbuilder.ceph.com/mod_fastcgi-rpm-centos6-x86_64-basic/ref/master
enabled=1
priority=2
gpgcheck=1
type=rpm-md
gpgkey=https://ceph.com/git/?p=ceph.git;a=blob_plain;f=keys/autobuild.asc

[fastcgi-ceph-source]
name=FastCGI source packages for Ceph
baseurl=http://gitbuilder.ceph.com/mod_fastcgi-rpm-centos6-x86_64-basic/ref/master
enabled=0
priority=2
gpgcheck=1
type=rpm-md
gpgkey=https://ceph.com/git/?p=ceph.git;a=blob_plain;f=keys/autobuild.asc
[root@ceph-rgw ~]#
```

3. Create the `ceph.repo` file under the `/etc/yum.repos.d` directory:

```
# vim /etc/yum.repos.d/ceph.repo
## You can grab this code at publishers website.
[Ceph]
name=Ceph packages for $basearch
baseurl=http://ceph.com/rpm-firefly/el6/$basearch
enabled=1
gpgcheck=1
type=rpm-md
gpgkey=https://ceph.com/git/?p=ceph.git;a=blob_plain;f=keys/re
lease.asc

[Ceph-noarch]
name=Ceph noarch packages
baseurl=http://ceph.com/rpm-firefly/el6/noarch
enabled=1
gpgcheck=1
type=rpm-md
gpgkey=https://ceph.com/git/?p=ceph.git;a=blob_plain;f=keys/re
lease.asc

[ceph-source]
name=Ceph source packages
baseurl=http://ceph.com/rpm-firefly/el6/SRPMS
enabled=1
gpgcheck=1
type=rpm-md
gpgkey=https://ceph.com/git/?p=ceph.git;a=blob_plain;f=keys/re
lease.asc
```

4. Install yum-plugin-priorities:

```
# yum install yum-plugin-priorities
```

5. Install the apache (httpd), fastcgi (mod_fastcgi), ceph-radosgw, and ceph packages:

```
# yum install httpd mod_fastcgi ceph-radosgw ceph
```

6. Set FQDN for ceph-rgw host:

  ° Edit /etc/hosts and add IP, FQDN, and hostname in the # <rgw_ip_addr> <FQDN> <Hostname> format:

        192.168.57.110 ceph-rgw.objectstore.com ceph-rgw

  ° Edit /etc/sysconfig/network and set HOSTNAME as FQDN:

        HOSTNAME=ceph-rgw.objectstore.com

  ° Check hostname and FQDN:

        # hostname

        # hostname -f

```
[root@ceph-rgw ~]# cat /etc/hosts | grep rgw
192.168.57.110  ceph-rgw.objectstore.com
[root@ceph-rgw ~]#
[root@ceph-rgw ~]# cat /etc/sysconfig/network | grep rgw
HOSTNAME=ceph-rgw.objectstore.com
[root@ceph-rgw ~]#
[root@ceph-rgw ~]# hostname
ceph-rgw.objectstore.com
[root@ceph-rgw ~]#
[root@ceph-rgw ~]# hostname -f
ceph-rgw.objectstore.com
[root@ceph-rgw ~]#
```

Configuring the RADOS gateway

The configuration of the RADOS gateway includes Apache and FastCGI configuration and Ceph key generation. Perform the following steps:

1. Configure Apache by editing /etc/httpd/conf/httpd.conf:

  ° Set ServerName <FQDN>

  ° Ensure the following line is present and uncommented:

        LoadModule rewrite_module modules/mod_rewrite.so

```
[root@ceph-rgw ~]# cat /etc/httpd/conf/httpd.conf | egrep "rgw|rewrite"
LoadModule rewrite_module modules/mod_rewrite.so
ServerName ceph-rgw.objectstore.com
[root@ceph-rgw ~]#
```

2. Configure FastCGI by editing `/etc/httpd/conf.d/fastcgi.conf`:
   - ° Ensure that the FastCGI modules are enabled:

     ```
     LoadModule fastcgi_module modules/mod_fastcgi.so
     ```

   - ° Turn off `FastCgiWrapper`

```
[root@ceph-rgw ~]# cat /etc/httpd/conf.d/fastcgi.conf | egrep -i "FastCgiWrapper|fastcgi_module"
LoadModule fastcgi_module modules/mod_fastcgi.so
FastCgiWrapper Off
[root@ceph-rgw ~]#
```

3. Create a Ceph object gateway script with the following content, change ownership, and allow executable permission. You can match the changes from the author's version of the `s3gw.fcgi` file provided with this book:

   ```
   # vim /var/www/html/s3gw.fcgi

   #!/bin/sh

   exec /usr/bin/radosgw -c /etc/ceph/ceph.conf -n
   client.radosgw.gateway


   # chmod +x /var/www/html/s3gw.fcgi

   # chown apache:apache /var/www/html/s3gw.fcgi
   ```

   ```
   [root@ceph-rgw /]# cat  /var/www/html/s3gw.fcgi
   #!/bin/sh
   exec /usr/bin/radosgw -c /etc/ceph/ceph.conf -n client.radosgw.gateway
   [root@ceph-rgw /]#
   [root@ceph-rgw /]# chmod +x /var/www/html/s3gw.fcgi
   [root@ceph-rgw /]# chown apache:apache /var/www/html/s3gw.fcgi
   [root@ceph-rgw /]#
   ```

4. Create the gateway configuration file `rgw.conf` under `/etc/httpd/conf.d` with the following contents. Replace `{fqdn}` with servers fqdn (`hostname -f`) and `{email.address}` with the e-mail address of the server administrator. You can match the changes from the author's version of the `rgw.conf` file provided with this book:

   ```
   FastCgiExternalServer /var/www/html/s3gw.fcgi -socket
   /var/run/ceph/ceph.radosgw.gateway.fastcgi.sock

   <VirtualHost *:80>
           ServerName {fqdn}
           <!--Remove the comment. Add a server alias with
   *.{fqdn} for S3 subdomains-->
           <!--ServerAlias *.{fqdn}-->
           ServerAdmin {email.address}
   ```

```
        DocumentRoot /var/www/html
        RewriteEngine On
        RewriteRule  ^/(.*) /s3gw.fcgi?%{QUERY_STRING}
[E=HTTP_AUTHORIZATION:%{HTTP:Authorization},L]
        <IfModule mod_fastcgi.c>
        <Directory /var/www/html>
                    Options +ExecCGI
                    AllowOverride All
                    SetHandler fastcgi-script
                    Order allow,deny
                    Allow from all
                    AuthBasicAuthoritative Off
            </Directory>
        </IfModule>
        AllowEncodedSlashes On
        ErrorLog /var/log/httpd/error.log
        CustomLog /var/log/httpd/access.log combined
        ServerSignature Off
    </VirtualHost>
# vim /etc/httpd/conf.d/rgw.conf
```

```
[root@ceph-rgw /]# cat /etc/httpd/conf.d/rgw.conf
FastCgiExternalServer /var/www/html/s3gw.fcgi -socket /var/run/ceph/ceph.radosgw.gateway.fastcgi.sock
<VirtualHost *:80>
        ServerName ceph-rgw.objectstore.com
        ServerAlias *.ceph-rgw.objectstore.com
        ServerAdmin test@ceph-rgw.objectstore.com
        DocumentRoot /var/www/html
        RewriteEngine On
        RewriteRule  ^/(.*) /s3gw.fcgi?%{QUERY_STRING} [E=HTTP_AUTHORIZATION:%{HTTP:Authorization},L]
        <IfModule mod_fastcgi.c>
        <Directory /var/www/html>
                    Options +ExecCGI
                    AllowOverride All
                    SetHandler fastcgi-script
                    Order allow,deny
                    Allow from all
                    AuthBasicAuthoritative Off
            </Directory>
        </IfModule>
        AllowEncodedSlashes On
        ErrorLog /var/log/httpd/error.log
        CustomLog /var/log/httpd/access.log combined
        ServerSignature Off
</VirtualHost>
[root@ceph-rgw /]#
```

5. Create the RADOS gateway user and keyring for Ceph, log in to any of the Ceph monitor nodes, and execute the following:

   ° Create the keyring:

      ```
      # ceph-authtool --create-keyring
      /etc/ceph/ceph.client.radosgw.keyring

      # chmod +r /etc/ceph/ceph.client.radosgw.keyring
      ```

   ° Generate the gateway user and key for the RADOS gateway instance; our RADOS gateway instance name is `gateway`:

      ```
      # ceph-authtool /etc/ceph/ceph.client.radosgw.keyring -n
      client.radosgw.gateway --gen-key
      ```

   ° Add capabilities to the key:

      ```
      # ceph-authtool -n client.radosgw.gateway --cap osd
      'allow
      rwx' --cap mon 'allow rw'
      /etc/ceph/ceph.client.radosgw.keyring
      ```

   ° Add the key to the Ceph cluster:

      ```
      # ceph -k /etc/ceph/ceph.client.admin.keyring auth add
      client.radosgw.gateway -i
      /etc/ceph/ceph.client.radosgw.keyring
      ```

   ° Distribute the key to the Ceph RADOS gateway node:

      ```
      # scp /etc/ceph/ceph.client.radosgw.keyring ceph-
      rgw:/etc/ceph/ceph.client.radosgw.keyring
      ```

   ° Create a pool for the RADOS gateway

      ```
      # ceph osd pool create .rgw 128 128
      ```

```
[root@ceph-node1 ~]# ceph-authtool --create-keyring /etc/ceph/ceph.client.radosgw.keyring
creating /etc/ceph/ceph.client.radosgw.keyring
[root@ceph-node1 ~]# chmod +r /etc/ceph/ceph.client.radosgw.keyring
[root@ceph-node1 ~]# ceph-authtool /etc/ceph/ceph.client.radosgw.keyring -n client.radosgw.gateway --gen-key
[root@ceph-node1 ~]# ceph-authtool -n client.radosgw.gateway --cap osd 'allow rwx' --cap mon 'allow rw' /etc/ceph/ceph.client.radosgw.keyring
[root@ceph-node1 ~]# ceph -k /etc/ceph/ceph.client.admin.keyring auth add client.radosgw.gateway -i /etc/ceph/ceph.client.radosgw.keyring
added key for client.radosgw.gateway
[root@ceph-node1 ~]# scp /etc/ceph/ceph.client.radosgw.keyring ceph-rgw:/etc/ceph/ceph.client.radosgw.keyring
ceph.client.radosgw.keyring                                                        100%  120     0.1KB/s   00:00
[root@ceph-node1 ~]#
```

6. Create the Ceph RADOS gateway data directory:

```
# mkdir -p /var/lib/ceph/radosgw/ceph-radosgw.gateway
```

7. Add a gateway configuration to Ceph, add the following configuration to Ceph monitor's ceph.conf file, and move this ceph.conf file to the RADOS gateway node. Make sure that the hostname is the RADOS gateway hostname, and not FQDN:

```
[client.radosgw.gateway]

host = ceph-rgw

keyring = /etc/ceph/ceph.client.radosgw.keyring

rgw socket path = /var/run/ceph/ceph.radosgw.gateway.fastcgi.sock

log file = /var/log/ceph/client.radosgw.gateway.log

rgw dns name = ceph-rgw.objectstore.com   ## This would be used
for S3 API

rgw print continue = false

# scp /etc/ceph/ceph.conf ceph-rgw:/etc/ceph/ceph.conf
```

```
[root@ceph-node1 ceph]# tail -6 /etc/ceph/ceph.conf
[client.radosgw.gateway]
host = ceph-rgw.objectstore.com
keyring = /etc/ceph/ceph.client.radosgw.keyring
rgw socket path = /var/run/ceph/ceph.radosgw.gateway.fastcgi.sock
log file = /var/log/ceph/client.radosgw.gateway.log
rgw print continue = false
[root@ceph-node1 ceph]#
[root@ceph-node1 ceph]# scp /etc/ceph/ceph.conf ceph-rgw:/etc/ceph/ceph.conf
ceph.conf                                                    100%  828     0.8KB/s   00:00
[root@ceph-node1 ceph]#
```

8. Adjust the ownership and permission on the RADOS gateway node for /var/log/httpd, /var/run/ceph, and /var/log/ceph. Set SELinux to Permissive:

```
# chown apache:apache /var/log/httpd

# chown apache:apache /var/run/ceph

# chown apache:apache /var/log/ceph

# setenforce 0
```

9. Start the Apache and Ceph RADOS gateway services. If you encounter any warning, you can ignore them at this point:

   ° Start the Apache service:

      ```
      # service httpd start
      ```

   ° Start the ceph-radosgw service:

      ```
      # service ceph-radosgw start
      ```

```
[root@ceph-rgw ceph]# service httpd start
Starting httpd:                                    [  OK  ]
[root@ceph-rgw ceph]# service ceph-radosgw start
Starting radosgw instance(s)...
bash: line 0: ulimit: open files: cannot modify limit: Operation not permitted
2014-06-22 04:04:26.930208 7fa1b8d45820 -1 WARNING: libcurl doesn't support curl_multi_wait()
2014-06-22 04:04:26.930369 7fa1b8d45820 -1 WARNING: cross zone / region transfer performance may be affected
Starting client.radosgw.gateway...                 [  OK  ]
/usr/bin/radosgw is running.
[root@ceph-rgw ceph]#
```

10. Verify the configuration:

    ° Perform an HTTP GET request on radosgw FQDN using curl:

       ```
       # curl http://ceph-rgw.objectstore.com
       ```

    ° You should get a response similar to the one shown in the following snippet. It shows that your configuration is correct:

       ```
       <?xml version="1.0" encoding="UTF-8"?>

       <ListAllMyBucketsResult xmlns="http://s3.amazonaws.com/
       doc/2006-03-01/">

       <Owner>

       <ID>anonymous</ID>

       <DisplayName></DisplayName>

       </Owner><Buckets></Buckets>

       </ListAllMyBucketsResult>
       ```

11. Submitting an HTTP request to the browser of an radosgw node can also do the verification.

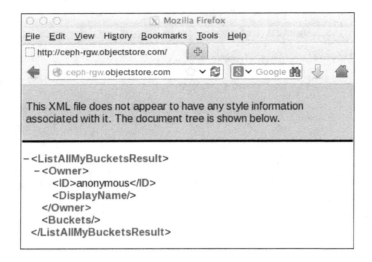

Creating a radosgw user

To use the Ceph object storage, we need to create users for the RADOS gateway. These user accounts will be identified by access and secret keys, which can be used by clients to perform operations on the Ceph object storage.

Now, let's create a RADOS gateway user and access object storage:

1. Make sure the RADOS gateway machine (ceph-rgw) is able to access a Ceph cluster. Copy the Ceph keyring to the RADOS gateway machine from the monitor node:

```
# scp ceph.client.admin.keyring ceph-rgw:/etc/ceph
```

2. Execute Ceph cluster commands from ceph-rgw to ensure cluster accessibility:

```
# ceph -s
```

3. Create a RADOS gateway user. This will also create an `access_key` and `secret_key` for the user, which will be required to access the Ceph object storage:

```
#  radosgw-admin user create --uid=mona --display-name="Monika
Singh" --email=mona@example.com
```

```
[root@ceph-rgw ~]# radosgw-admin user create --uid=mona --display-name="Monika Singh" --email=mona@example.com
{ "user_id": "mona",
  "display_name": "Monika Singh",
  "email": "mona@example.com",
  "suspended": 0,
  "max_buckets": 1000,
  "auid": 0,
  "subusers": [],
  "keys": [
        { "user": "mona",
          "access_key": "PZM9Y0JSTNB5DCRDNBH0",
          "secret_key": "8R8saOONCE+IR2vZ6DFDubXfT8vn9Cesow5uiFem"}],
  "swift_keys": [],
  "caps": [],
  "op_mask": "read, write, delete",
  "default_placement": "",
  "placement_tags": [],
  "bucket_quota": { "enabled": false,
      "max_size_kb": -1,
      "max_objects": -1},
  "user_quota": { "enabled": false,
      "max_size_kb": -1,
      "max_objects": -1},
  "temp_url_keys": []}
[root@ceph-rgw ~]#
```

Accessing the Ceph object storage

The Ceph object storage supports S3- and Swift-compatible APIs; to make use of object storage capabilities of Ceph, we need to configure S3 or Swift interfaces. We will now perform a basic configuration for these interfaces one by one. For advanced configurations, check their respective documentations.

S3 API-compatible Ceph object storage

Amazon offers **Simple Storage Service (S3)** to provide storage through web interfaces such as REST. Ceph extends its compatibility with S3 through RESTful API. S3 client applications can access the Ceph object storage based on access and secret keys. Let's now see how to configure this. Perform the following commands on the ceph-rgw node until otherwise specified:

1. Radosgw users should have enough capabilities to allow S3 requests. Add the required capabilities to the radosgw user ID (mona):

    ```
    # radosgw-admin caps add --uid=mona   --caps="users=*"
    ```

    ```
    # radosgw-admin caps add --uid=mona   --caps="buckets=*"
    ```

    ```
    # radosgw-admin caps add --uid=mona   --caps="metadata=*"
    ```

    ```
    radosgw-admin caps add --uid=mona --caps="zone=*"
    ```

    ```
    [root@ceph-rgw ~]# radosgw-admin caps add --uid=mona  --caps="zone=*"
    { "user_id": "mona",
      "display_name": "Monika Singh",
      "email": "mona@example.com",
      "suspended": 0,
      "max_buckets": 1000,
      "auid": 0,
      "subusers": [],
      "keys": [
          { "user": "mona",
            "access_key": "PZM9Y0JSTNB5DCRDNBHO",
            "secret_key": "8R8saOONCE+IR2vZ6DFDubXfT8vn9Cesow5uiFem"}],
      "swift_keys": [],
      "caps": [
          { "type": "buckets",
            "perm": "*"},
          { "type": "metadata",
            "perm": "*"},
          { "type": "users",
            "perm": "*"},
          { "type": "zone",
            "perm": "*"}],
      "op_mask": "read, write, delete",
      "default_placement": "",
      "placement_tags": [],
      "bucket_quota": { "enabled": false,
          "max_size_kb": -1,
          "max_objects": -1},
      "user_quota": { "enabled": false,
          "max_size_kb": -1,
          "max_objects": -1},
      "temp_url_keys": []}
    [root@ceph-rgw ~]#
    ```

2. S3 also requires a DNS service in place as it uses the virtual host bucket naming convention <object_name>.<RGW_Fqdn>. For example, if you have a bucket named jupiter, it will be accessible over HTTP via the URL http://jupiter.ceph-rgw.objectstore.com.

    Perform the following steps to configure DNS on the ceph-rgw node. If you have an existing DNS server, you can use it with slight modifications.

    1. Install bind packages on the ceph-rgw node:

        ```
        # yum install bind* -y
        ```

2. Edit /etc/named.conf, the IP address, and the IP range and zone as mentioned in the following code. You can match the changes from the author's version of the named.conf file provided with this book's code bundle:

```
listen-on port 53 { 127.0.0.1;192.168.57.110; };   ###
Add
DNS IP ###


allow-query    { localhost;192.168.57.0/24; };     ###
Add
IP Range ###


### Add new zone for domain objectstore.com before EOF
###
zone "objectstore.com" IN {
type master;
file "db.objectstore.com";
allow-update { none; };
};
```

3. Save and exit your editor from /etc/named.conf.

4. Create the zone file /var/named/db.objectstore.com with the following content. You can match the changes from the author's version of the db.objectstore.com file provided with this book:

```
@ 86400 IN SOA objectstore.com. root.objectstore.com. (
        20091028 ; serial yyyy-mm-dd
        10800 ; refresh every 15 min
        3600 ; retry every hour
        3600000 ; expire after 1 month +
        86400 ); min ttl of 1 day
@ 86400 IN NS objectstore.com.
@ 86400 IN A 192.168.57.110
* 86400 IN CNAME @
```

5. Disable the firewall, or you can allow DNS rules from the firewall:

```
# service iptables stop
```

6. Edit /etc/resolve.conf and add the following content:

```
search objectstore.com
nameserver 192.168.57.110
```

7. Start the named service:

```
# service named start
```

8. Test DNS configuration files for any syntax errors:

```
# named-checkconf /etc/named.conf
```

```
# named-checkzone objectstore.com
/var/named/db.objectstore.com
```

9. Test the DNS server:

```
# dig ceph-rgw.objectstore.com
```

```
# nslookup ceph-rgw.objectstore.com
```

10. Apply the same DNS settings to ceph-client1, which will be our S3 client machine. Edit /etc/resolve.conf on ceph-client1 and add the following content:

```
search objectstore.com
nameserver 192.168.57.110
```

11. Test the DNS settings on ceph-client1:

```
# dig ceph-rgw.objectstore.com
```

```
# nslookup ceph-rgw.objectstore.com
```

12. The ceph-client1 machine should be able to resolve all the subdomains for ceph-rgw.objectstore.com.

```
[root@ceph-client1 ~]# ping mona.ceph-rgw.objectstore.com -c 1
PING objectstore.com (192.168.57.110) 56(84) bytes of data.
64 bytes from ceph-rgw.objectstore.com (192.168.57.110): icmp_seq=1 ttl=64 time=0.368 ms

--- objectstore.com ping statistics ---
1 packets transmitted, 1 received, 0% packet loss, time 1ms
rtt min/avg/max/mdev = 0.368/0.368/0.368/0.000 ms
[root@ceph-client1 ~]#
[root@ceph-client1 ~]# ping anything.ceph-rgw.objectstore.com -c 1
PING objectstore.com (192.168.57.110) 56(84) bytes of data.
64 bytes from ceph-rgw.objectstore.com (192.168.57.110): icmp_seq=1 ttl=64 time=1.12 ms

--- objectstore.com ping statistics ---
1 packets transmitted, 1 received, 0% packet loss, time 2ms
rtt min/avg/max/mdev = 1.129/1.129/1.129/0.000 ms
[root@ceph-client1 ~]#
```

3. Configure the S3 client (s3cmd) on ceph-client1:

1. Install s3cmd:

```
# yum install s3cmd
```

2. Configuring s3cmd will require an `access _key` and `secret_key` for a user; in our case, the user ID is `mona` that we created in the first step:

   # **s3cmd --configure**

```
[root@ceph-client1 ~]# s3cmd --configure

Enter new values or accept defaults in brackets with Enter.
Refer to user manual for detailed description of all options.

Access key and Secret key are your identifiers for Amazon S3
Access Key: PZM9Y0JSTNB5DCRDNBHO
Secret Key: 8R8saOONCE+IR2vZ6DFDubXfT8vn9Cesow5uiFem

Encryption password is used to protect your files from reading
by unauthorized persons while in transfer to S3
Encryption password: packtpub
Path to GPG program [/usr/bin/gpg]:

When using secure HTTPS protocol all communication with Amazon S3
servers is protected from 3rd party eavesdropping. This method is
slower than plain HTTP and can't be used if you're behind a proxy
Use HTTPS protocol [No]:

On some networks all internet access must go through a HTTP proxy.
Try setting it here if you can't conect to S3 directly
HTTP Proxy server name:

New settings:
  Access Key: PZM9Y0JSTNB5DCRDNBHO
  Secret Key: 8R8saOONCE+IR2vZ6DFDubXfT8vn9Cesow5uiFem
  Encryption password: packtpub
  Path to GPG program: /usr/bin/gpg
  Use HTTPS protocol: False
  HTTP Proxy server name:
  HTTP Proxy server port: 0

Test access with supplied credentials? [Y/n] n

Save settings? [y/N] y
Configuration saved to '/root/.s3cfg'
[root@ceph-client1 ~]#
```

3. The s3cmd configure command will create the `.s3cfg` file under `/root`; edit this file for the RADOS gateway host details. Modify `host_base` and `host_bucket`, as shown in the following snippet. Make sure these lines do not have trailing spaces at the end:

```
host_base = ceph-rgw.objectstore.com
host_bucket = %(bucket)s.ceph-rgw.objectstore.com
```

You can match the changes from the author's version of the `.s3cfg` file provided with this book.

```
[root@ceph-client1 ~]# cat .s3cfg
[default]
access_key = PZM9Y0JSTNB5DCRDNBH0
bucket_location = US
cloudfront_host = cloudfront.amazonaws.com
cloudfront_resource = /2010-07-15/distribution
default_mime_type = binary/octet-stream
delete_removed = False
dry_run = False
encoding = UTF-8
encrypt = False
follow_symlinks = False
force = False
get_continue = False
gpg_command = /usr/bin/gpg
gpg_decrypt = %(gpg_command)s -d --verbose --no-use-agent --batch --yes --passphrase-fd %(passphrase_fd)s -o %(output_file)s %(input_file)s
gpg_encrypt = %(gpg_command)s -c --verbose --no-use-agent --batch --yes --passphrase-fd %(passphrase_fd)s -o %(output_file)s %(input_file)s
gpg_passphrase = packtpub
guess_mime_type = True
host_base = ceph-rgw.objectstore.com
host_bucket = %(bucket)s.ceph-rgw.objectstore.com
human_readable_sizes = False
list_md5 = False
log_target_prefix =
preserve_attrs = True
progress_meter = True
proxy_host =
proxy_port = 0
recursive = False
recv_chunk = 4096
reduced_redundancy = False
secret_key = 8R8saOONCE+IR2vZ6DFDubXfT8vn9Cesow5uiFem
send_chunk = 4096
simpledb_host = sdb.amazonaws.com
skip_existing = False
socket_timeout = 300
urlencoding_mode = normal
use_https = False
verbosity = WARNING
[root@ceph-client1 ~]#
```

4. Finally, we will create S3 buckets and put objects into it:

```
# s3cmd ls
```

```
# s3cmd mb s3://first-bucket
```

```
# s3cmd put /etc/hosts s3://first-bucket
```

```
[root@ceph-client1 ~]# s3cmd ls
[root@ceph-client1 ~]# s3cmd mb s3://first-bucket
Bucket 's3://first-bucket/' created
[root@ceph-client1 ~]# s3cmd ls
2014-06-25 08:43  s3://first-bucket
[root@ceph-client1 ~]#
```

Swift API-compatible Ceph object storage

Ceph supports a RESTful API that is compatible with the basic data access model of the Swift API. To use Ceph object storage using the Swift API, we need to create a Swift subuser on the Ceph RADOS gateway, which will allow the Swift API to access Ceph object storage:

1. Log in to ceph-rgw and create a subuser for Swift access. The subuser will have its own secret key:

   ```
   # radosgw-admin subuser create --uid=mona --subuser=mona:swift
   --access=full --secret=secretkey --key-type=swift
   ```

```
[root@ceph-rgw ~]# radosgw-admin subuser create --uid=mona --subuser=mona:swift --access=full --secret=secretkey --key-type=swift
{ "user_id": "mona",
  "display_name": "Monika Singh",
  "email": "mona@example.com",
  "suspended": 0,
  "max_buckets": 1000,
  "auid": 0,
  "subusers": [
        { "id": "mona:swift",
          "permissions": "full-control"}],
  "keys": [
        { "user": "mona",
          "access_key": "PZM9Y0JSTNB5DCRDNBH0",
          "secret_key": "8R8saOONCE+IR2vZ6DFDubXfT8vn9Cesow5uiFem"}],
  "swift_keys": [
        { "user": "mona:swift",
          "secret_key": "secretkey"}],
  "caps": [
        { "type": "buckets",
          "perm": "*"},
        { "type": "metadata",
          "perm": "*"},
        { "type": "users",
          "perm": "*"},
        { "type": "zone",
          "perm": "*"}],
  "op_mask": "read, write, delete",
  "default_placement": "",
  "placement_tags": [],
  "bucket_quota": { "enabled": false,
      "max_size_kb": -1,
      "max_objects": -1},
  "user_quota": { "enabled": false,
      "max_size_kb": -1,
      "max_objects": -1},
  "temp_url_keys": []}
[root@ceph-rgw ~]#
```

2. Install a swift client on the ceph-client1 node:

   ```
   # yum install python-setuptools
   ```

   ```
   # easy_install pip
   ```

   ```
   # pip install --upgrade setuptools
   ```

   ```
   # pip install python-swiftclient
   ```

3. Finally, create and list buckets using the swift client:

```
#  swift -V 1.0 -A http://ceph-rgw.objectstore.com/auth -U
mona:swift -K secretkey post example-bucket
```

```
#  swift -V 1.0 -A http://ceph-rgw.objectstore.com/auth -U
mona:swift -K secretkey list
```

Summary

Storage provisioning is the most frequent operation a storage administration has to perform. As compared to traditional enterprise storage systems, you no longer need to procure and manage multiple storage systems for different storage types. Ceph uniquely delivers object, block, and file storage from a single unified system. In this chapter, we learned how to configure and provision RADOS block devices, Ceph filesystems, and the Ceph object storage. It's been more than two decades that the block device and filesystem storage types exist; however, object storage is fairly new is gaining momentum now due to Amazon S3 and Swift. Ceph extends its support to S3 and Swift APIs. In this chapter, we also learned the configuration of S3 and Swift separately, followed by their usage. In the next chapter, we will learn about Ceph service management and the Ceph cluster.

7
Ceph Operations and Maintenance

As a Ceph storage administrator, it will be quite useful for you to manage your enterprise Ceph cluster effectively. In this chapter, we will cover the following topics:

- Ceph service management
- Scaling out a Ceph cluster
- Scaling down a Ceph cluster
- Replacing a failed drive
- Managing a CRUSH map

Ceph service management

As soon as you have your first Ceph cluster set up, you will need to manage it. As a Ceph storage administrator, one should know about Ceph services and how to use them. On Red Hat-based distributions, Ceph daemons can be managed in two ways, as a traditional sysvinit or as a service. Now, let's learn more about these methods of service management.

Running Ceph with sysvinit

sysvinit is a traditional, yet still recommended, method of managing Ceph daemons on RedHat-based systems as well as some older Debian/Ubuntu-based distributions. The general syntax to manage Ceph daemons using sysvinit is as follows:

```
/etc/init.d/ceph [options] [command] [daemons]
```

The Ceph options include:

- `--verbose` (`-v`): Used for verbose logging
- `--allhosts` (`-a`): Executes on all nodes mentioned in `ceph.conf`, otherwise on localhost
- `--conf` (`-c`): Uses alternate configuration file

The Ceph commands include:

- `status`: Shows the status of the daemon
- `start`: Starts the daemon
- `stop`: Stops the daemon
- `restart`: Stops, and then starts the daemon
- `forcestop`: Forces the daemon to stop; this is similar to `kill -9`

The Ceph daemons include:

- mon
- osd
- mds
- ceph-radosgw

Starting daemons by type

During your cluster administration, you might require to manage Ceph services by their types. In this section, we will learn how to start daemons by their types.

To start Ceph monitor daemons on localhost, execute Ceph with the `start` command:

```
# /etc/init.d/ceph start mon
```

To start all of the Ceph monitor daemons on local as well as remote hosts, execute Ceph with the `start` command and the `-a` option:

```
# /etc/init.d/ceph -a start mon
```

The -a option will perform the requested operation on all the nodes mentioned in the ceph.conf file. Have a look at the following screenshot:

```
[root@ceph-node1 ~]# /etc/init.d/ceph -a start mon
=== mon.ceph-node1 ===
Starting Ceph mon.ceph-node1 on ceph-node1...
Starting ceph-create-keys on ceph-node1...
=== mon.ceph-node2 ===
Starting Ceph mon.ceph-node2 on ceph-node2...
Starting ceph-create-keys on ceph-node2...
=== mon.ceph-node3 ===
Starting Ceph mon.ceph-node3 on ceph-node3...
Starting ceph-create-keys on ceph-node3...
[root@ceph-node1 ~]#
```

Similarly, you can start daemons of other types, such as mon and mds:

```
# /etc/init.d/ceph start osd
```

```
# /etc/init.d/ceph start mds
```

 If you are using the -a option while starting services of any type, make sure your ceph.conf file has all your Ceph hosts defined there. If the -a option is not used, the command will only be executed on localhost.

Stopping daemons by type

In this section, we will learn about stopping Ceph daemons by their types.

To stop Ceph monitor daemons on localhost, execute Ceph with the stop command:

```
# /etc/init.d/ceph stop mon
```

To stop Ceph monitor daemons on all hosts, execute Ceph with the stop command and the -a option:

```
# /etc/init.d/ceph -a stop mon
```

The -a option will perform the requested operation on all the nodes mentioned in the ceph.conf file. The following screenshot shows these commands in action:

```
[root@ceph-node1 ~]# /etc/init.d/ceph -a stop mon
=== mon.ceph-node3 ===
Stopping Ceph mon.ceph-node3 on ceph-node3...kill 9679...done
=== mon.ceph-node2 ===
Stopping Ceph mon.ceph-node2 on ceph-node2...kill 12758...done
=== mon.ceph-node1 ===
Stopping Ceph mon.ceph-node1 on ceph-node1...kill 12331...done
[root@ceph-node1 ~]#
```

Similarly, you can stop daemons of other types, such as mon and mds:

```
# /etc/init.d/ceph stop osd
```

```
# /etc/init.d/ceph stop mds
```

 If you are using the -a option while starting services of any type, make sure your ceph.conf file has all your Ceph hosts defined there. If hosts are not defined in the ceph.conf file, the command will only be executed on localhost.

Starting and stopping all daemons

To start your Ceph cluster, execute Ceph with the start command. This command will start all Ceph services that you have deployed for all the hosts mentioned in the ceph.conf file:

```
# /etc/init.d/ceph -a start
```

To stop your Ceph cluster, execute Ceph with the stop command. This command will stop all Ceph services that you have deployed for all the hosts mentioned in the ceph.conf file:

```
# /etc/init.d/ceph -a stop
```

Starting and stopping a specific daemon

To start a specific daemon for your Ceph cluster, execute Ceph with the start command and daemon ID:

```
# /etc/init.d/ceph start osd.0
```

To check the status of a specific daemon for your Ceph cluster, execute Ceph with the `status` command and daemon ID:

```
# /etc/init.d/ceph status osd.0
```

To stop a specific daemon for your Ceph cluster, execute Ceph with the `stop` command and daemon ID:

```
# /etc/init.d/ceph stop osd.0
```

This screenshot shows the output of the preceding commands:

```
[root@ceph-node1 ~]# /etc/init.d/ceph start osd.0
=== osd.0 ===
create-or-move updated item name 'osd.0' weight 0.01 at location {host=ceph-node1,root=default} to crush map
Starting Ceph osd.0 on ceph-node1...
starting osd.0 at :/0 osd_data /var/lib/ceph/osd/ceph-0 /var/lib/ceph/osd/ceph-0/journal
[root@ceph-node1 ~]#
[root@ceph-node1 ~]# /etc/init.d/ceph status osd.0
=== osd.0 ===
osd.0: running {"version":"0.80.1"}
[root@ceph-node1 ~]#
[root@ceph-node1 ~]# /etc/init.d/ceph stop  osd.0
=== osd.0 ===
Stopping Ceph osd.0 on ceph-node1...kill 20792...done
[root@ceph-node1 ~]#
```

Similarly, you can manage specific daemons for the monitor and mds of your Ceph cluster.

Running Ceph as a service

Depending on your Linux working style, you can choose to manage your Ceph services either by `sysvinit` or by the Linux `service` command. Starting from Ceph Argonaut and Bobtail, you can mange Ceph daemons using the Linux `service` command:

```
service ceph [options] [command] [daemons]
```

The Ceph options include:

- `--verbose` (`-v`): Used for verbose logging
- `--allhosts` (`-a`): Executes on all nodes that are mentioned in `ceph.conf`, otherwise on localhost
- `--conf` (`-c`): Uses and alternates configuration files

The Ceph commands include:

- `status`: Shows the status of the daemon
- `start`: Starts the daemon
- `stop`: Stops the daemon
- `restart`: Stops, and then starts the daemon
- `forcestop`: Forces the daemon to stop; this is similar to `kill -9`

The Ceph daemons include:

- mon
- osd
- mds
- ceph-radosgw

Starting and stopping all daemons

To start your Ceph cluster, execute Ceph with the `start` command. This command will start all Ceph services that you have deployed for all the hosts mentioned in the `ceph.conf` file:

```
# service ceph -a start
```

To stop your Ceph cluster, execute Ceph with the `stop` command. This command will stop all Ceph services that you have deployed for all the hosts mentioned in the `ceph.conf` file:

```
# service ceph -a stop
```

Starting and stopping a specific daemon

To start a specific daemon for your Ceph cluster, execute Ceph with the `start` command and daemon ID:

```
# service ceph start osd.0
```

To check the status of a specific daemon for your Ceph cluster, execute Ceph with the `status` command and daemon ID:

```
# service ceph status osd.0
```

To stop a specific daemon for your Ceph cluster, execute Ceph with the `stop` command and daemon ID:

```
# service ceph stop osd.0
```

The following is the screenshot showing the command outputs:

```
[root@ceph-node1 ~]# service ceph start osd.0
=== osd.0 ===
create-or-move updated item name 'osd.0' weight 0.01 at location {host=ceph-node1,root=default} to crush map
Starting Ceph osd.0 on ceph-node1...
starting osd.0 at :/0 osd_data /var/lib/ceph/osd/ceph-0 /var/lib/ceph/osd/ceph-0/journal
[root@ceph-node1 ~]#
[root@ceph-node1 ~]# service ceph status osd.0
=== osd.0 ===
osd.0: running {"version":"0.80.1"}
[root@ceph-node1 ~]#
[root@ceph-node1 ~]# service ceph stop osd.0
=== osd.0 ===
Stopping Ceph osd.0 on ceph-node1...kill 22435...done
[root@ceph-node1 ~]#
```

Scaling out a Ceph cluster

When you are building a storage solution, scalability is one of the most important design aspects. Your storage solution should be scalable to accommodate your future data needs. Usually, a storage system starts with small to medium capacity and grows gradually over a period of time. Traditional storage systems are based on scale-up designs and are bound to a certain capacity. If you try to expand your storage system over a certain limit, you might need to compromise with performance and reliability. The scale-up design methodology for storage involves adding disk resources to the existing device, which becomes a bottleneck for performance, capacity, and manageability when it reaches a certain level.

On the other hand, scale-out designs focus on adding entire new node, including disk, CPU, and memory, to the existing cluster. In this type of design, you will not end up with limited storage; rather, you will get benefited by the performance and robustness. Have a look at the following architecture:

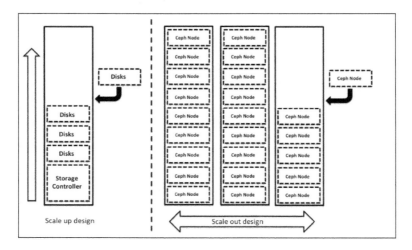

Ceph is a seamless scalable storage system based on the scale-out design, where you can add any off-the-shelf server node to a Ceph cluster and extend your storage system beyond the limits of a traditional system. Ceph allows on-the-fly addition of monitor and OSD nodes to an existing Ceph cluster. Now, let's see how to add nodes to a Ceph cluster.

Adding OSD nodes to a Ceph cluster

Adding an OSD node to a Ceph cluster is an online process. To demonstrate this, we require a new virtual machine named `ceph-node4` with three disks; we will add this node to our existing Ceph cluster.

Create a new node `ceph-node4` with three disks (OSDs). You can follow the process of creating a new virtual machine with disks, OS configuration, and Ceph installation as mentioned in *Chapter 2*, *Ceph Instant Deployment*, and *Chapter 5*, *Deploying Ceph – the Way You Should Know*.

Once you have the new node ready for addition to a Ceph cluster, check the current Ceph OSD details:

```
# ceph osd tree
```

This is what you will get once this command is run:

```
[root@ceph-node1 ceph]# ceph osd tree
# id    weight  type name       up/down reweight
-1      0.08995 root default
-2      0.02998         host ceph-node1
0       0.009995                        osd.0   up      1
1       0.009995                        osd.1   up      1
2       0.009995                        osd.2   up      1
-3      0.02998         host ceph-node2
3       0.009995                        osd.3   up      1
5       0.009995                        osd.5   up      1
4       0.009995                        osd.4   up      1
-4      0.02998         host ceph-node3
6       0.009995                        osd.6   up      1
7       0.009995                        osd.7   up      1
8       0.009995                        osd.8   up      1

[root@ceph-node1 ceph]#
```

Expanding a Ceph cluster is an online process, and to demonstrate this, we will perform some operations on our Ceph cluster; we will also expand the cluster in parallel. In *Chapter 5, Deploying Ceph – the Way You Should Know*, we deployed the Ceph RADOS block device on a ceph-client1 machine. We will use the same machine to generate traffic to our Ceph cluster. Make sure that ceph-client1 has mounted RBD:

```
# df -h /mnt/ceph-vol1
```

```
[root@ceph-client1 ~]# df -h /mnt/ceph-vol1
Filesystem              Size  Used Avail Use% Mounted on
/dev/rbd0               10G   33M   10G   1% /mnt/ceph-vol1
[root@ceph-client1 ~]#
```

Log in on ceph-node1 from a separate cli terminal and list the disks available to add as OSDs for ceph-node4. The ceph-node4 machine should have Ceph installed and the ceph.conf file copied to it. You will notice three disks, sdb, sdc, and sdd, listed when you execute the following command:

```
# ceph-deploy disk list ceph-node4
```

As mentioned earlier, scaling up a Ceph cluster is a seamless and online process. To demonstrate this, we will generate some load to the cluster and perform the scaling-up operation simultaneously. Note that this is an optional step.

Make sure the host running the VirtualBox environment has adequate disk space as we will write data to the Ceph cluster. Open the ceph-client1 cli terminal and generate some write traffic to the Ceph cluster. As soon as you start generating traffic to the cluster, start expanding it by performing next steps.

```
# dd if=/dev/zero of=/mnt/ceph-vol1/file1 count=10240 bs=1M
```

Switch to the ceph-node1 cli terminal and expand the Ceph cluster by adding ceph-node4 disks as new Ceph OSDs:

```
# ceph-deploy disk zap ceph-node4:sdb ceph-node4:sdc ceph-node4:sdd
```

```
# ceph-deploy osd create ceph-node4:sdb ceph-node4:sdc ceph-node4:sdd
```

By the time OSD addition is under progress, you should monitor your Ceph cluster status from a separate terminal window. You will notice that the Ceph cluster performs the write operation while simultaneously scaling out its capacity:

```
# watch ceph status
```

Finally, once ceph-node4 disk addition is complete; you can check your Ceph cluster status using the preceding command. The following is what you will see after running this command:

```
[root@ceph-node1 /]# ceph status
    cluster 07a92ca3-347e-43db-87ee-e0a0a9f89e97
     health HEALTH_OK
     monmap e3: 3 mons at {ceph-node1=192.168.57.101:6789/0,ceph-node2=192.168.57.102:6789/0,
ceph-node3=192.168.57.103:6789/0}, election epoch 938, quorum 0,1,2 ceph-node1,ceph-node2,cep
h-node3
     mdsmap e61: 1/1/1 up {0=ceph-node2=up:active}
     osdmap e807: 12 osds: 12 up, 12 in
      pgmap v3998: 1472 pgs, 13 pools, 78568 kB data, 2687 objects
            828 MB used, 107 GB / 107 GB avail
                1472 active+clean
[root@ceph-node1 /]#
```

At this point, if you list out all OSDs, it will give you a better understanding:

```
# ceph osd tree
```

This command outputs some valuable information related to OSD, such as OSD weight, which the Ceph node hosts. The OSD, status of OSD (up/down), and OSD IN/OUT status are represented by 1 or 0. Have a look at the following screenshot:

```
[root@ceph-node1 tmp]# ceph osd tree
# id    weight  type name           up/down reweight
-1      0.12       root default
-2      0.009995              host ceph-node1
0       0.009995                    osd.0   up      1
1       0.009995                    osd.1   up      1
2       0.009995                    osd.2   up      1
-3      0.03                  host ceph-node2
3       0.009995                    osd.3   up      1
5       0.009995                    osd.5   up      1
4       0.009995                    osd.4   up      1
-4      0.03                  host ceph-node3
6       0.009995                    osd.6   up      1
7       0.009995                    osd.7   up      1
8       0.009995                    osd.8   up      1
-5      0.04999               host ceph-node4
9       0.009995                    osd.9   up      1
10      0.009995                    osd.10  up      1
11      0.009995                    osd.11  up      1
[root@ceph-node1 tmp]#
```

Scaling down a Ceph cluster

A storage solution is rated on the basis of its flexibility; a good storage solution should be flexible enough to support its expansion and reduction without causing any downtime to the services. Traditional storage systems are very limited when it comes to flexibility; they do support storage capacity addition, but to a very small extent, and there's no support for online capacity reduction. You are locked with storage capacity and cannot perform changes as per your needs.

Ceph is an absolute, flexible storage system providing online and on-the-fly changes to storage capacity either by expansion or reduction. In the last section, we saw how easy the scale-out operation with Ceph is. We added a new node, ceph-node4, with three OSDs to the Ceph cluster. Now, we will demonstrate the scaling-down operation on a Ceph cluster, without any impact on its accessibility, by removing ceph-node4 out of the Ceph cluster.

Bringing an OSD out and down from a Ceph cluster

Before proceeding with a cluster's size reduction or scaling it down, make sure the cluster has enough free space to accommodate all the data present on the node you are moving out. The cluster should not be at its near-to-full ratio.

From the ceph-client1 node, generate some load on the Ceph cluster. This is an optional step to demonstration on-the-fly scale-down operations of a Ceph cluster. Make sure the host running the VirtualBox environment has adequate disk space since we will write data to a Ceph cluster.

```
# dd if=/dev/zero of=/mnt/ceph-vol1/file1 count=3000 bs=1M
```

As we need to scale down the cluster, we will remove ceph-node4 and all of its associated OSDs out of the cluster. Ceph OSDs should be set out so that Ceph can perform data recovery. From any of the Ceph nodes, take the OSDs out of the cluster:

```
# ceph osd out osd.9
# ceph osd out osd.10
# ceph osd out osd.11
```

```
[root@ceph-node1 /]# ceph osd out osd.9
marked out osd.9.
[root@ceph-node1 /]# ceph osd out osd.10
marked out osd.10.
[root@ceph-node1 /]# ceph osd out osd.11
marked out osd.11.
```

As soon as you mark OSDs out of the cluster, Ceph will start rebalancing the cluster by migrating the placement groups out of the OSDs that were made out to other OSDs inside the cluster. Your cluster state will become unhealthy for some time, but it will be good to serve data to clients. Based on the number of OSDs removed, there might be some drop in cluster performance till the time recovery is completed. Once the cluster is healthy again, it should perform as usual. Have a look at the following screenshot:

```
[root@ceph-node1 /]# ceph -s
    cluster 07a92ca3-347e-43db-87ee-e0a0a9f89e97
     health HEALTH_WARN 517 pgs peering; 16 pgs recovering; 4 pgs recovery_wait; 363 pgs stuck
inactive; 379 pgs stuck unclean; 43 requests are blocked > 32 sec; recovery 1401/5290 objects
degraded (26.484%)
     monmap e3: 3 mons at {ceph-node1=192.168.57.101:6789/0,ceph-node2=192.168.57.102:6789/0,c
eph-node3=192.168.57.103:6789/0}, election epoch 938, quorum 0,1,2 ceph-node1,ceph-node2,ceph-
node3
     mdsmap e61: 1/1/1 up {0=ceph-node2=up:active}
     osdmap e824: 12 osds: 12 up, 9 in
      pgmap v4077: 1472 pgs, 13 pools, 161 MB data, 2618 objects
            748 MB used, 82095 MB / 82844 MB avail
            1401/5290 objects degraded (26.484%)
                437 inactive
                 10 active
                511 peering
                  4 active+recovery_wait
                487 active+clean
                 16 active+recovering
                  1 remapped
                  6 remapped+peering
recovery io 0 B/s, 52 objects/s
  client io 517 B/s rd, 78962 kB/s wr, 398 op/s
[root@ceph-node1 /]#
```

In the preceding screenshot, you can see that the cluster is under a recovery mode while also serving data to clients at the same time. You can observe the recovery process using the following command:

```
# ceph -w
```

As we marked osd.9, osd.10, and osd.11 out of the cluster, they are not a member of the cluster, but their services still run. Next, log in on a ceph-node4 machine and stop the OSD services:

```
# service ceph stop osd.9
# service ceph stop osd.10
# service ceph stop osd.11
```

Once OSDs are down, check the OSD tree, as shown in the following screenshot. You will observe that the OSDs are down and out:

```
[root@ceph-node4 ~]# ceph osd tree
# id    weight  type name        up/down reweight
-1      0.12      root default
-2      0.009995                    host ceph-node1
0       0.009995                        osd.0   up      1
1       0.009995                        osd.1   up      1
2       0.009995                        osd.2   up      1
-3      0.03              host ceph-node2
3       0.009995                        osd.3   up      1
5       0.009995                        osd.5   up      1
4       0.009995                        osd.4   up      1
-4      0.03              host ceph-node3
6       0.009995                        osd.6   up      1
7       0.009995                        osd.7   up      1
8       0.009995                        osd.8   up      1
-5      0.04999           host ceph-node4
9       0.009995                        osd.9   down    0
10      0.009995                        osd.10  down    0
11      0.009995                        osd.11  down    0
[root@ceph-node4 ~]#
```

Removing the OSD from a Ceph cluster

The process of removing OSDs from a Ceph cluster involves removing all the entries of these OSDs from cluster maps.

Remove the OSDs from the CRUSH map. For this, log in to any of the cluster nodes and perform the following commands:

```
# ceph osd crush remove osd.9
```

```
# ceph osd crush remove osd.10
```

```
# ceph osd crush remove osd.11
```

```
[root@ceph-node1 ~]# ceph osd crush remove osd.9
removed item id 9 name 'osd.9' from crush map
[root@ceph-node1 ~]# ceph osd crush remove osd.10
removed item id 10 name 'osd.10' from crush map
[root@ceph-node1 ~]# ceph osd crush remove osd.11
removed item id 11 name 'osd.11' from crush map
[root@ceph-node1 ~]#
```

As soon as OSDs are removed from the CRUSH map, the Ceph cluster becomes healthy. You should also observe the OSD map; since we have not removed the OSDs, it will show as 12 OSD, 9 UP, 9 IN:

```
[root@ceph-node1 /]# ceph status
    cluster 07a92ca3-347e-43db-87ee-e0a0a9f89e97
     health HEALTH_OK
     monmap e3: 3 mons at {ceph-node1=192.168.57.101:6789/0,ceph-node2=192.168.57.102:
6789/0,ceph-node3=192.168.57.103:6789/0}, election epoch 938, quorum 0,1,2 ceph-node1,
ceph-node2,ceph-node3
     mdsmap e61: 1/1/1 up {0=ceph-node2=up:active}
     osdmap e898: 12 osds: 9 up, 9 in
     pgmap v4400: 1472 pgs, 13 pools, 683 MB data, 2838 objects
            1876 MB used, 80968 MB / 82844 MB avail
                 1472 active+clean
[root@ceph-node1 /]#
```

Remove the OSD authentication key:

```
# ceph auth del osd.9
# ceph auth del osd.10
# ceph auth del osd.11
```

Finally, remove the OSD and check your cluster status. You should see 9 OSD, 9 UP, 9 IN, and the cluster health should be OK:

```
[root@ceph-node1 /]# ceph osd rm osd.9
removed osd.9
[root@ceph-node1 /]# ceph osd rm osd.10
removed osd.10
[root@ceph-node1 /]# ceph osd rm osd.11
removed osd.11
[root@ceph-node1 /]# ceph status
    cluster 07a92ca3-347e-43db-87ee-e0a0a9f89e97
     health HEALTH_OK
     monmap e3: 3 mons at {ceph-node1=192.168.57.101:6789/0,ceph-node2=192.168.57.102:
6789/0,ceph-node3=192.168.57.103:6789/0}, election epoch 938, quorum 0,1,2 ceph-node1,
ceph-node2,ceph-node3
     mdsmap e61: 1/1/1 up {0=ceph-node2=up:active}
     osdmap e901: 9 osds: 9 up, 9 in
     pgmap v4413: 1472 pgs, 13 pools, 683 MB data, 2838 objects
            1879 MB used, 80965 MB / 82844 MB avail
                 1472 active+clean
[root@ceph-node1 /]#
```

To keep your cluster clean, perform some housekeeping. As we have removed all the OSDs from the CRUSH map, ceph-node4 does not hold any item. Remove ceph-node4 from the CRUSH map to remove all traces of this node from the Ceph cluster:

```
# ceph osd crush remove ceph-node4
```

Replacing a failed disk drive

Being a Ceph storage admin, you will need to manage Ceph clusters with multiple physical disks. As the physical disk count increases for your Ceph cluster, the frequency of disk failures might also increase. Hence, replacing a failed disk drive might become a repetitive task for a Ceph storage administrator. There is generally no need to worry if one or more disks fail in your Ceph cluster as Ceph will take care of the data by its replication and high availability feature. The process of removing OSDs from a Ceph cluster relies on Ceph's data replication and removing all the entries of failed OSDs from CRUSH cluster maps. We will now see the failed disk replacement process on ceph-node1 and osd.0.

Firstly, check the status of your Ceph cluster. Since this cluster does not have any failed disk, the status will be HEALTH_OK:

```
# ceph status
```

Since we are demonstrating this exercise on virtual machines, we need to forcefully fail a disk by bringing ceph-node1 down, detaching a disk and powering up the VM:

```
# VBoxManage  controlvm ceph-node1 poweroff
```

```
# VBoxManage storageattach ceph-node1 --storagectl "SATA Controller"
--port 1 --device 0 --type hdd --medium none
```

```
# VBoxManage startvm ceph-node1
```

In the following screenshot, you will notice that ceph-node1 contains a failed osd.0 that should be replaced:

```
[root@ceph-node1 ~]# ceph osd tree
# id    weight  type name       up/down reweight
-1      0.06999 root default
-2      0.009995                host ceph-node1
0       0.009995                        osd.0   down    1
1       0.009995                        osd.1   up      1
2       0.009995                        osd.2   up      1
-3      0.03            host ceph-node2
3       0.009995                        osd.3   up      1
5       0.009995                        osd.5   up      1
4       0.009995                        osd.4   up      1
-4      0.03            host ceph-node3
6       0.009995                        osd.6   up      1
7       0.009995                        osd.7   up      1
8       0.009995                        osd.8   up      1
[root@ceph-node1 ~]#
```

Once the OSD is down, Ceph will mark this OSD out of the cluster in some time; by default, it is after 300 seconds. If not, you can make it out manually:

```
# ceph osd out osd.0
```

Remove the failed OSD from the CRUSH map:

```
# ceph osd crush rm osd.0
```

Delete Ceph authentication keys for the OSD:

```
# ceph auth del osd.0
```

Finally, remove the OSD from the Ceph cluster:

```
# ceph osd rm osd.0
```

```
[root@ceph-node1 ~]# ceph osd out osd.0
marked out osd.0.
[root@ceph-node1 ~]# ceph osd crush rm osd.0
removed item id 0 name 'osd.0' from crush map
[root@ceph-node1 ~]# ceph auth del osd.0
updated
[root@ceph-node1 ~]# ceph osd rm osd.0
removed osd.0
[root@ceph-node1 ~]#
```

Since one of your OSDs is unavailable, the cluster health will not be OK, and it will perform recovery; there is nothing to worry about, this is a normal Ceph operation.

Now, you should physically replace the failed disk with the new disk on your Ceph node. These days, almost all the server hardware and operating systems support disk hot swapping, so you will not require any downtime for disk replacement. Since we are using a virtual machine, we need to power off the VM, add a new disk, and restart the VM. Once the disk is inserted, make a note of its OS device ID:

```
# VBoxManage  controlvm ceph-node1 poweroff
```

```
# VBoxManage storageattach ceph-node1 --storagectl "SATA Controller"
--port 1 --device 0 --type hdd --medium ceph-node1-osd1.vdi
```

```
# VBoxManage startvm ceph-node1
```

Perform the following commands to list disks; the new disk generally does not have any partition:

```
# ceph-deploy disk list ceph-node1
```

Before adding the disk to the Ceph cluster, perform disk zap:

```
# ceph-deploy disk zap ceph-node1:sdb
```

Finally, create an OSD on the disk, and Ceph will add it as osd.0:

```
# ceph-deploy --overwrite-conf osd create  ceph-node1:sdb
```

Once an OSD is created, Ceph will perform a recovery operation and start moving placement groups from secondary OSDs to the new OSD. The recovery operation might take a while, after which your Ceph cluster will be HEALTHY_OK again:

```
[root@ceph-node1 /]# ceph status
    cluster 07a92ca3-347e-43db-87ee-e0a0a9f89e97
    health HEALTH_OK
    monmap e3: 3 mons at {ceph-node1=192.168.57.101:6789/0,ceph-node2=192.168.57.102:
6789/0,ceph-node3=192.168.57.103:6789/0}, election epoch 938, quorum 0,1,2 ceph-node1,
ceph-node2,ceph-node3
    mdsmap e61: 1/1/1 up {0=ceph-node2=up:active}
    osdmap e901: 9 osds: 9 up, 9 in
    pgmap v4413: 1472 pgs, 13 pools, 683 MB data, 2838 objects
        1879 MB used, 80965 MB / 82844 MB avail
            1472 active+clean
[root@ceph-node1 /]#
```

Manipulating CRUSH maps

We already covered Ceph CRUSH maps in *Chapter 4, Ceph Internals*. In this section, we will dive into the details of CRUSH maps, including their layouts, as well as defining custom CRUSH maps. When you deploy a Ceph cluster using the procedure mentioned in this book, it will create a default CRUSH map for your Ceph cluster. This default CRUSH map is good to go for sandbox and testing environments. However, if you run Ceph clusters in production or at a large scale, consider developing a custom CRUSH map for your environment to ensure better performance, reliability, and data security.

Identifying CRUSH locations

A CRUSH location is the location of an OSD in a CRUSH map. For instance, an organization named mona-labs.com has a Ceph cluster with the CRUSH location of osd.156, which belongs to the host ceph-node15. This host is physically present in chassis-3, which is installed in rack-16, which is a part of room-2 and datacentre-1-north-FI.

This osd.156 will be a part of a CRUSH map, as shown in the following diagram:

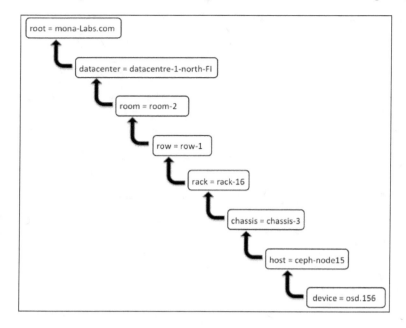

In the preceding diagram, keys are shown on the left-hand side of =; these are also known as CRUSH types. The default CRUSH map includes `root`, `datacentre`, `room`, `row`, `pod`, `pdu`, `rack`, `chassis`, and `host`. It is not mandatory to use all the CRUSH types while defining a CRUSH map, but the used CRUSH type must be valid, else you might get compilation errors. CRUSH is quite flexible; you can even define your custom CRUSH types and use it across the CRUSH map in your own way.

CRUSH map internals

To know what's inside a CRUSH map, we need to extract it and decompile it to convert it into a human-readable form and for easy editing. We can perform all the necessary changes to a CRUSH map at this stage, and to make the changes take effect, we should compile and inject it back to the Ceph cluster. The change to Ceph clusters by the new CRUSH map is dynamic, that is, once the new CRUSH map is injected into the Ceph cluster, the change will come into effect immediately on the fly. We will now take a look at the CRUSH map of our Ceph cluster that we deployed in this book.

Extract the CRUSH map from any of the monitor nodes:

```
# ceph osd getcrushmap -o crushmap_compiled_file
```

Once you have the CRUSH map, decompile it to make it human readable and editable:

```
# crushtool -d crushmap_compiled_file -o crushmap_decompiled_file
```

At this point, the output file, crushmap_decompiled_file, can be viewed/edited in your favorite editor.

In the next section, we will learn how to perform changes to a CRUSH map.

Once the changes are done, you should compile the changes with -c command option:

```
# crushtool -c crushmap_decompiled_file -o newcrushmap
```

Finally, inject the new compiled CURSH map into the Ceph cluster with -i command option:

```
# ceph osd setcrushmap  -i newcrushmap
```

A CRUSH map file contains four sections; they are as follows:

- **Crush map devices**: The device section contains a list of all the OSDs present in a Ceph cluster. Whenever any new OSD is added or removed from a Ceph cluster, the CRUSH map's devices section is updated automatically. Usually, you do not require changing this section; Ceph takes care of this. However, if you need to add a new device, add a new line at the end of the device section with a unique device number followed by the OSD. The following screenshot shows the devices section of a CRUSH map from our sandbox Ceph cluster:

```
# devices
device 0 osd.0
device 1 osd.1
device 2 osd.2
device 3 osd.3
device 4 osd.4
device 5 osd.5
device 6 osd.6
device 7 osd.7
device 8 osd.8
```

- **Crush map bucket types**: This section defines the types of buckets that can be used in a CRUSH map. The default CRUSH map contains several bucket types, which is usually enough for most of the Ceph clusters. However, based on your requirement, you can add or remove bucket types from this section. To add a bucket type, add a new line in the bucket type section of the CRUSH map file, enter the type, and type the ID (next numeric number) followed by the bucket name. The default bucket list from our sandbox Ceph cluster looks like the following:

```
# types
type 0 osd
type 1 host
type 2 rack
type 3 row
type 4 room
type 5 datacenter
type 6 root
```

- **Crush map bucket definition**: Once the bucket type is declared, it is defined for hosts and other failure domains. In this section, you can do hierarchical changes to your Ceph cluster architecture, for example, defining hosts, row, racks, chassis, room, and datacenter. You can also define what type of algorithm the bucket should use. The bucket definition contains several parameters; you can use the following syntax to create a bucket definition:

```
[bucket-type] [bucket-name] {
        id [a unique negative numeric ID]
        weight [the relative capacity/capability of the
        item(s)]
        alg [the bucket type: uniform | list | tree | straw
        ]
        hash [the hash type: 0 by default]
        item [item-name] weight [weight]
}
```

The following is the bucket definition section from our sandbox Ceph cluster:

```
# buckets
host ceph-node1 {
        id -2              # do not change unnecessarily
        # weight 0.030
        alg straw
        hash 0  # rjenkins1
        item osd.1 weight 0.010
        item osd.2 weight 0.010
        item osd.0 weight 0.010
}
host ceph-node2 {
        id -3              # do not change unnecessarily
        # weight 0.030
        alg straw
        hash 0  # rjenkins1
        item osd.3 weight 0.010
        item osd.5 weight 0.010
        item osd.4 weight 0.010
}
host ceph-node3 {
        id -4              # do not change unnecessarily
        # weight 0.030
        alg straw
        hash 0  # rjenkins1
        item osd.6 weight 0.010
        item osd.7 weight 0.010
        item osd.8 weight 0.010
}
root default {
        id -1              # do not change unnecessarily
        # weight 0.090
        alg straw
        hash 0  # rjenkins1
        item ceph-node1 weight 0.030
        item ceph-node2 weight 0.030
        item ceph-node3 weight 0.030
}
```

- **Crush map rules**: It defines the way to select an appropriate bucket for data placement in pools. For a larger Ceph cluster, there might be multiple pools, and each pool will have its one CRUSH ruleset. CRUSH map rules require several parameters; you can use the following syntax to create a CRUSH ruleset:

```
rule <rulename> {
ruleset <ruleset>
      type [ replicated | raid4 ]
      min_size <min-size>
```

```
        max_size <max-size>
        step take <bucket-type>
        step [choose|chooseleaf] [firstn|indep] <N>
        <bucket-type>
        step emit
}
```

```
# rules
rule data {
        ruleset 0
        type replicated
        min_size 1
        max_size 10
        step take default
        step chooseleaf firstn 0 type host
        step emit
}
rule metadata {
        ruleset 1
        type replicated
        min_size 1
        max_size 10
        step take default
        step chooseleaf firstn 0 type host
        step emit
}
rule rbd {
        ruleset 2
        type replicated
        min_size 1
        max_size 10
        step take default
        step chooseleaf firstn 0 type host
        step emit
}

# end crush map
```

Different pools on different OSDs

Ceph seamlessly runs on heterogeneous commodity hardware. There are possibilities that you can use for your existing hardware systems for Ceph and develop a storage cluster of different hardware types. As a Ceph storage administrator, your use case might require creating multiple Ceph pools on multiple types of drives. The most common use case is to provide a fast storage pool based on SSD disk types where you can get high performance out of your storage cluster. The data, which do not require higher I/O is usually stored on pools backed by slower magnetic drives.

Our next hands-on demonstration will focus on creating two Ceph pools, ssd-pools backed by faster SSD disks, and sata-pools backed by slower SATA disks. To achieve this, we will edit CRUSH maps and do the necessary configurations.

The sandbox Ceph cluster that we deployed in the earlier chapters is hosted on virtual machines and does not have real SSD disks backing it. Hence, we will be considering a few disks as SSD disks for learning purposes. If you perform this exercise on real SSD disk-based Ceph clusters, there will be no changes in the steps we will perform. You should be able to use the same steps without any modifications.

In the following demonstration, we assume that ceph-node1 is our SSD node hosting three SSDs. The ceph-node2 and ceph-node3 nodes host SATA disks. We will modify the default CRUSH map and create two pools, namely SSD and SATA. The SSD pool's primary copy will be hosed on ceph-node1, while the secondary and tertiary copies will be on other nodes. Similarly, SATA pool's primary copy will be on either ceph-node2 or ceph-node3 as we have two nodes backing the SATA pool. At any step of this demonstration, you can refer to the updated CRUSH map file provided with this book on the Packt Publishing website.

Extract the CRUSH map from any of the monitor nodes and compile it:

```
# ceph osd getcrushmap -o crushmap-extract
```

```
# crushtool -d crushmap-extract -o crushmap-decompiled
```

```
[root@ceph-node1 tmp]# ceph osd getcrushmap -o crushmap-extract
got crush map from osdmap epoch 1045
[root@ceph-node1 tmp]# crushtool -d crushmap-extract -o crushmap-decompiled
[root@ceph-node1 tmp]# ls -l crushmap-decompiled
-rw-r--r--. 1 root root 1591 Jul 25 00:18 crushmap-decompiled
[root@ceph-node1 tmp]#
```

Use your favorite editor to edit the default CRUSH map:

```
# vi crushmap-decompiled
```

Replace the root default bucket with the root ssd and root sata buckets. Here, the root ssd bucket contains one item, ceph-node1. Similarly, the root sata bucket has two hosts defined. Have a look at the following screenshot:

```
root ssd {
        id -1
        alg straw
        hash 0
        item ceph-node1  weight  0.030
}
root sata {
        id -5
        alg straw
        hash 0
        item ceph-node2  weight  0.030
        item ceph-node3  weight  0.030
}
```

Adjust the existing rules to work with new buckets. For this, change `step take default` to `step take sata` for data, metadata, and RBD rules. This will instruct these rules to use the `sata root` bucket instead of the default `root` bucket as we removed it in the previous step.

Finally, add new rules for the `ssd` and `sata` pools, as shown in the following screenshot:

```
rule sata {
        ruleset 3
        type replicated
        min_size 1
        max_size 10
        step take sata
        step chooseleaf firstn 0 type host
        step emit
}
rule ssd {
        ruleset 4
        type replicated
        min_size 1
        max_size 10
        step take ssd
        step chooseleaf firstn 0 type host
        step emit
}
```

Once the changes are done, compile the CRUSH file and inject it back to the Ceph cluster:

```
# crushtool -c crushmap-decompiled -o crushmap-compiled
# ceph osd setcrushmap -i crushmap-compiled
```

As soon as you inject the new CRUSH map to the Ceph cluster, the cluster will undergo data reshuffling and data recovery, but it should attain the `HEALTH_OK` status soon. Check the status of your cluster as follows:

```
[root@ceph-node1 tmp]# ceph -s
    cluster 07a92ca3-347e-43db-87ee-e0a0a9f89e97
     health HEALTH_WARN 18 pgs recovering; 1309 pgs stuck unclean; recovery 1670/5738 objects degraded (29.104%)
     monmap e3: 3 mons at {ceph-node1=192.168.57.101:6789/0,ceph-node2=192.168.57.102:6789/0,ceph-node3=192.168.57.103:6789/0}, election epoch 1040, quorum 0,1,2 ceph-node1,ceph-node2,ceph-node3
     mdsmap e93: 1/1/1 up {0=ceph-node2=up:active}
     osdmap e1079: 9 osds: 9 up, 9 in
      pgmap v4804: 1472 pgs, 13 pools, 683 MB data, 2838 objects
            2106 MB used, 80738 MB / 82844 MB avail
            1670/5738 objects degraded (29.104%)
                  11 active
                1280 active+remapped
                 163 active+clean
                  18 active+recovering
recovery io 17308 kB/s, 134 objects/s
[root@ceph-node1 tmp]#
```

Once your cluster is healthy, create two pools for `ssd` and `sata`:

```
# ceph osd pool create sata 64 64
# ceph osd pool create ssd 64 64
```

Assign `crush_ruleset` for the `sata` and `ssd` rules, as defined in the CRUSH map:

```
# ceph osd pool set sata crush_ruleset 3
# ceph osd pool set ssd crush_ruleset 4
# ceph osd dump | egrep -i "ssd|sata"
```

```
[root@ceph-node1 /]# ceph osd pool create sata 64 64
pool 'sata' created
[root@ceph-node1 /]# ceph osd pool create ssd 64 64
pool 'ssd' created
[root@ceph-node1 /]# ceph osd pool set sata crush_ruleset 3
set pool 16 crush_ruleset to 3
[root@ceph-node1 /]# ceph osd pool set ssd crush_ruleset 4
set pool 17 crush_ruleset to 4
[root@ceph-node1 /]# ceph osd dump | egrep -i "ssd|sata"
pool 16 'sata' replicated size 3 min_size 2 crush_ruleset 3 object_hash rjenkins pg_num 64 pgp_num 64 last_change 1093
 owner 0 flags hashpspool stripe_width 0
pool 17 'ssd' replicated size 3 min_size 2 crush_ruleset 4 object_hash rjenkins pg_num 64 pgp_num 64 last_change 1094
owner 0 flags hashpspool stripe_width 0
[root@ceph-node1 /]#
```

To test these newly created pools, we will put some data on them and verify which OSD the data gets stored on. Create some data files:

```
# dd if=/dev/zero of=sata.pool bs=1M count=32 conv=fsync
# dd if=/dev/zero of=ssd.pool bs=1M count=32 conv=fsync
```

```
[root@ceph-node1 /]# dd if=/dev/zero of=sata.pool bs=1M count=32 conv=fsync
32+0 records in
32+0 records out
33554432 bytes (34 MB) copied, 0.240931 s, 139 MB/s
[root@ceph-node1 /]# dd if=/dev/zero of=ssd.pool bs=1M count=32 conv=fsync
32+0 records in
32+0 records out
33554432 bytes (34 MB) copied, 0.179995 s, 186 MB/s
[root@ceph-node1 /]#
[root@ceph-node1 /]# ls -l *.pool
-rw-r--r--. 1 root root 33554432 Jul 25 01:00 sata.pool
-rw-r--r--. 1 root root 33554432 Jul 25 01:01 ssd.pool
[root@ceph-node1 /]#
```

Put these files to Ceph storage on respective pools:

```
#  rados -p ssd put ssd.pool.object   ssd.pool
#  rados -p sata put sata.pool.object   sata.pool
Finally check the OSD map for pool objects
# ceph osd map ssd ssd.pool.object
# ceph osd map sata sata.pool.object
```

```
[root@ceph-node1 /]# ceph osd map ssd ssd.pool.object
osdmap e1097 pool 'ssd' (17) object 'ssd.pool.object' -> pg 17.82fd0527 (17.27) -> up ([2], p2) acting ([2,5,6], p2)
[root@ceph-node1 /]#
[root@ceph-node1 /]# ceph osd map sata sata.pool.object
osdmap e1097 pool 'sata' (16) object 'sata.pool.object' -> pg 16.f71bcbc2 (16.2) -> up ([4,8], p4) acting ([4,8], p4)
[root@ceph-node1 /]#
```

Let's diagnose the preceding output; the first output for the SSD pool represents the object's primary copy that is located on osd.2; the other copies are located on osd.5 and osd.6. This is because of the way we configured our CRUSH map. We defined an SSD pool to use ceph-node1, which contains osd.0, osd.1, and osd.2.

This is just a basic demonstration for custom CRUSH maps. You can do a lot of things with CRUSH. There are a lot of possibilities for effectively and efficiently managing all the data of your Ceph cluster using custom CRUSH maps.

Summary

In this chapter, we covered operations and maintenance tasks that need to be performed on a Ceph cluster. This chapter gives us an understanding of Ceph service management, scaling out, and scaling down a running Ceph cluster. The latter part of this chapter deals with failed disk drive replacement procedure for your Ceph cluster, which is something quite common for a medium to large cluster. Finally, you learned about powerful CRUSH maps and how to customize a CRUSH map. CRUSH map modification and tuning is quite an interesting and important part of Ceph; with it comes an enterprise-grade production storage solution. You can always get more information related to Ceph CRUSH maps at http://ceph.com/docs/master/rados/operations/crush-map/.

In the next chapter, we will learn about Ceph monitoring as well as logging and debugging your Ceph cluster with some troubleshooting tips.

8
Monitoring Your Ceph Cluster

Ceph cluster monitoring is one of the prime responsibilities of Ceph storage administration. Monitoring plays a vital role in troubleshooting cluster and fixes the problem when a cluster is unhealthy.

In this chapter, we will cover the following topics:

- Monitoring a Ceph cluster
- Monitoring MON and MDS
- Monitoring OSD and PG
- Open source dashboards for Ceph such as Kraken, ceph-dash, and Calamari

Monitoring a Ceph cluster

Monitoring is one of the most important responsibilities for a storage administrator. System monitoring usually comes after cluster designing, deployment, and service implementation. As a storage administrator, you will need to keep an eye on your Ceph storage cluster and find out what's going on at any given time. Regular and disciplined monitoring keeps you updated with your cluster health. Based on monitoring notifications, you will get a bit more time to take necessary actions before service outages. Monitoring a Ceph cluster is an everyday task, which includes monitoring of MON, OSD, MDS, and PG, storage provisioning services such as RBD, radosgw, and CephFS, and Ceph clients. Ceph comes with a rich set of native command-line tools and API to monitor these components. In addition to this, there are open source projects, which are intentionally developed to monitor Ceph clusters on a GUI one-view dashboard.

Monitoring has a wider scope, which should not be limited to the software layer of Ceph. It should be extended to the underlying infrastructure, including hardware, networking, and other related systems which power your Ceph cluster. Usually, the manufacturer of these hardware systems provides a rich monitoring interface, which may or may not involve cost. We recommend you to use such tools for system monitoring at an infrastructure level. Remember that the more stable your underlying infrastructure is, the better results you can get out of your Ceph cluster. We will now focus on Ceph-based monitoring tools as well as some other open source projects for monitoring. Ceph comes with powerful CLI tools for cluster monitoring and troubleshooting. You can use the `ceph` tool to monitor your cluster.

Checking cluster health

To check the health of your cluster, use the `ceph` command followed by `health` as the command option:

```
# ceph health
```

The output of this command will be divided into several sections separated by semicolons:

```
[root@ceph-node1 ~]# ceph health
HEALTH_WARN 64 pgs degraded; 1408 pgs stuck unclean; recovery 1/5744 objects degraded (0.017%)
[root@ceph-node1 ~]#
```

The first section of the output shows that your cluster is in the warning state, HEALTH_WARN, as 64 **placement groups** (**PGs**) are degraded. The second section shows that 1,408 PGs are not clean, and the third section of the output shows that cluster recovery is in process for one out of 5,744 objects and the cluster is 0.017 percent degraded. If your cluster is healthy, you will receive the output as HEALTH_OK.

To know the health details of your Ceph cluster, use the `ceph health detail` command; this command will tell you all the placement groups that are not active and clean, that is, all the PGs that are unclean, inconsistent, and degraded will be listed here with their details. If your cluster is healthy, you will receive the output as HEALTH_OK. The following screenshot shows the health details of `ceph`:

```
[root@ceph-node2 ceph]# ceph health detail
HEALTH_ERR 61 pgs degraded; 6 pgs inconsistent; 1312 pgs stuck unclean; recovery 3/5746 objects degraded (0.052%); 8 scrub errors
pg 9.76 is stuck unclean since forever, current state active+remapped, last acting [7,3,2]
pg 8.77 is stuck unclean since forever, current state active+remapped, last acting [4,6,8]
pg 7.78 is stuck unclean for 788849.714074, current state active+remapped, last acting [6,5,1]
pg 6.79 is stuck unclean since forever, current state active+remapped, last acting [4,7,8]
pg 5.7a is stuck unclean since forever, current state active+remapped, last acting [7,4,2]
pg 4.7b is stuck unclean since forever, current state active+remapped, last acting [7,3,1]
pg 11.74 is stuck unclean for 788413.925336, current state active+remapped, last acting [4,7,8]
pg 10.75 is stuck unclean for 788412.797947, current state active+remapped, last acting [7,3,0]
```

Watching cluster events

You can monitor cluster events using the ceph command with the -w option. This command will display all the cluster events, including INF (information), WRN (warning), and ERR (errors), in real time. This command will generate a continuous output of live cluster changes; you can use *Ctrl* + *C* to get on to the shell:

```
# ceph -w
```

```
[root@ceph-node1 ~]# ceph -w
    cluster 07a92ca3-347e-43db-87ee-e0a0a9f89e97
    health HEALTH_OK
    monmap e3: 3 mons at {ceph-node1=192.168.57.101:6789/0,ceph-node2=192.168.57.102:6789/0,
ceph-node3=192.168.57.103:6789/0}, election epoch 904, quorum 0,1,2 ceph-node1,ceph-node2,cep
h-node3
    mdsmap e55: 1/1/1 up {0=ceph-node2=up:active}
    osdmap e664: 9 osds: 9 up, 9 in
     pgmap v3528: 1472 pgs, 13 pools, 1352 kB data, 2650 objects
            525 MB used, 82319 MB / 82844 MB avail
                1472 active+clean

2014-07-19 19:04:44.384956 mon.0 [INF] osd.0 192.168.57.101:6810/3280 failed (511 reports fro
m 3 peers after 1025.991577 >= grace 1023.635244)
2014-07-19 19:04:53.531842 mon.0 [INF] osdmap e665: 9 osds: 8 up, 9 in
2014-07-19 19:04:53.638975 mon.0 [INF] pgmap v3529: 1536 pgs: 64 creating, 176 stale+active+c
lean, 1296 active+clean; 1352 kB data, 525 MB used, 82319 MB / 82844 MB avail
2014-07-19 19:04:54.531821 mon.0 [INF] osdmap e666: 9 osds: 8 up, 9 in
2014-07-19 19:04:54.688132 mon.0 [INF] pgmap v3530: 1536 pgs: 64 creating, 176 stale+active+c
lean, 2 peering, 1294 active+clean; 1352 kB data, 525 MB used, 82319 MB / 82844 MB avail
2014-07-19 19:04:58.619026 mon.0 [INF] pgmap v3531: 1536 pgs: 53 creating, 148 stale+active+c
lean, 21 active+degraded, 56 peering, 1258 active+clean; 1352 kB data, 523 MB used, 82321 MB
/ 82844 MB avail; 79/5266 objects degraded (1.500%)
2014-07-19 19:04:59.958947 mon.0 [INF] pgmap v3532: 1536 pgs: 5 inactive, 70 degraded, 28 cre
ating, 3 active, 111 active+degraded, 333 peering, 986 active+clean; 1352 kB data, 524 MB use
d, 82319 MB / 82844 MB avail; 260/4716 objects degraded (5.513%)
```

There are other options as well that can be used with the ceph command to gather different types of event details:

- --watch-debug: This is used to watch debug events

- --watch-info: This is used to watch info events

- --watch-sec: This is used to watch security events

- --watch-warn: This is used to watch warning events

- --watch-error: This is used to watch error events

Cluster utilization statistics

To know your cluster's space utilization statistics, use the `ceph` command with the `df` option. This command will show the total cluster size, available size, used size, and percentage. This will also display pool information such as pool name, ID, utilization, and number of objects in each pool:

```
# ceph df
```

```
[root@ceph-node1 ~]# ceph df
GLOBAL:
    SIZE        AVAIL       RAW USED      %RAW USED
    82844M      82349M      495M          0.60
POOLS:
    NAME                    ID      USED      %USED      OBJECTS
    data                    0       0         0          0
    metadata                1       5052      0          20
    rbd                     2       1344k     0          2568
    .rgw                    3       1040      0          6
    .rgw.root               4       822       0          3
    .rgw.control            5       0         0          8
    .rgw.gc                 6       0         0          32
    .users.uid              7       787       0          3
    .users.email            8       8         0          1
    .users                  9       20        0          2
    .rgw.buckets.index      10      0         0          5
    .rgw.buckets            11      365       0          1
    .users.swift            12      8         0          1
[root@ceph-node1 ~]#
```

Checking the cluster status

Checking the cluster status is the most common and frequent operation when managing a Ceph cluster. You can check the status of your cluster using the `ceph` command and the `status` option. Instead of the `status` subcommand, you can also use a shorter version, `-s`, as an option:

```
# ceph status
```

Alternatively, you can use:

```
# ceph -s
```

The following screenshot shows the status of our cluster:

```
[root@ceph-node1 ~]# ceph -s
    cluster 07a92ca3-347e-43db-87ee-e0a0a9f89e97
    health HEALTH_OK
    monmap e3: 3 mons at {ceph-node1=192.168.57.101:6789/0,ceph-node2=192.168.57.102:6789/0
,ceph-node3=192.168.57.103:6789/0}, election epoch 908, quorum 0,1,2 ceph-node1,ceph-node2,c
eph-node3
    mdsmap e57: 1/1/1 up {0=ceph-node2=up:active}
    osdmap e671: 9 osds: 9 up, 9 in
     pgmap v3553: 1536 pgs, 13 pools, 1352 kB data, 2650 objects
         495 MB used, 82349 MB / 82844 MB avail
             1536 active+clean
[root@ceph-node1 ~]#
```

This command will dump a lot of useful information for your Ceph cluster. The following is the explanation:

- cluster: This represents the Ceph unique cluster ID.
- health: This shows the cluster health.
- monmap: This represents the monitor map epoch version, information, election epoch version, and quorum status.
- mdsmap: This represents the mdsmap epoch version and status.
- osdmap: This represents osdmap epoch and OSD's UP and IN count.
- pgmap: This shows the pgmap version, total number of PGs, pool count, and total objects. It also displays information about cluster utilization, including the used size, free size, and total size. Finally, it displays the PG status.

In order to view the real-time cluster status, you can use ceph status with Unix's watch command to get a continuous output:

```
# watch ceph -s
```

Cluster authentication keys

Ceph works on a strong authentication system based on keys. All cluster components interact with one other once they undergo a key-based authentication system. As a Ceph administrator, you might need to check key lists managed by clusters. You can use the ceph command with the auth list subcommand to get a list of all keys:

```
# ceph auth list
```

To know more about command operations, you can use `help` as a suboption, for instance, `# ceph auth --help`. Use the command as directed by the `help` option.

Monitoring Ceph MON

Usually, a Ceph cluster is deployed with more than one MON instance for increased reliability and availability. Since there are a large number of monitors, they should attain a quorum to make the cluster function properly. Monitoring of MONs regularly is of utmost importance.

The MON status

To display the cluster MON status and MON map, use the `ceph` command with either `mon stat` or `mon dump` as the suboption:

```
# ceph mon stat
```

```
# ceph mon dump
```

The following figure displays the output of this command:

```
[root@ceph-node1 ~]# ceph mon stat
e3: 3 mons at {ceph-node1=192.168.57.101:6789/0,ceph-node2=192.168.57.102:6789/0,ceph-node3
=192.168.57.103:6789/0}, election epoch 912, quorum 0,1,2 ceph-node1,ceph-node2,ceph-node3
[root@ceph-node1 ~]#
[root@ceph-node1 ~]# ceph mon dump
dumped monmap epoch 3
epoch 3
fsid 07a92ca3-347e-43db-87ee-e0a0a9f89e97
last_changed 2014-06-04 21:07:47.147923
created 2014-06-02 00:51:00.765090
0: 192.168.57.101:6789/0 mon.ceph-node1
1: 192.168.57.102:6789/0 mon.ceph-node2
2: 192.168.57.103:6789/0 mon.ceph-node3
[root@ceph-node1 ~]#
```

The MON quorum status

To maintain a quorum between Ceph MONs, the cluster should always have more than 51 percent of available monitors in a Ceph cluster. Checking the quorum status of a cluster is very useful at the time of MON troubleshooting. You can check the quorum status by using the `ceph` command and the `quorum_status` subcommand:

```
# ceph quorum_status
```

```
[root@ceph-node1 ~]# ceph quorum_status

{ "election_epoch": 914,
  "quorum": [
        0,
        1,
        2],
  "quorum_names": [
        "ceph-node1",
        "ceph-node2",
        "ceph-node3"],
  "quorum_leader_name": "ceph-node1",
  "monmap": { "epoch": 3,
        "fsid": "07a92ca3-347e-43db-87ee-e0a0a9f89e97",
        "modified": "2014-06-04 21:07:47.147923",
        "created": "2014-06-02 00:51:00.765090",
        "mons": [
              { "rank": 0,
                "name": "ceph-node1",
                "addr": "192.168.57.101:6789\/0"},
              { "rank": 1,
                "name": "ceph-node2",
                "addr": "192.168.57.102:6789\/0"},
              { "rank": 2,
                "name": "ceph-node3",
                "addr": "192.168.57.103:6789\/0"}]}}
[root@ceph-node1 ~]#
```

The quorum status displays `election_epoch`, which is the election version number, and `quorum_leader_name`, which denotes the hostname of the quorum leader. It also displays the MON map epoch, cluster ID, and cluster creation date. Each cluster monitor is allocated with a rank. For I/O operations, clients first connect to quorum lead monitors if the leader MON is unavailable; the client then connects to the next rank monitor.

Monitoring Ceph OSD

OSD in a Ceph cluster are the workhorses; they perform all the work at the bottom layer and store the user data. Monitoring OSDs is a crucial task and requires a lot of attention as there are a lot of OSDs to monitor and take care of. The bigger your cluster, the more OSDs it will have, and the more rigorous monitoring it requires. Generally, a Ceph cluster hosts a lot of disks, so the chances of getting OSD failure is quite high. We will now focus on Ceph commands for OSD monitoring.

OSD tree view

The tree view of OSD is quite useful to view OSD status such as IN or OUT and UP or DOWN. The tree view of OSD displays each node with all its OSDs and its location in a CRUSH map. You can check the tree view of OSD using the following command:

```
# ceph osd tree
```

This will display the following output:

```
[root@ceph-node1 ~]# ceph osd tree
# id    weight  type name          up/down reweight
-1      0.08995 root default
-2      0.02998         host ceph-node1
0       0.009995                    osd.0   up      1
1       0.009995                    osd.1   up      1
2       0.009995                    osd.2   up      1
-3      0.02998         host ceph-node2
3       0.009995                    osd.3   up      1
5       0.009995                    osd.5   up      1
4       0.009995                    osd.4   up      1
-4      0.02998         host ceph-node3
6       0.009995                    osd.6   up      1
7       0.009995                    osd.7   up      1
8       0.009995                    osd.8   up      1
[root@ceph-node1 ~]#
[root@ceph-node1 ~]#
```

This command displays various useful information for Ceph OSDs, such as weight, the UP/DOWN status, and the IN/OUT status. The output will be beautifully formatted as per your Ceph CRUSH map. If you maintain a big cluster, this format will be beneficial for you to locate your OSDs and their hosting servers from a long list.

OSD statistics

To check OSD statistics, use # `ceph osd stat`; this command will help you to get the OSD map epoch, total OSD count, and their IN and UP statuses.

To get detailed information about the Ceph cluster and OSD, execute the following command:

```
# ceph osd dump
```

This is a very useful command that will output OSD map epochs, pool details, including the pool ID, pool name, and pool type that is replicated or erasure, the CRUSH ruleset, and placement groups.

This command will also display information such as OSD ID, status, weight, and a clean interval epoch for each OSD. This information is extremely helpful for cluster monitoring and troubleshooting.

To display blacklisted clients, use the following command:

```
# ceph osd blacklist ls
```

Checking the CRUSH map

We can query a CRUSH map directly from the `ceph osd` commands. The CRUSH map command-line utility can save a lot of time for a system administrator compared to manual way of viewing and editing a CRUSH map.

To view the CRUSH map, execute the following command:

```
# ceph osd crush dump
```

To view CRUSH map rules, execute:

```
# ceph osd crush rule list
```

To view a detailed CRUSH rule, execute:

```
# ceph osd crush rule dump  <crush_rule_name>
```

```
[root@ceph-node1 /]# ceph osd crush rule list
[
    "data",
    "metadata",
    "rbd"]
[root@ceph-node1 /]#
[root@ceph-node1 /]#
[root@ceph-node1 /]# ceph osd crush rule dump data
{ "rule_id": 0,
  "rule_name": "data",
  "ruleset": 0,
  "type": 1,
  "min_size": 1,
  "max_size": 10,
  "steps": [
        { "op": "take",
          "item": -1,
          "item_name": "default"},
        { "op": "chooseleaf_firstn",
          "num": 0,
          "type": "host"},
        { "op": "emit"}]}
[root@ceph-node1 /]#
```

If you are managing a large Ceph cluster with several hundred OSDs, it's sometimes difficult to find the location of a specific OSD in the CRUSH map. It's also difficult if your CRUSH map contains multiple bucket hierarchies. You can use `ceph osd find` to search an OSD and its location in a CRUSH map:

```
# ceph osd find  <Numeric_OSD_ID>
# ceph osd find 1
```

```
[root@ceph-node1 /]# ceph osd find 1
{ "osd": 1,
  "ip": "192.168.57.101:6805\/2583",
  "crush_location": { "host": "ceph-node1",
      "root": "default"}}[root@ceph-node1 /]#
[root@ceph-node1 /]#
[root@ceph-node1 /]# ceph osd find 2
{ "osd": 2,
  "ip": "192.168.57.101:6800\/2311",
  "crush_location": { "host": "ceph-node1",
      "root": "default"}}[root@ceph-node1 /]#
[root@ceph-node1 /]#
```

Monitoring placement groups

OSDs store placement groups, and placement groups contain objects. The overall health of a cluster majorly depends on placement groups. The cluster will remain in a HEALTH_OK status only if all the placement groups are on the active + clean status. If your Ceph cluster is not healthy, there are chances that the placement groups are not active + clean. Placement groups can exhibit multiple states:

- **Peering**: Under peering, the placement groups of the OSDs that are in the acting set, storing the replica of the placement group, come into agreement about the state of the object and its metadata in the PG. Once peering is completed, OSDs that store the PG agree about the current state of it.

- **Active**: Once the peering operation is complete, Ceph makes the PG active. Under the active state, the data in the PG is available on the primary PG and its replica for an I/O operation.

- **Clean**: Under the clean state, the primary and secondary OSDs have successfully peered, no PG moves away from their correct location, and the objects are replicated correct number of times.

- **Degraded**: Once an OSD goes down, Ceph changes the state of all its PGs that are assigned to this OSD as degraded. After the OSD comes UP, it has to peer again to make the degraded PGs clean. If the OSD remains down and out for more than 300 seconds, Ceph recovers all the PGs that are degraded from their replica PGs to maintain the replication count. Clients can perform I/O even after PGs are in a degraded stage. There can be one more reason why a placement group can be degraded; this is when one or more objects inside a PG become unavailable. Ceph assumes the object should be in the PG, but it's not actually available. In such cases, Ceph marks the PG as degraded and tries to recover the PG form its replica.

- **Recovering**: When an OSD goes down, the content of its placement groups fall behind the contents of its replica PGs on other OSDs. Once the OSD comes UP, Ceph initiates a recovery operation on the PGs to keep them up to date with replica PGs in other OSDs.

- **Backfilling**: As soon as a new OSD is added to a cluster, Ceph tries to rebalance the data by moving some PGs from other OSDs to this new OSD; this process is known as backfilling. Once backfilling is completed for the placement groups, the OSD can participate in client I/O. Ceph performs backfilling smoothly in the background and makes sure not to overload the cluster.

- **Remapped**: Whenever there is a change in a PG acting set, data migration happens from the old acting set OSD to the new acting set OSD. This operation might take some time based on the data size that gets migrated to the new OSD. During this time, the old primary OSD of the old acting group serves the client request. As soon as the data migration operation completes, Ceph uses new primary OSDs from the acting group.

- **Stale**: Ceph OSD reports its statistics to a Ceph monitor every 0.5 seconds; by any chance, if the primary OSDs of the placement group acting set fail to report their statistics to the monitors, or if other OSDs report their primary OSDs down, the monitor will consider these PGs as stale.

You can monitor placement groups using the commands explained here. The following is the command to get a placement group status:

```
# ceph pg stat
```

```
[root@ceph-node1 ~]# ceph pg stat

v4430: 1536 pgs: 1536 active+clean; 1352 kB data, 518 MB used, 82326 MB / 82844 MB avail
[root@ceph-node1 ~]#
```

The output of the pg stat command will display a lot of information in a specific format:

```
vNNNN: X pgs: Y active+clean; R bytes data, U MB used, F GB / T GB
avail
```

The variables here are:

- vNNNN: This is the PG map version number
- X: This is the total number of placement groups
- Y: This states the number of PGs with their states
- R: This specifies the raw data stored
- U: This specifies the real data stored after replication
- F: This is the remaining free capacity
- T: This is the total capacity

To get a placement group list, execute:

```
# ceph pg dump
```

This command will generate a lot of essential information, such as the PG map version, PG ID, PG state, acting set, and acting set primary, with respect to placement groups. The output of this command can be huge depending on the number of PGs in your cluster.

To query a particular PG for detailed information, execute the following command that has the ceph pg <PG_ID> query syntax:

```
# ceph pg 2.7d query
```

To list the stuck placement group, execute the following command that has the ceph pg dump_stuck < unclean | Inactive | stale > syntax:

```
# ceph pg dump_stuck unclean
```

Monitoring MDS

Metadata servers are used only for CephFS, which is not production ready at the time of writing this book. A metadata server has several states, such as UP, DOWN, ACTIVE, and INACTIVE. While performing monitoring of MDS, you should make sure that the state of MDS is UP and ACTIVE. The following commands will help you get information related to Ceph MDS.

To check the MDS status, execute:

```
# ceph mds stat
```

To display the details of the metadata server, execute:

```
# ceph mds dump
```

The output is shown in the following screenshot:

```
[root@ceph-node1 ~]# ceph mds stat
e85: 1/1/1 up {0=ceph-node2=up:active}
[root@ceph-node1 ~]#
[root@ceph-node1 ~]# ceph mds dump
dumped mdsmap epoch 85
epoch    85
flags    0
created 2014-06-02 01:05:20.199702
modified        2014-08-08 17:18:40.563408
tableserver     0
root    0
session_timeout 60
session_autoclose       300
max_file_size   1099511627776
last_failure    0
last_failure_osd_epoch  794
compat  compat={},rocompat={},incompat={1=base v0.20,2=client writeable ranges,3=default file layo
uts on dirs,4=dir inode in separate object,5=mds uses versioned encoding,6=dirfrag is stored in om
ap}
max_mds 1
in      0
up      {0=15699}
failed
stopped
data_pools      0
metadata_pool   1
inline_data     disabled
15699:  192.168.57.102:6800/2046 'ceph-node2' mds.0.13 up:active seq 4252
[root@ceph-node1 ~]#
```

Monitoring Ceph using open source dashboards

A Ceph storage administrator will perform most of the cluster monitoring using CLI via commands provided by the Ceph interface. Ceph also provides a rich interface for admin APIs that can be used natively to monitor the entire Ceph cluster. There are a couple of open source projects that make use of Ceph's REST admin API and represent the monitoring results in a GUI dashboard where you can have a quick look at your entire cluster. We will now take a look at such open source projects and their installation procedures.

Kraken

Kraken is an open source Ceph dashboard written in Python for stats and monitoring of a Ceph cluster, initially developed by Donald Talton, and later joined by David Moreau Simard.

Donald is the owner of Merrymack, an IT consulting company. He is an expert engineer with over 20 years of experience and has worked for companies such as Apollo Group, Wells Fargo, PayPal, and Cisco. During his tenure in PayPal and Cisco, he focused primarily on OpenStack and Ceph. During the time he was working for Cisco, he kickstarted the development of Kraken. Fortunately, Donald is one of the technical reviewers of this book, too.

David Simard started his career in 2006 when he was studying in college; he started working for iWeb, a web-hosting company, as a temporary employee during his summer holidays; later, when his job got converted to a full-time position, he had no other option than to leave his studies and continue working on amazing stuff at iWeb. It has now been 8 years since he started working with iWeb as an IT architecture specialist. He deals with cloud storage, cloud computing, and other interesting fields.

There are a few key reasons behind the development of Kraken. The first is that when it was conceived, Ceph's Calamari tool was only available to commercial customers of Inktank. Donald believes that it's necessary to have a good open source dashboard to monitor the Ceph cluster and its components from a single window; this will lead to better management and speed up the adoption of Ceph as a whole. He took this as a challenge and kicked off the development of Kraken. Donald decided to use ceph-rest-api to extract all the necessary cluster data for monitoring and reporting. To converge all this cluster data in a presentable dashboard format, Donald used several other tools such as Python, Django, humanize, and python-cephclient.

The roadmap for Kraken has been divided into several milestones. Currently, Kraken is at its first milestone, which consists of the following feature sets:

- Cluster data usage
- The MON status
- The OSD status
- The PG status
- Better user interface
- Support for multiple MONs

The next development stage of Kraken will be the inclusion of operational changes for OSD, live CRUSH map configuration, Ceph user authentication, pool operations, block device management, and system metrics such as CPU and memory usage. You can follow the Kraken roadmap on the GitHub page at `https://github.com/krakendash/krakendash` or on Kraken's readme file. Kraken is fully open source and follows BSD-licensing. Developers who want to contribute to Kraken can send a pull request to Donald and can contact him at `don@merrymack.com`.

The building blocks of Kraken consist of several open source projects such as:

- **Python 2.7 or later**: This is required for libraries such as collections.
- **ceph-rest-api**: This is included with Ceph binaries.
- **Django 1.6.2 or later**: This is the core framework for Kraken.
- **humanize 0.5 or later**: This is required for data-free display conversion.
- **python-cephclient 0.1.0.4 or later**: Recently used in Kraken, it is the client wrapper for ceph-rest-api. In the previous releases, Kraken made use of ceph-rest-api directly without any wrapper. This has been written by David to wrap ceph-rest-api, which gives us additional capabilities, such as being able to support multiple clusters in the future.
- **djangorestframework 2.3.12 or later**: This is used for some custom API additions that might or might not stay in Kraken.
- **django-filter 0.7 or later**: This is required by Django.

Deploying Kraken

In this section, we will learn how to deploy Kraken to monitor your Ceph cluster. It is a lightweight application that requires a significantly lower amount of system resources. In this deployment, we will use the ceph-node1 machine; you can use any Ceph cluster node that has access to a Ceph cluster. Follow the listed steps:

1. Install dependencies for Kraken, such as python-pip, screen, and the Firefox browser, using the following command. If you have any other browser, you can skip installing Firefox packages. Python-pip is a package manager used to install Python packages, which is required to install dependencies. Kraken will use separate screen sessions to initiate subprocess required for dashboards; these screens will be provided by the screen package:

    ```
    # yum install python-pip screen firefox
    ```

2. Install the required development libraries:

    ```
    # yum install gcc python-devel libxml2-devel.x86_64 libxslt-
    devel.x86_64
    ```

3. Create a directory for Kraken:

    ```
    # mkdir /kraken
    ```

4. Clone the Kraken repository from GitHub:

    ```
    # git clone https://github.com/krakendash/krakendash
    ```

5. Use the Python package manager to install the required packages for Kraken, such as Django, python-cephclient, djangorestframework, markdown, and humanize:

    ```
    # cd krakendash
    # pip install -r requirements.txt
    ```

6. Once these packages are installed, execute api.sh and django.sh, which will invoke the ceph-rest-api and django python dashboards, respectively. These scripts will execute in independent screen environments; you can use screen commands to manage these sessions. Press *Ctrl + D* to detach screen sessions and move them to the background:

    ```
    # cp ../krakendash/contrib/*.sh .
    # ./api.sh
    # ./django.sh
    ```

7. You can check the screen sessions using the ps command and reattach to the screen session using the -r command:

    ```
    # ps -ef | grep -i screen
    ```

    The output is shown in the following screenshot:

```
[root@ceph-client1 kraken]# ll
total 12
-rwxr-xr-x. 1 root root  100 Aug  8 04:46 api.sh
-rwxr-xr-x. 1 root root   93 Aug  8 04:46 django.sh
drwxr-xr-x. 7 root root 4096 Aug  8 04:45 krakendash
[root@ceph-client1 kraken]#
[root@ceph-client1 kraken]#
[root@ceph-client1 kraken]# ./api.sh
[detached from 30167.api]
[root@ceph-client1 kraken]# ./django.sh
[detached from 30203.django]
[root@ceph-client1 kraken]#
[root@ceph-client1 kraken]# ps -ef | grep -i screen
root     30167    1  0 05:44 ?        00:00:00 SCREEN -S api sudo ceph-rest-api -c /etc/ceph/ceph.conf --cluster ceph -i admin
root     30203    1  0 05:45 ?        00:00:00 SCREEN -S django sudo python krakendash/manage.py runserver 0.0.0.0:8000
root     30209 6858  0 05:45 pts/0    00:00:00 grep --color=auto -i screen
[root@ceph-client1 kraken]#
```

8. Finally, when api.sh and django.sh are running, open your web browser and navigate to http://localhost:8000/; you should be able to view your Ceph cluster status on the Kraken dashboard:

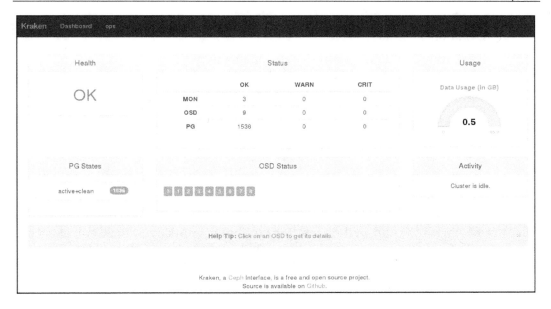

The ceph-dash tool

The ceph-dash is another free open source dashboard/monitoring API for a Ceph cluster, which has been developed by Christian Eichelmann, who is working fulltime for 1&1 Internet AG, Germany as a senior software developer. Christian started the development of this project at the time when there were very few open source dashboards available for Ceph. Moreover, the other dashboards that were available had complex architectures and did not work well with large clusters. So, Christian focused on developing a simple REST API-based dashboard that allows cluster monitoring via simple REST calls that should work well with large Ceph clusters.

The ceph-dash tool has been designed with a keep-it-simple approach to provide an overall Ceph cluster health status via a RESTful JSON API as well as web GUI. It is a lightweighted application that does not have any dependencies on ceph-rest-api. It is a pure Python wsgi application that talks to the cluster directly via librados. Currently, ceph-dash provides a clean and simple web GUI that is able to show the following information about the Ceph cluster:

- The overall cluster status with detailed problem description
- Support for multiple monitors and the status of every monitor
- The OSD status with count for IN, OUT, and unhealthy OSD
- Graphical storage capacity visualization

- The current throughput, including writes/second, reads/second, and operations/second
- Graphical placement group status visualization
- Cluster recovery state

In continuation to this, ceph-dash also provides REST endpoint that generates all the cluster information in JSON format, which can further be used in various creative ways. Since ceph-dash is an open source project, anyone can contribute by sending pull requests to Christian via `https://github.com/Crapworks/ceph-dash`.

If you run ceph-dash tests/development purposes, you can run it independently. For production usage, it is strongly recommended to deploy the application on a wsgi capable web server (Apache, nginx, and so on). The ceph-dash tool uses Flask microframework and ceph-python bindings to connect directly to the Ceph cluster. The access to Ceph cluster by ceph-dash is purely read only and doesn't require any write privileges. The ceph-dash tool uses the `ceph status` command via the Python `Rados` class. The returned JSON output is then either exposed via the REST API or via a web GUI that refreshes itself every 5 seconds.

Deploying ceph-dash

In this section, we will learn how to deploy ceph-dash for a Ceph cluster. Proceed with the following steps:

1. The ceph-dash tool must be installed on a machine that has access to a Ceph cluster. Since it is not resource hungry, you can designate any of your monitor machines for it.

2. Create a directory for ceph-dash and clone its repository from GitHub:

    ```
    # mkdir /ceph-dash
    # git clone https://github.com/Crapworks/ceph-dash.git
    ```

3. Install python-pip:

    ```
    # yum install python-pip
    ```

4. Install Jinja2 package:

    ```
    # easy_install Jinja2
    ```

5. Once the installation is complete, you are good to launch the ceph-dash GUI. To start ceph-dash, execute:

    ```
    # ./ceph-dash.py
    ```

The output is shown in the following screenshot:

```
[root@ceph-node1 ceph-dash]# ./ceph-dash.py
 * Running on http://0.0.0.0:5000/
127.0.0.1 - - [08/Aug/2014 13:15:52] "GET / HTTP/1.1" 200 -
127.0.0.1 - - [08/Aug/2014 13:15:55] "GET / HTTP/1.1" 200 -
127.0.0.1 - - [08/Aug/2014 13:15:55] "GET /static/css/bootstrap.min.slate.css HTTP/1.1" 304 -
127.0.0.1 - - [08/Aug/2014 13:15:55] "GET /static/js/jquery-2.0.3.min.js HTTP/1.1" 304 -
127.0.0.1 - - [08/Aug/2014 13:15:55] "GET /static/js/bootstrap.min.js HTTP/1.1" 304 -
127.0.0.1 - - [08/Aug/2014 13:15:55] "GET /static/js/globalize.min.js HTTP/1.1" 304 -
127.0.0.1 - - [08/Aug/2014 13:15:55] "GET /static/js/dx.chartjs.js HTTP/1.1" 304 -
127.0.0.1 - - [08/Aug/2014 13:15:55] "GET /static/js/ceph.dash.js HTTP/1.1" 304 -
127.0.0.1 - - [08/Aug/2014 13:15:56] "GET / HTTP/1.1" 200 -
```

6. Open the web browser, point it to http://localhost:5000/, and start monitoring your cluster using ceph-dash:

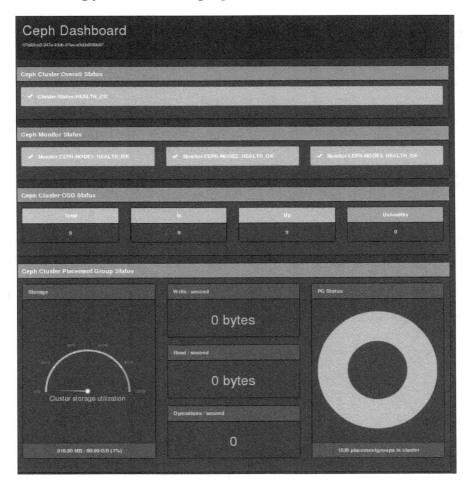

Calamari

Calamari is the management platform for Ceph, an attractive dashboard to monitor and manage your Ceph cluster. It was initially developed by Inktank as a proprietary software that ships with the Inktank Ceph Enterprise product for their customers. Just after the acquisition of Inktank by Red Hat, it was open sourced on May 30, 2014 by Red Hat. Calamari has several great feature sets, and its future roadmap is quite impressive. Calamari has two parts and each part has its own repositories.

Fronted is the browser-based graphical user interface that is majorly implemented in JavaScript. The fronted part makes use of Calamari's REST API and is constructed in a modular approach so that each component of the fronted can be updated or can undergo maintenance independently. The Calamari frontend has been open sourced with an MIT license. You can find the repository at `https://github.com/ceph/calamari-clients`.

Calamari backend is the core part of the platform, which is written in Python. It also makes use of other components such as SaltStack, ZeroRPC, graphite, djangorestframework, Django, and gevent, and provides a new REST API for integration with Ceph and other systems. Calamari has been reinvented in its new version, where it uses the new Calamari REST API to interact with Ceph clusters. The pervious release of Calamari uses the Ceph REST API, which is a bit restrictive for this purpose. The Calamari backend has been open sourced with the LGPL2+ license; you can find the repository at `https://github.com/ceph/calamari`.

Calamari has a good documentation available at `http://calamari.readthedocs.org`. Whether you are a Calamari operator, a developer working on Calamari, or a developer using the Calamari REST API, this documentation is a good source of information to get you started with Calamari. Like Ceph, Calamari has also been developed upstream; you can get involved with Calamari on IRC `irc://irc.oftc.net/ceph` by registering to the mailing list `ceph-calamari@ceph.com` or sending pull requests on Calamari GitHub accounts at `https://github.com/ceph/calamari` and `https://github.com/ceph/calamari-clients`.

If you want to install Calamari and are curious to see what it looks like, you can follow my blog about Calamari's step-by-step installation at `http://karan-mj.blogspot.fi/2014/09/ceph-calamari-survival-guide.html`.

Summary

In this chapter, we covered the monitoring aspect of Ceph, including cluster monitoring and monitoring of different Ceph components such as MON, OSD, and MDS. We also learned about monitoring placement groups, including their various states. The states of placement groups are very much dynamic and require keen monitoring. Most of the changes that happen on a Ceph cluster are in its placement groups. This chapter also covered some open source GUI monitoring dashboard projects such as Kraken and ceph-dash. These projects are separate from the Ceph community, managed and developed by individual efforts, yet they are open source, so you can contribute to these projects. We also covered an overview of Calamari, which is a management and monitoring service for Ceph, which has been recently open sourced by Red Hat (Inktank). In the next chapter, we will learn about how Ceph extends its benefits to cloud platforms such as OpenStack. We will also focus on integrating Ceph with OpenStack.

9
Integrating Ceph with OpenStack

Every cloud platform requires a robust, reliable, scalable, and all-in-one storage solution that suffices all their workload requirements. Ceph has been emerging amazingly fast as a cloud storage solution, which seamlessly integrates with OpenStack and other cloud platforms. Ceph's unique, unified, and distributed architecture makes it the right choice for being a cloud storage backend.

In this chapter, we will cover the following topics:

- Introduction to OpenStack
- Ceph – the best match for OpenStack
- Creating OpenStack environments
- Integrating Ceph and OpenStack

Introduction to OpenStack

OpenStack is a free and open source software platform for building and managing public and private cloud computing platforms. It is governed by an independent, nonprofit foundation known as OpenStack foundation. It has the largest and most active community backed by technology giants such as HP, Red Hat, Dell, Cisco, IBM, Rackspace, and many more. OpenStack's idea for cloud is that it should be simple to implement and massively scalable.

OpenStack is considered as the cloud operating system that allows users to instantly deploy hundreds of virtual machines in an automated way. It also provides an efficient, hassle-free management of these machines. OpenStack is known for its dynamic scale up, scale out, and distributed architecture capabilities, making your cloud environment robust and future ready.

OpenStack provides the enterprise class **Infrastructure-as-a-service (IaaS)** platform for all your cloud needs. The following is the architecture of OpenStack:

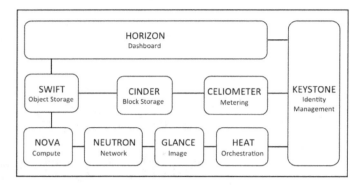

OpenStack is made up of several different software components that work together to provide cloud services. The OpenStack community has identified nine key components that make the core part of OpenStack:

- **Nova**: This is the compute part that is designed to manage and automate pools of computer resources and can work with a variety of virtualization technologies such as QEMU/KVM, Xen, Hyper-VMware, bare metal, and Linux containers.
- **Swift**: This provides object storage facility to OpenStack.
- **Cinder**: This is the block storage component providing persistent volumes to OpenStack instances.
- **Glance**: This is the image service for OpenStack, which makes virtual machine deployment easy and quick.
- **Neutron**: This is the network component of OpenStack.
- **Horizon**: This is the dashboard for managing OpenStack.
- **Keystone**: This provides identity services to OpenStack and manages authentication for OpenStack.
- **Ceilometer**: This provides the telemetry service and allows cloud providers with billing and autoscaling services.
- **Heat**: This is the orchestration component of OpenStack.

 For more information on OpenStack, visit http://www.openstack.org/.

Ceph – the best match for OpenStack

In the last few years, OpenStack has been getting amazingly popular as it's based on software-defined everything, whether it's compute, networking, or even storage. When you talk about storage for OpenStack, Ceph will get all the attraction. Ceph provides a robust, reliable storage backend that OpenStack was looking for. It's a seamless integration with OpenStack components such as Cinder, Glance, Nova, and keystone, which provides all-in-one cloud storage backend for OpenStack. Here are some key benefits that make Ceph the best match for OpenStack:

- Ceph provides enterprise-grade, feature-rich storage backend at a very low cost per gigabyte, which helps to keep the OpenStack cloud deployment price down.

- Ceph is a unified storage solution of block, file, or object storage for OpenStack, allowing applications to use storage as they need.

- Ceph provides advance block storage capabilities for OpenStack clouds that include easy-and-quick spin up, backup, and cloning of VMs.

- It provides default persistent volumes for OpenStack instances that can work like traditional servers, where data will not flush on rebooting the VMs.

- Ceph supports OpenStack for being host independent by supporting VM migrations and scaling up storage components without affecting VMs.

- It provides the snapshot feature to OpenStack volumes that can be used as a means of backup as well.

- Ceph's copy-on-write cloning feature provides OpenStack to spin up several instances at once, which helps the provisioning mechanism big time.

- Ceph supports rich APIs for both Swift and S3 object storage interfaces.

Ceph and OpenStack communities are working closely since last few years to make integration more seamless and use new features as they are landed. In future, we can expect OpenStack and Ceph to be more close to each other due to Red Hat's acquisition of Inktank, the company behind Ceph, as Red Hat is one of the major contributors of the OpenStack project.

Creating an OpenStack test environment

In this section, we will deploy a single-node test OpenStack environment that will be used to integrate with Ceph later in this chapter. For OpenStack deployment, we will use the Red Hat distribution of OpenStack known as RDO, which is Red Hat's open source community version of OpenStack. For more information on RDO OpenStack, visit http://openstack.redhat.com/.

Setting up an OpenStack machine

To perform single-node OpenStack installation, we will create a new virtual machine named os-node1. We need to install an OS on this new VM. In our case, we will install CentOS 6.4; you can also choose any other RHEL-based OS instead of CentOS if you like. Proceed with the following steps:

1. Create a new VirtualBox virtual machine for OpenStack installation:

   ```
   # VBoxManage createvm --name os-node1 --ostype RedHat_64 --
   register
   ```

   ```
   # VBoxManage modifyvm os-node1 --memory 4096 --nic1 nat  --
   nic2 hostonly --hostonlyadapter2 vboxnet1
   ```

   ```
   # VBoxManage storagectl os-node1 --name "IDE Controller" --add
   ide --controller PIIX4 --hostiocache on --bootable on
   ```

   ```
   # VBoxManage storageattach os-node1 --storagectl "IDE
   Controller" --type dvddrive --port 0 --device 0 --medium
   CentOS-6.4-x86_64-bin-DVD1.iso
   ```

    You must provide the correct absolute path of CentOS ISO file with --medium option for the previous command.

   ```
   # VBoxManage storagectl os-node1 --name "SATA Controller" --
   add sata --controller IntelAHCI --hostiocache on --bootable on
   ```

   ```
   # VBoxManage createhd --filename OS-os-node1.vdi --size 10240
   ```

   ```
   # VBoxManage storageattach os-node1 --storagectl "SATA
   Controller" --port 0 --device 0 --type hdd --medium OS-os-
   node1.vdi
   ```

   ```
   # VBoxManage startvm os-node1  --type gui
   ```

2. Once the virtual machine is created and started, install the CentOS operating system by following the OS installation documentation available at https://access.redhat.com/site/documentation/en-US/Red_Hat_Enterprise_Linux/6/html/Installation_Guide/index.html. During the installation process, provide the hostname as os-node1.

3. Once you have successfully installed the operating system, edit the network configuration of the machine. Make sure you edit the correct network device filename; in our case, the network devices are eth2 and eth3 (there are chances that the device names might change in your environment, but it should not create problems). Once the network device configuration files are updated, restart the network services. Proceed with the following steps to edit the network configuration:

- ° Edit the `/etc/sysconfig/network-scripts/ifcfg-eth2` file and add:

  ```
  ONBOOT=yes
  BOOTPROTO=dhcp
  ```

- ° Edit the `/etc/sysconfig/network-scripts/ifcfg-eth3` file and add:

  ```
  ONBOOT=yes
  BOOTPROTO=static
  IPADDR=192.168.57.201
  NETMASK=255.255.255.0
  ```

- ° Edit the `/etc/hosts` file and add:

  ```
  192.168.57.101 ceph-node1
  192.168.57.102 ceph-node2
  192.168.57.103 ceph-node3
  192.168.57.200 ceph-client1
  192.168.57.201 os-node1
  ```

4. Make sure the new node, os-node1, can communicate with the Ceph cluster nodes:

   ```
   # ping ceph-node1
   # ping ceph-node2
   # ping ceph-node3
   ```

5. Since this is a test setup, you should disable firewall and set `selinux` to `permissive` to avoid complexity:

   ```
   # setenforce 0
   # service iptables stop
   ```

Installing OpenStack

In this section, we will give you step-by-step instructions to install the Icehouse release of OpenStack RDO. If you are curious to learn about RDO OpenStack installation, visit `http://openstack.redhat.com/Quickstart`.

1. Update the current OS packages to avoid any warnings/errors due to package version incompatibility:

   ```
   # yum update -y
   ```

2. Install RDO packages:

   ```
   # yum install -y https://repos.fedorapeople.org/repos/openstack/
   openstack-icehouse/rdo-release-icehouse-4.noarch.rpm
   ```

3. Install OpenStack packsack packages:

    ```
    # yum install -y openstack-packstack
    ```

4. Finally, start the installation of OpenStack components using `packstack`, which performs absolute hands-free installation of OpenStack:

    ```
    # packstack --allinone
    ```

    ```
    Applying 10.0.2.15_ring_swift.pp
    10.0.2.15_ring_swift.pp:                    [ DONE ]
    Applying 10.0.2.15_swift.pp
    Applying 10.0.2.15_provision_demo.pp
    10.0.2.15_swift.pp:                         [ DONE ]
    10.0.2.15_provision_demo.pp:                [ DONE ]
    Applying 10.0.2.15_mongodb.pp
    10.0.2.15_mongodb.pp:                       [ DONE ]
    Applying 10.0.2.15_ceilometer.pp
    Applying 10.0.2.15_nagios.pp
    Applying 10.0.2.15_nagios_nrpe.pp
    10.0.2.15_ceilometer.pp:                    [ DONE ]
    10.0.2.15_nagios.pp:                        [ DONE ]
    10.0.2.15_nagios_nrpe.pp:                   [ DONE ]
    Applying 10.0.2.15_postscript.pp
    10.0.2.15_postscript.pp:                    [ DONE ]
    Applying Puppet manifests                   [ DONE ]
    Finalizing                                  [ DONE ]

    **** Installation completed successfully ******
    ```

5. Once `packstack` completes the installation, it will display some additional information, including the OpenStack Horizon dashboard URL and credentials that will be used to operate OpenStack:

```
Additional information:
 * A new answerfile was created in: /root/packstack-answers-20140823-195321.txt
 * Time synchronization installation was skipped. Please note that unsynchronized time on s
erver instances might be problem for some OpenStack components.
 * File /root/keystonerc_admin has been created on OpenStack client host 10.0.2.15. To use
the command line tools you need to source the file.
 * To access the OpenStack Dashboard browse to http://10.0.2.15/dashboard .
Please, find your login credentials stored in the keystonerc_admin in your home directory.
 * To use Nagios, browse to http://10.0.2.15/nagios username: nagiosadmin, password: bd9321
71484e4e16
 * Because of the kernel update the host 10.0.2.15 requires reboot.
 * The installation log file is available at: /var/tmp/packstack/20140823-195320-YSt3Kn/ope
nstack-setup.log
 * The generated manifests are available at: /var/tmp/packstack/20140823-195320-YSt3Kn/mani
fests
[root@os-node1 ~]#
```

6. The login credentials for an admin account will be stored under the `/root/keystone_rc` file:

```
[root@os-node1 ~]# cat /root/keystonerc_admin
export OS_USERNAME=admin
export OS_TENANT_NAME=admin
export OS_PASSWORD=1da01eb3782e4b88
export OS_AUTH_URL=http://10.0.2.15:5000/v2.0/
export PS1='[\u@\h \W(keystone_admin)]\$ '
[root@os-node1 ~]#
```

7. Finally, open the web browser, navigate to the OpenStack Horizon dashboard URL, and supply the credentials of the admin user:

8. Now, you have successfully deployed a single node OpenStack environment that is ready for Ceph integration. You will be presented with the following screen:

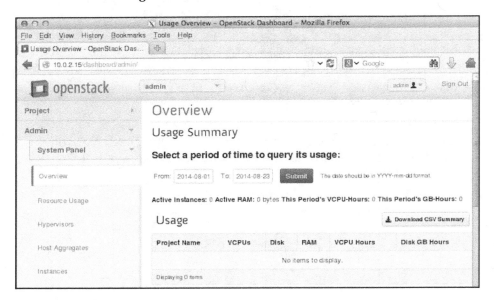

Ceph with OpenStack

OpenStack is a modular system, which has unique components for a specific set of tasks. There are several components that require a reliable storage backend such as Ceph and extend full integration to it, as shown in the following diagram. Each of these components uses Ceph in its own way to store block devices and objects. A majority of the cloud deployment based on OpenStack and Ceph uses Cinder, Glance, and Swift integration with Ceph. Keystone integration is used when you need S3-compatible object storage on Ceph backend. Nova integration allows booting from Ceph volume capabilities to your OpenStack cloud.

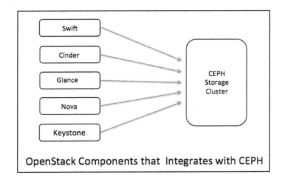

OpenStack Components that Integrates with CEPH

Installing Ceph on an OpenStack node

OpenStack nodes should be Ceph clients in order to be able to access a Ceph cluster. For this, install Ceph packages on OpenStack nodes and make sure they can access Ceph clusters:

1. To install Ceph packages on OpenStack nodes, use the ceph-deploy utility from any of the Ceph monitor nodes. In our case, we will use ceph-node1 to install Ceph packages using the ceph-deploy tool:

   ```
   # ceph-deploy install os-node1
   ```

2. Use ceph-deploy to copy Ceph client admin keyrings to OpenStack nodes:

   ```
   # ceph-deploy admin os-node1
   ```

3. Verify the Ceph keyring and configuration file under /etc/ceph of the OpenStack node, and try to connect to cluster:

```
[root@os-node1 ~]# ls -l /etc/ceph
total 12
-rw-r--r--. 1 root root 137 Aug 24 00:25 ceph.client.admin.keyring
-rw-r--r--. 1 root root 573 Aug 24 00:25 ceph.conf
-rwxr-xr-x. 1 root root  92 Jul 30 04:36 rbdmap
[root@os-node1 ~]#
[root@os-node1 ~]# ceph -s
    cluster 07a92ca3-347e-43db-87ee-e0a0a9f89e97
     health HEALTH_OK
     monmap e3: 3 mons at {ceph-node1=192.168.57.101:6789/0,ceph-node2=192.168.57.102:6789/0,
ceph-node3=192.168.57.103:6789/0}, election epoch 1060, quorum 0,1,2 ceph-node1,ceph-node2,ce
ph-node3
     mdsmap e96: 1/1/1 up {0=ceph-node2=up:active}
     osdmap e869: 9 osds: 9 up, 9 in
      pgmap v4931: 1536 pgs, 13 pools, 1352 kB data, 2650 objects
            509 MB used, 82335 MB / 82844 MB avail
                 1536 active+clean
[root@os-node1 ~]#
```

Configuring Ceph for OpenStack

At this point, your OpenStack node, os-node1, can connect to your Ceph cluster. We will next configure Ceph for OpenStack. To do this, execute the following commands from os-node1, unless otherwise specified:

1. Create dedicated Ceph pools for OpenStack Cinder and Glance. Make sure to use an appropriate number of PGs for your environment:

   ```
   # ceph osd pool create volumes 128

   # ceph osd pool create images 128
   ```

2. Create new users for Cinder and Glance to use the cephx authentication:

```
# ceph auth get-or-create client.cinder mon 'allow r' osd
'allow class-read object_prefix rbd_children, allow rwx
pool=volumes,allow rx pool=images'
```

```
# ceph auth get-or-create client.glance mon 'allow r' osd
'allow class-read object_prefix rbd_children, allow rwx
pool=images'
```

3. Create keyring files for newly created users client.cinder and client.glance, and allow them to be accessible by Cinder and Glance OpenStack users:

```
# ceph auth get-or-create client.cinder | tee /etc/ceph/ceph.
client.cinder.keyring
```

```
# chown cinder:cinder /etc/ceph/ceph.client.cinder.keyring
```

```
# ceph auth get-or-create client.glance | tee /etc/ceph/ceph.
client.glance.keyring
```

```
# chown glance:glance /etc/ceph/ceph.client.glance.keyring
```

 Make sure that the `/etc/ceph/ceph.conf` file has read permission for Cinder users. Usually, it should have permission of 644.

4. The libvirt process requires accessing a Ceph cluster while attaching or detaching a block device from Cinder and creating a temporary copy of the client.cinder key that will be added to libvirt in the next step:

```
# ceph auth get-key client.cinder | tee /tmp/client.cinder.key
```

5. Add the secret key to libvirt and remove the temporary copy of the client.cinder key:

    1. Generate a UUID:

       ```
       # uuidgen
       ```

    2. Create a secret file with the following content, and make sure you use the unique UUID that you generated in the last step:

       ```
       cat > secret.xml <<EOF
       <secret ephemeral='no' private='no'>
         <uuid>63b033bb-3305-479d-854b-cf3d0cb6a50c</uuid>
         <usage type='ceph'>
           <name>client.cinder secret</name>
         </usage>
       </secret>
       EOF
       ```

3. Define the secret and keep the generated secret value safe. We will require this secret value in the further steps:

```
# virsh secret-define --file secret.xml
```

```
[root@os-node1 ceph]# uuidgen
63b033bb-3305-479d-854b-cf3d0cb6a50c
[root@os-node1 ceph]#
[root@os-node1 ceph]# cat > secret.xml <<EOF
> <secret ephemeral='no' private='no'>
>    <uuid>63b033bb-3305-479d-854b-cf3d0cb6a50c</uuid>
>    <usage type='ceph'>
>      <name>client.cinder secret</name>
>    </usage>
> </secret>
> EOF
[root@os-node1 ceph]# virsh secret-define --file secret.xml
Secret 63b033bb-3305-479d-854b-cf3d0cb6a50c created
```

 The secret key generated in this step is usually similar to the UUID.

4. Set the secret value and delete temporary files. Deleting the files is optional; it is just to keep the system clean:

```
# virsh secret-set-value --secret 63b033bb-3305-479d-
854b-
cf3d0cb6a50c --base64 $(cat /tmp/client.cinder.key) &&
rm
/tmp/client.cinder.key secret.xml
```

```
[root@os-node1 ceph]# virsh secret-set-value --secret 63b033bb-3305-479d-854b-cf3d0cb6a50c --base64 $(cat
/tmp/client.cinder.key) && rm /tmp/client.cinder.key secret.xml
Secret value set

rm: remove regular file `/tmp/client.cinder.key'? y
rm: remove regular file `secret.xml'? y
[root@os-node1 ceph]#
```

Configuring OpenStack Cinder

At this point, we have covered configuration from Ceph's point of view. Next, we will configure the OpenStack components Cinder, Glance, and Nova to use Ceph. Cinder supports multiple backends. To configure Cinder to use Ceph, edit the Cinder configuration file and define the RBD driver that OpenStack Cinder should use.

To do this, you must also specify the pool name that we created for Cinder volumes previously. On your OpenStack node, edit `/etc/cinder/cinder.conf` and perform the following changes:

1. Navigate to the `Options defined in cinder.volume.manager` section of the `/etc/cinder/cinder.conf` file and add an RBD driver for Cinder:

   ```
   volume_driver=cinder.volume.drivers.rbd.RBDDriver
   ```

2. Navigate to the `Options defined in cinder.volume.drivers.rbd` section of the `/etc/cinder/cinder.conf` file and add (replace the secret UUID with your environment's value) the following:

   ```
   rbd_pool=volumes
   rbd_user=cinder
   rbd_ceph_conf=/etc/ceph/ceph.conf
   rbd_flatten_volume_from_snapshot=false
   rbd_secret_uuid=63b033bb-3305-479d-854b-cf3d0cb6a50c
   rbd_max_clone_depth=5
   ```

3. Navigate to the `Options defined in cinder.common.config` section of the `/etc/cinder/cinder.conf` file and add:

   ```
   glance_api_version=2
   ```

 If you are using multiple backends, this option should be placed in the [default] section of the `/etc/cinder/cinder.conf` file.

4. Save the Cinder configuration file and exit the editor.

Configuring OpenStack Nova

To boot OpenStack instances directly into Ceph, that is, to boot from volume feature, you must configure the ephemeral backend for Nova. To achieve this, edit `/etc/nova/nova.conf`:

1. Navigate to the `Options defined in nova.virt.libvirt.imagebackend` section and add:

   ```
   images_type=rbd
   images_rbd_pool=rbd
   images_rbd_ceph_conf=/etc/ceph/ceph.conf
   ```

2. Navigate to the `Options defined in nova.virt.libvirt.volume` section and add (replace the secret UUID with your environment's value):

   ```
   rbd_user=cinder
   rbd_secret_uuid=63b033bb-3305-479d-854b-cf3d0cb6a50c
   ```

Configuring OpenStack Glance

OpenStack Glance is capable of supporting multiple storage backends. In this section, we will learn to configure OpenStack Glance to use Ceph to store Glance images:

1. To use Ceph block devices to store Glance images, edit the `/etc/glance/ glance-api.conf` file and add:

    ◦   The `default_store=rbd` statement to the default section of the `glance-api.conf` file

    ◦   Navigate to the `RBD Store Options` section of the `glance-api.conf` file and add:

        ```
        rbd_store_user=glance
        rbd_store_pool=images
        ```

    ◦   If you want copy-on-write cloning of images, then set `show_image_ direct_url=True`

2. Save the Glance configuration file and exit the editor.

Restarting OpenStack services

To bring all the changes into effect, you must restart OpenStack services using the following commands:

```
# service openstack-glance-api restart
# service openstack-nova-compute restart
# service openstack-cinder-volume restart
```

Testing OpenStack Cinder

You can operate Cinder from either CLI or GUI. We will now test Cinder from each of these interfaces.

Using Cinder CLI

Perform the following steps:

1. Source the OpenStack RDO `keystonerc_admin` file that will be autocreated post OpenStack installation:

    ```
    # source /root/keystonerc_admin
    ```

2. Create your first Cinder volume of 10 GB, which should be created on your default Ceph storage backend:

```
# cinder create --display-name ceph-volume01 --display-
description "Cinder volume on CEPH storage" 10
```

```
[root@os-node1 ~(keystone_admin)]# cinder create --display-name ceph-volume01 --display-description "Cinder volume on CEPH storage" 10
+---------------------+--------------------------------------+
|       Property      |                Value                 |
+---------------------+--------------------------------------+
|     attachments     |                  []                  |
|  availability_zone  |                 nova                 |
|       bootable      |                false                 |
|      created_at     |      2014-08-24T00:09:48.299357       |
|  display_description |     Cinder volume on CEPH storage    |
|     display_name    |             ceph-volume01            |
|      encrypted      |                False                 |
|          id         | 00a90cd9-c2ea-4154-b045-6a837ac343da |
|       metadata      |                  {}                  |
|         size        |                  10                  |
|     snapshot_id     |                 None                 |
|     source_volid    |                 None                 |
|        status       |               creating               |
|     volume_type     |                 None                 |
+---------------------+--------------------------------------+
[root@os-node1 ~(keystone_admin)]#
```

3. While OpenStack Cinder is creating your volume, you can monitor your Ceph cluster using `#ceph -s`, where you observe cluster write operations.

4. Finally, check the status of your Cinder volume; make sure you have the status of your Cinder volume as available:

```
# cinder list
```

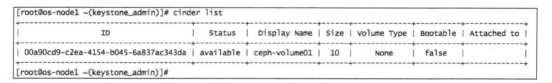

```
[root@os-node1 ~(keystone_admin)]# cinder list
+--------------------------------------+-----------+---------------+------+-------------+----------+-------------+
|                  ID                  |   Status  |  Display Name | Size | Volume Type | Bootable | Attached to |
+--------------------------------------+-----------+---------------+------+-------------+----------+-------------+
| 00a90cd9-c2ea-4154-b045-6a837ac343da | available |  ceph-volume01 |  10  |     None    |   false  |             |
+--------------------------------------+-----------+---------------+------+-------------+----------+-------------+
[root@os-node1 ~(keystone_admin)]#
```

Using Horizon GUI

You can also create and manage your Cinder volumes from the OpenStack Horizon dashboard. Open the web interface of OpenStack Horizon and navigate to the volume section:

1. Click on **Create volume** and provide the volume details.

2. Once you create the volume from Horizon GUI, it will display the status of all your volumes:

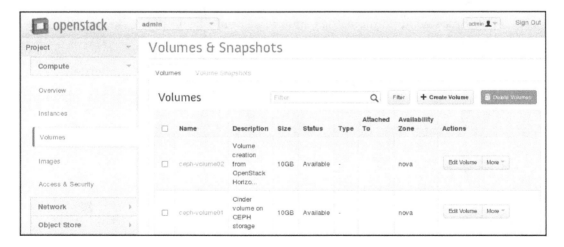

3. Finally, check your Ceph volumes pool; you will find objects in your Ceph pool containing the volume ID. For instance, you can identify the object name, which is `rbd_id.volume-00a90cd9-c2ea-4154-b045-6a837ac343da`, for the Cinder volume named `ceph-volume01` having the ID `00a90cd9-c2ea-4154-b045-6a837ac343da` in Ceph volume pools:

```
[root@os-node1 ~(keystone_admin)]# cinder list
+--------------------------------------+-----------+---------------+------+-------------+----------+-------------+
|                  ID                  |  Status   | Display Name  | Size | Volume Type | Bootable | Attached to |
+--------------------------------------+-----------+---------------+------+-------------+----------+-------------+
| 00a90cd9-c2ea-4154-b045-6a837ac343da | available | ceph-volume01 |  10  |    None     |  false   |             |
| ce8b1344-80d8-42d6-8e22-8c4d17abcfeb | available | ceph-volume02 |  10  |    None     |  false   |             |
+--------------------------------------+-----------+---------------+------+-------------+----------+-------------+
[root@os-node1 ~(keystone_admin)]#
[root@os-node1 ~(keystone_admin)]# rados -p volumes ls
rbd_directory
rbd_header.4c381910a0d0
rbd_header.4a885399b49f
rbd_id.volume-ce8b1344-80d8-42d6-8e22-8c4d17abcfeb
rbd_id.volume-00a90cd9-c2ea-4154-b045-6a837ac343da
[root@os-node1 ~(keystone_admin)]#
```

4. You can attach these volumes to OpenStack VM instances as block storage and access them based on your requirements.

Testing OpenStack Glance

You can use OpenStack Glance to store operating system images for instances. These images will eventually be stored on storage backed by Ceph.

Perform the following steps to test OpenStack Glance:

1. Before adding a Glance image, check the Ceph images pool. Since we have not imported any image, the Ceph pool should be empty:

   `# rados -p images ls`

2. Download images that can be used with OpenStack from the Internet:

   `# wget http://cloud-images.ubuntu.com/precise/current/precise-server-cloudimg-amd64-disk1.img`

```
[root@os-node1 glance(keystone_admin)]# wget http://cloud-images.ubuntu.com/precise/current/precise-server-cloudimg-amd64-disk1.img
--2014-08-26 19:39:26--  http://cloud-images.ubuntu.com/precise/current/precise-server-cloudimg-amd64-disk1.img
Resolving cloud-images.ubuntu.com... 91.189.88.141
Connecting to cloud-images.ubuntu.com|91.189.88.141|:80... connected.
HTTP request sent, awaiting response... 200 OK
Length: 261227008 (249M) [application/octet-stream]
Saving to: "precise-server-cloudimg-amd64-disk1.img"

100%[==============================================================>] 261,227,008 6.46M/s   in 52s

2014-08-26 19:40:19 (4.76 MB/s) - "precise-server-cloudimg-amd64-disk1.img" saved [261227008/261227008]

[root@os-node1 glance(keystone_admin)]#
```

3. Create a Glance image:

```
# glance image-create --name="ubuntu-precise-image" --is-
public=True --disk-format=qcow2 --container-format=ovf  <
precise-server-cloudimg-amd64-disk1.img
```

```
[root@os-node1 glance(keystone_admin)]# glance image-create --name="ubuntu-precise-image" --is-public=True
--disk-format=qcow2 --container-format=ovf  < precise-server-cloudimg-amd64-disk1.img
+------------------+--------------------------------------+
| Property         | Value                                |
+------------------+--------------------------------------+
| checksum         | 23034c4e06f9f012099d61d4a4e5248d     |
| container_format | ovf                                  |
| created_at       | 2014-08-26T16:49:33                  |
| deleted          | False                                |
| deleted_at       | None                                 |
| disk_format      | qcow2                                |
| id               | 249cc4be-474d-4137-80f6-dc03f77b3d49 |
| is_public        | True                                 |
| min_disk         | 0                                    |
| min_ram          | 0                                    |
| name             | ubuntu-precise-image                 |
| owner            | a84af521b50f41bba704f8dc0e1ae15d     |
| protected        | False                                |
| size             | 261227008                            |
| status           | active                               |
| updated_at       | 2014-08-26T16:50:18                  |
| virtual_size     | None                                 |
+------------------+--------------------------------------+
[root@os-node1 glance(keystone_admin)]#
```

4. Check the Glance image list as well as query your Ceph image pool for the Glance image ID:

```
# glance image-list

# rados -p images ls | grep -i  249cc4be-474d-4137-80f6-
dc03f77b3d49
```

```
[root@os-node1 glance(keystone_admin)]# glance image-list
+--------------------------------------+----------------------+-------------+------------------+-----------+--------+
| ID                                   | Name                 | Disk Format | Container Format | Size      | Status |
+--------------------------------------+----------------------+-------------+------------------+-----------+--------+
| d1184d23-b568-49f2-9aa7-1e4d2e915224 | cirros               | qcow2       | bare             | 13147648  | active |
| 249cc4be-474d-4137-80f6-dc03f77b3d49 | ubuntu-precise-image | qcow2       | ovf              | 261227008 | active |
+--------------------------------------+----------------------+-------------+------------------+-----------+--------+
[root@os-node1 glance(keystone_admin)]#
[root@os-node1 glance(keystone_admin)]# rados -p images ls | grep -i  249cc4be-474d-4137-80f6-dc03f77b3d49
rbd_id.249cc4be-474d-4137-80f6-dc03f77b3d49
[root@os-node1 glance(keystone_admin)]#
```

5. The output of the preceding commands confirms that we have imported an Ubuntu image into OpenStack Glance, which has been stored on Ceph image volumes.

Summary

In this chapter, we discussed OpenStack and its components and how seamlessly they integrate with Ceph. The demonstration section would have helped you to learn the step-by-step integration of OpenStack followed by testing each OpenStack component. In the next chapter, we will focus on some general performance-tuning tricks for your Ceph cluster as well as benchmarking your cluster.

10
Ceph Performance Tuning and Benchmarking

In this chapter, we will cover the following topics:

- Ceph performance overview
- General Ceph performance consideration – hardware level
- Ceph performance tuning – software level
- Ceph erasure coding
- Ceph cache tiering
- Ceph benchmarking using RADOS bench

Ceph performance overview

Data and information always keep on changing and increasing. Every organization, whether small or large, faces data growth challenges with time, and most of the time, these data growth challenges bring performance problems with them. In this era, where the world is generating enormous amount of data, organizations have to look for a storage solution that is highly scalable, distributed, extremely reliable, and on top of that, well performing for all of their workload needs.

One of the several biggest advantages of Ceph is that it possesses scalable, distributed architecture. Due to its distributed nature, all the workload that comes to Ceph is evenly distributed and allocated to the entire cluster for storage, which makes Ceph a good performing storage system. You can imagine storing a data file on a traditional storage system is quite limited in scalability, almost nondistributed, and has only a limited numbers of data storage nodes and disks. In such a kind of traditional setup, performance problems might occur with data growth and increasing user requests.

These days, when applications serve a huge number of clients, they require a better-performing backend storage system. A typical Ceph setup contains numerous nodes, and each node contains several OSDs. Since Ceph is distributed, when data arrives to Ceph for storage, it's distributed across several nodes and OSDs beneath, delivering an accumulative performance of several nodes. Moreover, the traditional systems are limited to a certain performance when you add more capacity to them, that is, you will not get added performance with increasing capacity. In some scenarios, the performance degrades on increasing the capacity. With Ceph, you will never see performance degradation with increase in the capacity. When you increase the capacity of a Ceph storage system, that is, when you add new nodes full of OSDs, the performance of the entire storage cluster increases linearly since we now get more OSD workhorses and added CPU, memory, and network per new node. This is something that makes Ceph unique and differentiates Ceph from other storage systems.

Ceph performance consideration – hardware level

When it comes to performance, the underlying hardware plays a major role. Traditional storage systems run specifically on their vendor-manufactured hardware, where users do not have any flexibility in terms of hardware selection based on their needs and unique workload requirements. It's very difficult for organizations that invest in such vendor-locked systems to overcome problems generated due to incapable hardware.

Ceph, on the other hand, is absolutely vendor-free; organizations are no longer tied up with hardware manufacturers, and they are free to use any hardware of their choice, budget, and performance requirements. They have full control over their hardware and the underlying infrastructure.

The other advantage of Ceph is that it supports heterogeneous hardware, that is, Ceph can run on cluster hardware from multiple vendors. Customers are allowed to mix hardware brands while creating their Ceph infrastructure. For example, while purchasing hardware for Ceph, customers can mix the hardware from different manufacturers such as HP, Dell, IBM, Fujitsu, Super Micro, and even off-the-shelf hardware. In this way, customers can achieve huge money-savings, their desired hardware, full control, and decision-making rights.

Hardware selection plays a vital role in the overall Ceph storage performance. Since the customers have full rights to select the hardware type for Ceph, it should be done with extra care, with proper estimation of the current and future workloads.

One should keep in mind that hardware selection for Ceph is totally dependent on the workload that you will put on your cluster, the environment, and all features you will use. In this section, we will learn some general practices for selecting hardware for your Ceph cluster.

Processor

Some of the Ceph components are not processor hungry. Like Ceph, monitor daemons are lightweight, as they maintain copies of cluster and do not serve any data to clients. Thus, for most cases, a single core processor for monitor will do the job. You can also think of running monitor daemons on any other server in your environment that has free resources. Make sure you have system resources such as memory, network, and disk space available in an adequate quantity for monitor daemons.

Ceph OSD daemons might require a fair amount of CPU as they serve data to clients and hence require some data processing. A dual-core processor for OSD nodes will be nice. From a performance point of view, it's important to know how you will use OSDs, whether it's in a replicated fashion or erasure coded. If you use OSDs in erasure coding, you should consider a quad-core processor as erasure-coding operations require a lot of computation. In the event of cluster recovery, the processor consumption by OSD daemons increases significantly.

Ceph MDS daemons are more process hungry as compared to MON and OSD. They need to dynamically redistribute their load that is CPU intensive; you should consider a quad-core processor for Ceph MDS.

Memory

Monitor and metadata daemons need to serve their data rapidly, hence they should have enough memory for faster processing. From a performance point of view, 2 GB or more per-daemon instance should be available for metadata and monitor. OSDs are generally not memory intensive. For an average workload, 1 GB of memory per-OSD-daemon instance should suffice; however, from a performance point of view, 2 GB per-OSD daemon will be a good choice. This recommendation assumes that you are using one OSD daemon for one physical disk. If you use more than one physical disk per OSD, your memory requirement will grow as well. Generally, more physical memory is good, since during cluster recovery, memory consumption increases significantly.

Network

All the cluster nodes should have dual-network interfaces for two different networks, that is, cluster network and client network. For a medium-size cluster of several hundred terabytes, 1 G network link should go well. However, if your cluster size is big and it serves several clients, you should think of 10 G or more bandwidth network. At the time of system recovery, network plays a vital role. If you have a good 10 G or more bandwidth network connection, your cluster will recover quickly, else it might take some time. So, from a performance point of view, 10 Gb or more dual network will be a good option. A well-designed Ceph cluster makes use of two physically separated networks, one for cluster network (internal network) and another for client network (external network); both these networks should be physically separated from the network switch; a point-of-availability setup will require a redundant dual network, as shown in the following diagram:

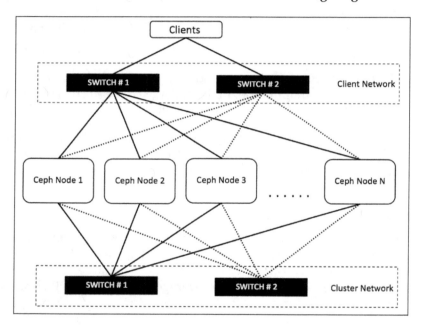

Disk

Disk drive selection for Ceph storage cluster holds a lot of importance with respect to overall performance and the total cluster cost. Before taking your final decision on disk drive selection, you should understand your workload and possible performance requirements. Ceph OSD consists of two different parts: the OSD journal part and the OSD data part. Every write operation is a two-step process.

When any OSD receives client requests to store an object, it first writes the object to the journal part, and then from the journal, it writes the same object to the data part before it sends an acknowledge signal to the client. In this way, all the cluster performance revolves around OSD journal and data partition. From a performance point of view, it's recommended to use SSD for journals. By using SSD, you can achieve significant throughput improvements by reducing access time and read latency. In most environments, where you are not concerned about extreme performance, you can consider configuring journal and data partition on the same hard disk drive. However, if you are looking for significant performance improvements out of your Ceph cluster, it's worth investing on SSD for journals.

To use SSD as journals, we create logical partitions on each physical SSD that will be used as journals, such that each SSD journal partition is mapped to one OSD data partition. In this type of setup, you should keep in mind not to overload SSDs by storing multiple journals beyond its limits. By doing this, you will impact the overall performance. To achieve good performance out of your SSDs, you should store no more than four OSD journals on each SSD disk.

The dark side of using a single SSD for multiple journals is that if you lose your SSD hosting multiple journals, all the OSDs associated with this SSD will fail and you might lose your data. However, you can overcome this situation by using RAID 1 for journals, but this will increase your storage cost. Also, SSD cost per gigabyte is nearly 10 times more compared to HDD. So, if you are building a cluster with SSDs, it will increase the cost per gigabyte for your Ceph cluster.

Filesystem type selection is also one of the aspects for cluster performance. Btrfs is an advance filesystem that can write the object in a single operation as compared to XFS and EXT4, which require two steps to write an object. Btrfs is copy-on-write filesystem, that is, while writing the object to journal, it can simultaneously write the same object on data partition, providing significant performance improvements. However, Btrfs is not production ready at the time of writing. You might face data inconsistency problems with Btrfs.

Ceph performance tuning – software level

The performance of any system is quantified by load and performance testing. The results of these tests help us to make the decision whether the current setup requires tuning or not. Performance tuning is the process of rectifying performance bottlenecks identified during performance tests. Performance tuning is a very vast topic, which requires a deep study of each and every component, whether it's internal or external to Ceph.

The recommended approach to fine-tune a Ceph cluster is to start investigation from one end of the cluster's smallest element up to the level of end users who use the storage services. In this section, we will cover some performance tuning parameters from a Ceph cluster's point of view. We will define these performance tuning parameters under a Ceph cluster configuration file so that each time any Ceph daemon starts, it should adhere to the tuning setting. We will first learn about Ceph configuration files and its various sections, and then we will focus on performance tuning settings.

Cluster configuration file

Most of the cluster-wide configuration settings are defined under a Ceph cluster configuration file. If you have not changed your cluster name and configuration file location for your cluster, the default name will be `ceph.conf` and the path will be `/etc/ceph/ceph.conf`. This configuration file has a global section as well as several sections for each service type. Whenever each Ceph service type starts, that is, MON, OSD, and MDS, it reads the configuration defined under the global section as well as their specific section.

Config sections

A Ceph configuration file has multiple sections; we will now discuss the role of each section of configuration file.

The global section

The global section is the section defined under `[global]`; all the settings under this section affect all the daemons of a Ceph cluster. The setting that needs to be applied for the entire cluster is defined here. The following is the example of the settings in this section:

```
public network = 192.168.0.0/24
```

The MON section

The settings mentioned under the `[MON]` section are applied to all ceph-mon daemons in the Ceph cluster. The configuration defined under this section overrides the same settings defined under the `[global]` section. The following is the example of the settings in this section:

```
mon initial members = ceph-mon1
```

The OSD section

The settings mentioned under the [OSD] section are applied to all ceph-osd daemons in the Ceph cluster. The configuration defined under this section overrides the same setting defined under the [global] section. The following is the example of the settings in this section:

```
osd mkfs type = xfs
```

The MDS section

The settings mentioned under the [MDS] section are applied to all ceph-mds daemons in the Ceph cluster. The configuration defined under this section overrides the same setting defined under the [global] section. The following is the example of the settings in this section:

```
mds cache size = 250000
```

The client section

The settings mentioned under the [client] section are applied to all Ceph clients. The configuration defined under this section overrides the same setting defined under the [global] section. The following is the example of the settings in this section:

```
rbd cache = true
```

Ceph cluster performance tuning

As mentioned earlier, performance tuning is mostly environment-specific. Your organization environment and hardware infrastructure for Ceph cluster will be a lot different from other organizations. Things you tune for your Ceph cluster may or may not work the same way as in other environments. In this section, we will discuss some general performance tuning parameters that you can tailor more specifically for your environment.

Global tuning parameters

The parameters mentioned in this section should be defined under the [global] section of your Ceph cluster configuration file.

Network

It's highly recommended that you use two physically separated networks for your Ceph cluster. Each of these networks has their own set of responsibilities. Under Ceph's terminology, these networks are referred to as public and cluster networks:

- The public network is also referred to as the client-side network that allows clients to communicate with Ceph clusters and access the cluster for their data storage. This network is dedicated to clients only, so no internal cluster communication happens on this network. You should define the public network for your Ceph cluster configuration as follows:

```
public network = {public network / netmask}
```

The example of this will be as follows:

```
public network = 192.168.100.0/24
```

- The cluster network is also referred to as the internal network, which is a dedicated network for all the internal cluster operations between Ceph nodes. From a performance point of view, this network should have a decent bandwidth of 10 Gb or 40 Gb as this network is responsible for high bandwidth cluster operations such as data replication, recovery, rebalancing, and heartbeat checks. You can define cluster network as follows:

```
cluster network = {cluster network / netmask}
```

The example of this will be as follows:

```
cluster network = 192.168.1.0/24
```

Max open files

If this parameter is in place and the Ceph cluster starts, it sets the max open file descriptors at the OS level. This helps OSD daemons from running out of file descriptors. The default vale of this parameter is 0; you can set it as up to a 64-bit integer.

Have a look at the following example:

```
max open files = 131072
```

OSD tuning parameters

The parameters mentioned in this section should be defined under the [OSD] section of your Ceph cluster configuration file:

- **Extended attributes**: These are also known as XATTRs, which are very valuable for storing file metadata. Some filesystems allow a limited set of bytes to store as XATTRs. In some cases, using well-defined extended attributes will help the filesystem. The XATTR parameters should be used with an EXT4 filesystem to achieve good performance. The following is the example:

```
filestore xattr use omap = true
```

- **Filestore sync interval**: In order to create a consistent commit point, the filestore needs to quiesce write operations and do a syncfs, which syncs data from the journal to the data partition, and thus frees the journal. A more frequent sync operation reduces the amount of data that is stored in a journal. In such cases, the journal becomes underutilized. Configuring less frequent syncs allows the filesystem to coalesce small writes better, and we might get an improved performance. The following parameters define the minimum and maximum time period between two syncs:

```
filestore min sync interval = 10
filestore max sync interval = 15
```

 You can set any other double-type value that better suits your environment for filestore min and filestore max.

- **Filestore queue**: The following settings allow a limit on the size of a filestore queue. These settings might have minimal impact on performance:

    ○ filestore queue max ops: This is the maximum number of operations that a filestore can accept before blocking new operations to join the queue. Have a look at the following example:

    ```
    filestore queue max ops = 25000
    ```

    ○ filestore queue max bytes: This is the maximum number of bytes of an operation. The following is the example:

    ```
    filestore queue max bytes = 10485760
    ```

    ○ filestore queue committing max ops: This is the maximum number of operations the filestores can commit. An example for this is as follows:

    ```
    filestore queue committing max ops = 5000
    ```

- ○ `filestore queue committing max bytes`: This is the maximum number of bytes the filestore can commit. Have a look at the following example:

  ```
  filestore queue committing max bytes = 10485760000
  ```

- ○ `filestore op threads`: This is the number of filesystem operation threads that can execute in parallel. The following is the example:

  ```
  filestore op threads = 32
  ```

- **OSD journal tuning**: Ceph OSD daemons support the following journal configurations:

  - ○ `journal max write bytes`: This is the maximum number of bytes the journal can write at once. The following is the example:

    ```
    journal max write bytes = 1073714824
    ```

  - ○ `journal max write entries`: This is the maximum number of entries the journal can write at once. Here is the example:

    ```
    journal max write entries = 10000
    ```

  - ○ `journal queue max ops`: This is the maximum number of operations allowed in the journal queue at one time. An example of this is as follows:

    ```
    journal queue max ops = 50000
    ```

  - ○ `journal queue max bytes`: This is the maximum number of bytes allowed in the journal queue at one time. Have a look at the following example:

    ```
    journal queue max bytes = 10485760000
    ```

- **OSD config tuning**: Ceph OSD daemons support the following OSD config settings:

  - ○ `osd max write size`: This is the maximum size in megabytes an OSD can write at a time. The following is the example:

    ```
    osd max write size = 512
    ```

  - ○ `osd client message size cap`: This is the maximum size of client data in megabytes that is allowed in memory. An example is as follows:

    ```
    osd client message size cap = 2048
    ```

- ° `osd deep scrub stride`: This is the size in bytes that is read by OSDs when doing a deep scrub. Have a look at the following example:

  ```
  osd deep scrub stride = 131072
  ```

- ° `osd op threads`: This is the number of operation threads used by a Ceph OSD daemon. For example:

  ```
  osd op threads = 16
  ```

- ° `osd disk threads`: This is the number of disk threads to perform OSD-intensive operations such as recovery and scrubbing. The following is the example:

  ```
  osd disk threads = 4
  ```

- ° `osd map cache size`: This is the size of OSD map cache in megabytes. The following is the example:

  ```
  osd map cache size = 1024
  ```

- ° `osd map cache bl size`: This is the size of OSD map caches stored in-memory in megabytes. An example is as follows:

  ```
  osd map cache bl size = 128
  ```

- ° `osd mount options xfs`: This allows us to supply xfs filesystem mount options. At the time of mounting OSDs, it will get mounted with supplied mount options. Have a look at the following example:

  ```
  osd mount options xfs =
  "rw,noatime,inode64,logbsize=256k,delaylog,allocsize=4M"
  ```

- **OSD recovery tuning**: These settings should be used when you like performance over recovery or vice versa. If your Ceph cluster is unhealthy and is under recovery, you might not get its usual performance as OSDs will be busy into recovery. If you still prefer performance over recovery, you can reduce recovery priority to keep OSDs less occupied with recovery. You can also set these values if you want a quick recovery for your cluster, helping OSDs to perform recovery faster.

  - ° `osd recovery op priority`: This is the priority set for recovery operation. Lower the number, higher the recovery priority. Higher recovery priority might cause performance degradation until recovery completes. The following is the example:

    ```
    osd recovery op priority = 4
    ```

- ○ `osd recovery max active`: This is the maximum number of active recover requests. Higher the number, quicker the recovery, which might impact the overall cluster performance until recovery finishes. The following is the example:

  ```
  osd recovery max active = 10
  ```

- ○ `osd max backfills`: This is the maximum number of backfill operations allowed to/from OSD. The higher the number, the quicker the recovery, which might impact overall cluster performance until recovery finishes. The following is the example:

  ```
  osd recovery max backfills = 4
  ```

Client tuning parameters

The user space implementation of a Ceph block device cannot take advantage of a Linux page cache, so a new in-memory caching mechanism has been introduced in Ceph Version 0.46, which is known as RBD Caching. By default, Ceph does not allow RBD caching; to enable this feature, you should update the `[client]` section of your Ceph cluster configuration file with the following parameters:

- `rbd cache = true`: This is to enable RBD caching.
- `rbd cache size = 268435456`: This is the RBD cache size in bytes.
- `rbd cache max dirty = 134217728`: This is the dirty limit in bytes; after this specified limit, data will be flushed to the backing store. If this value is set to `0`, Ceph uses the write-through caching method. If this parameter is not used, the default cache mechanism is write-back.
- `rbd cache max dirty age = 5`: This is the number of seconds during which dirty data will be stored on cache before it's flushed to the backing store.

General performance tuning

In the last section, we covered various tuning parameters that you can define under your cluster configuration file. These were absolute Ceph-based tuning tips. In this section, we will learn a few general tuning tips, which will be configured at OS- and network-level for your infrastructure:

- **Kernel pid max**: This is a Linux kernel parameter that is responsible for maximum number of threads and process IDs. A major part of the Linux kernel has a relatively small `kernel.pid_max` value. Configuring this parameter with a higher value on Ceph nodes having greater number of OSDs, that is, `OSD > 20`, might help spawning multiple threads for faster recovery and rebalancing. To use this parameter, execute the following command from the root user:

```
# echo 4194303 > /proc/sys/kernel/pid_max
```

- **Jumbo frames**: The Ethernet frames that are more than 1,500 bytes of payload MTU are known as jumbo frames. Enabling jumbo frames of all the network interfaces of your Ceph cluster node should provide better network throughput and overall improved performance. The jumbo frames are configured at an OS level, however, the network interface and backend network switch should support jumbo frames. To enable jumbo frames, you should configure your switch-side interfaces to accept them and then start configuring at the OS level. For instance, from an OS point of view, to enable jumbo frames on interface eth0, execute the following command:

```
# ifconfig eth0 mtu 9000
```

9,000 bytes of payload is the maximum limit of network interface MTU; you should also update your network interface configuration file, /etc/sysconfig/network-script/ifcfg-eth0, to MTU=9000, in order to make the change permanent.

- **Disk read_ahead**: The read_ahead parameter speeds up the disk read operation by prefetching data and loading it to random access memory. Setting up a relatively higher value for read_ahead will benefit clients performing sequential read operations. You can check the current read_ahead value using this command:

```
# cat /sys/block/vda/queue/read_ahead_kb
```

To set read_ahead to a higher value, execute the following command:

```
# echo "8192">/sys/block/vda/queue/read_ahead_kb
```

Typically, customized read_ahead settings are used on Ceph clients that use RBD. You should change read_ahead for all the RBDs mapped to this host; also make sure to use the correct device path name.

Ceph erasure coding

Data protection and redundancy technologies have existed for many decades. One of the most popular methods for data reliability is **replication**. The replication method involves storing the same data multiple times on different physical locations. This method proves to be good when it comes to performance and data reliability, but it increases the overall cost associated with a storage system. The TOC with a replication method is way too high.

This method requires double the amount of storage space to provide redundancy. For instance, if you are planning for a storage solution with 1 PB of data with a replication factor of one, you will require a 2 PB of physical storage to store 1 PB of replicated data. In this way, the replication cost per gigabyte of storage system increases significantly. You might ignore the storage cost for a small storage cluster, but imagine where the cost will hit if you build up a hyper-scale data storage solution based on replicated storage backend.

Erasure coding mechanism comes as a gift in such scenarios. It is the mechanism used in storage for data protection and data reliability, which is absolutely different from the replication method. It guarantees data protection by dividing each storage object into smaller chunks known as data chunks, expanding and encoding them with coding chunks, and finally storing all these chunks across different failure zones of a Ceph cluster.

The erasure coding feature has been introduced in Ceph Firefly, and it is based on a mathematical function to achieve data protection. The entire concept revolves around the following equation:

```
n = k + m
```

The following points explain these terms and what they stand for:

- **k**: This is the number of chunks the original data is divided into, also known as data chunks.
- **m**: This is the extra code added to original data chunks to provide data protection, also known as coding chunk. For ease of understanding, you can consider it as the reliability level.
- **n**: This is the total number of chunks created after the erasure coding process.

Based on the preceding equation, every object in an erasure-coded Ceph pool will be stored as $k+m$ chunks, and each chunk is stored in OSD in an acting set. In this way, all the chunks of an object are spread across the entire Ceph cluster, providing a higher degree of reliability. Now, let's discuss some useful terms with respect to erasure coding:

- **Recovery**: At the time of Ceph recovery, we will require any k chunks out of n chunks to recover the data
- **Reliability level**: With erasure coding, Ceph can tolerate failure up to m chunks
- **Encoding Rate (r)**: This can be calculated using the formula $r = k/n$, where $r < 1$
- **Storage required**: This is calculated as $1/r$

For instance, consider a Ceph pool with five OSDs that is created using the erasure code (3, 2) rule. Every object that is stored inside this pool will be divided into the following set of data and coding chunks:

```
n = k + m
similarly, 5 = 3 + 2
hence n = 5 , k = 3 and m = 2
```

So, every object will be divided into three data chunks, and two extra erasure-coded chunks will be added to it, making a total of five chunks that will be stored and distributed on five OSDs of erasure-coded pool in a Ceph cluster. In an event of failure, to construct the original file, we need any three chunks out of any five chunks to recover it. Thus, we can sustain failure of any two OSDs as the data can be recovered using three OSDs.

```
Encoding rate (r) = 3 / 5 = 0.6 < 1
Storage required = 1/r = 1 / 0.6 = 1.6 times of original file.
```

Suppose there is a data file of size 1 GB. To store this file in a Ceph cluster on a erasure coded (3, 5) pool, you will need 1.6 GB of storage space, which will provide you file storage with sustainability of two OSD failures.

In contrast to replication method, if the same file is stored on a replicated pool, then in order to sustain the failure of two OSDs, Ceph will need a pool of replica size 3, which eventually requires 3 GB of storage space to reliably store 1 GB of file. In this way, you can save storage cost by approximately 40 percent by using the erasure coding feature of Ceph and getting the same reliability as with replication.

Erasure-coded pools require less storage space compared to replicated pools; however, this storage saving comes at the cost of performance because the erasure coding process divides every object into multiple smaller data chunks, and few newer coding chunks are mixed with these data chunks. Finally, all these chunks are stored across different failure zones of a Ceph cluster. This entire mechanism requires a bit more computational power from the OSD nodes. Moreover, at the time of recovery, decoding the data chunks also requires a lot of computing. So, you might find the erasure coding mechanism of storing data somewhat slower than the replication mechanism. Erasure coding is mainly use-case dependent, and you can get the most out of erasure coding based on your data storage requirements.

Low-cost cold storage

With erasure coding, you can store more with less money. Cold storage can be a good use case for erasure code, where read and write operations on data are less frequent; for example, large data sets where images and genomics data is stored for a longer time without reading and writing them, or some kind of archival system where data is archived and is not accessed frequently.

Usually, such types of low-cost cold storage erasure pools are tiered with faster replicated pools so that data is initially stored on the replicated pool, and if the data is not accessible for a certain time period (some weeks), it will be flushed to low-cost erasure code, where performance is not a criteria.

Implementing erasure coding

Erasure code is implemented by creating Ceph pools of type erasure; each of these pools are based on an erasure code profile that defines erasure coding characteristics. We will now create an erasure code profile and erasure-coded pool based on this profile:

1. The command mentioned in this section will create an erasure code profile with the name EC-profile, which will have characteristics of $k=3$ and $m=2$, which are the number of data and coding chunks, respectively. So, every object that is stored in the erasure-coded pool will be divided into 3 (k) data chunks, and 2 (m) additional coding chunks are added to them, making a total of 5 $(k + m)$ chunks. Finally, these 5 $(k + m)$ chunks are spread across different OSD failure zones.

   ○ Create the erasure code profile:

   ```
   # ceph osd erasure-code-profile set EC-profile ruleset-
   failure-domain=osd k=3 m=2
   ```

   ○ List the profile:

   ```
   # ceph osd erasure-code-profile ls
   ```

   ○ Get the contents of your erasure code profile:

   ```
   # ceph osd erasure-code-profile get EC-profile
   ```

```
[root@ceph-node1 /]# ceph osd erasure-code-profile set EC-profile ruleset-failure-domain=osd k=3 m=2
[root@ceph-node1 /]# ceph osd erasure-code-profile ls
EC-profile
[root@ceph-node1 /]# ceph osd erasure-code-profile get EC-profile
directory=/usr/lib64/ceph/erasure-code
k=3
m=2
plugin=jerasure
ruleset-failure-domain=osd
technique=reed_sol_van
[root@ceph-node1 /]#
```

2. Create a Ceph pool of erasure type, which will be based on the erasure code profile that we created in step 1:

   ```
   # ceph osd pool create EC-pool 16 16 erasure EC-profile
   ```

Check the status of your newly created pool; you should find that the size of the pool is 5 (*k* + *m*), that is, erasure size 5. Hence, data will be written to five different OSDs:

```
# ceph osd dump | grep -i EC-pool
```

```
[root@ceph-node1 /]# ceph osd pool create EC-pool 16 16 erasure EC-profile
pool 'EC-pool' created
[root@ceph-node1 /]#
[root@ceph-node1 /]# ceph osd dump | grep -i EC-pool
pool 15 'EC-pool' erasure size 5 min_size 1 crush_ruleset 3 object_hash rjenkins pg_num 16 pgp_num 16
last_change 975 owner 0 flags hashpspool stripe_width 4128
[root@ceph-node1 /]#
```

 Use a relatively good number or PG_NUM and PGP_NUM for your Ceph pool, which is more appropriate for your setup.

3. Now we have a new Ceph pool, which is of type erasure. We should now put some data to this pool by creating a sample file with some random content and putting this file to a newly created erasure-coded Ceph pool:

```
[root@ceph-node1 /]# echo "Mona is now testing Ceph Erasure Coding" > file1.txt
[root@ceph-node1 /]# cat file1.txt
Mona is now testing Ceph Erasure Coding
[root@ceph-node1 /]# rados -p EC-pool ls
[root@ceph-node1 /]# rados put -p EC-pool object1 file1.txt
[root@ceph-node1 /]# rados -p EC-pool ls
object1
[root@ceph-node1 /]#
```

4. Check the OSD map for EC-pool and object1. The output of this command will make things clear by showing the OSD ID where the object chunks are stored. As explained in step 1, object1 is divided into 3 (*m*) data chunks and added with 2 (*k*) coded chunks; so, altogether, five chunks were stored on different OSDs across the Ceph cluster. In this demonstration, object1 has been stored on five OSDs, namely, osd.7, osd.6, osd.4, osd.8, and osd.5.

```
[root@ceph-node1 /]# ceph osd map EC-pool object1
osdmap e976 pool 'EC-pool' (15) object 'object1' -> pg 15.bac5debc (15.c) -> up ([7,6,4,8,5], p7)
acting ([7,6,4,8,5], p7)
[root@ceph-node1 /]#
```

At this stage, we have completed setting up an erasure pool in a Ceph cluster. Now, we will deliberately try to break OSDs to see how the erasure pool behaves when OSDs are unavailable.

5. As mentioned in the previous step, some of the OSDs for the erasure pool are osd.4 and osd.5; we will now test the erasure pool reliability by breaking these OSDs one by one.

 These are some optional steps and should not be performed on Ceph clusters serving critical data. Also, the OSD numbers might change for your cluster; replace wherever necessary.

Bring down osd.4 and check the OSD map for EC-pool and object1. You should notice that osd.4 is replaced by a random number 2147483647, which means that osd.4 is no longer available for this pool:

```
# ssh ceph-node2 service ceph stop osd.5
# ceph osd map EC-pool object1
```

```
[root@ceph-node1 /]# ssh ceph-node2 service ceph stop osd.4
=== osd.4 ===
Stopping Ceph osd.4 on ceph-node2...kill 4542...done
[root@ceph-node1 /]# ceph osd map EC-pool object1
osdmap e980 pool 'EC-pool' (15) object 'object1' -> pg 15.bac5debc (15.c) -> up ([7,6,2147483647,8,5], p7)
acting ([7,6,2147483647,8,5], p7)
[root@ceph-node1 /]#
```

6. Similarly, break one more osd, that is, osd.5, and notice the OSD map for EC-pool and object1. You should notice that osd.5 is replaced by the random number 2147483647, which means that osd.5 is also no longer available for this pool:

```
[root@ceph-node1 /]# ssh ceph-node2 service ceph stop osd.5
=== osd.5 ===
Stopping Ceph osd.5 on ceph-node2...kill 5437...done
[root@ceph-node1 /]#
[root@ceph-node1 /]#
[root@ceph-node1 /]# ceph osd map EC-pool object1
osdmap e982 pool 'EC-pool' (15) object 'object1' -> pg 15.bac5debc (15.c) -> up ([7,6,2147483647,8,2147483647], p7]
acting ([7,6,2147483647,8,2147483647], p7)
[root@ceph-node1 /]#
```

7. Now, the Ceph pool is running on three OSDs, which is the minimum requirement for this setup of erasure pool. As discussed earlier, the EC-pool will require any three chunks out of five in order to serve data. Now, we have only three chunks left, which are on osd.7, osd.6, and osd.8, and we can still access the data.

```
[root@ceph-node1 /]# rados -p EC-pool ls
object1
[root@ceph-node1 /]# rados get -p EC-pool object1 /tmp/file1
[root@ceph-node1 /]# cat /tmp/file1
Mona is not testing Ceph Erasure Coding
```

In this way, erasure coding provides reliability to Ceph pools, and at the same time, less amount of storage is required to provide the required reliability.

The Erasure code feature is greatly benefited by Ceph's robust architecture. When Ceph detects unavailability of any failure zone, it starts its basic operation of recovery. During the recovery operation, erasure pools rebuild themselves by decoding failed chunks on to new OSDs, and after that, they make all the chunks available automatically.

In the last two steps mentioned above, we intentionally broke osd.4 and osd.5. After a while, Ceph started recovery and regenerated missing chunks onto different OSDs. Once the recovery operation is complete, you should check the OSD map for EC-pool and object1; you will be amazed to see the new OSD ID as osd.1 and osd.3, and thus, an erasure pool becomes healthy without administrative input.

```
[root@ceph-node1 /]# ceph osd stat
     osdmap e1025: 9 osds: 7 up, 7 in
[root@ceph-node1 /]#
[root@ceph-node1 /]# ceph osd map EC-pool object1
osdmap e1025 pool 'EC-pool' (15) object 'object1' -> pg 15.bac5debc (15.c) -> up ([7,6,1,8,3], p7) acting ([7,6,1,8,3], p7)
[root@ceph-node1 /]#
```

This is how Ceph and erasure coding make a great combination. The erasure coding feature for a storage system such as Ceph, which is scalable to the petabyte level and beyond, will definitely give a cost-effective, reliable way of data storage.

Ceph cache tiering

Like erasure coding, the cache tiering feature has also been introduced in the Ceph Firefly release, and it has been one of the most talked about features of Ceph Firefly. Cache tiering creates a Ceph pool that will be constructed on top of faster disks, typically SSDs. This cache pool should be placed in front of a regular, replicated, or erasure pool such that all the client I/O operations are handled by the cache pool first; later, the data is flushed to existing data pools.

The clients enjoy high performance out of the cache pool, while their data is written to regular pools transparently.

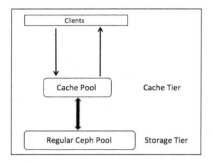

Generally, a cache tier is constructed on top of expensive/faster SSD disks, thus it provides clients with better I/O performance. The cache pool is backed up by a storage tier, which is made up of HDDs with type replicated or erasure. In this type of setup, clients submit I/O requests to the cache pool and get instant responses for their requests, whether it's a read or write; the faster cache tier serves the client request. After a while, the cache tier flushes all its data to the backing storage tier so that it can cache new requests from clients. All the data migration between the cache and storage tiers happens automatically and is transparent to clients. Cache tiering can be configured in two modes.

The writeback mode

When Ceph cache tiering is configured as a writeback mode, a Ceph client writes the data to the cache tier pool, that is, to the faster pool, and hence receives acknowledgement instantly. Based on the flushing/evicting policy that you have set for your cache tier, data is migrated from the cache tier to the storage tier, and eventually removed from the cache tier by a cache-tiering agent. During a read operation by the client, data is first migrated from the storage tier to the cache tier by the cache-tiering agent, and it is then served to clients. The data remains in the cache tier until it becomes inactive or cold.

The read-only mode

When Ceph cache tiering is configured as a read-only mode, it works only for a client's read operations. The client's write operation does not involve cache tiering, rather, all the client writes are done on the storage tier. During read operations by clients, a cache-tiering agent copies the requested data from the storage tier to the cache tier. Based on the policy that you have configured for the cache tier, stale objects are removed from them. This approach is idle when multiple clients need to read large amounts of similar data.

Implementing cache tiering

A cache tier is implemented on faster physical disks, generally SSDs, which makes a fast cache layer on top of slower regular pools made up of HDD. In this section, we will create two separate pools, a cache pool and a regular pool, which will be used as cache tier and storage tier, respectively:

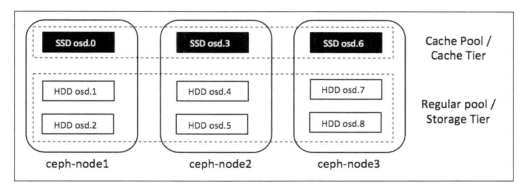

Creating a pool

In *Chapter 7, Ceph Operations and Maintenance,* we discussed the process of creating Ceph pools on top of specific OSDs by modifying a CRUSH map. Similarly, we will create a cache pool, which will be based on osd.0, osd.3, and osd.6. Since we do not have real SSDs in this setup, we will assume the OSDs as SSDs and create a cache pool on top of it. The following are the instructions to create a cache pool on osd.0, osd.3, and osd.4:

1. Get the current CRUSH map and decompile it:

```
# ceph osd getcrushmap -o crushmapdump
# crushtool -d crushmapdump -o crushmapdump-decompiled
```

2. Edit the decompiled CRUSH map file and add the following section after the root default section:

```
# vim crushmapdump-decompiled
root cache {
            id -5
            alg straw
            hash 0
            item osd.0 weight 0.010
            item osd.3 weight 0.010
            item osd.6 weight 0.010
}
```

You should change the CRUSH map layout based on your environment.

3. Create the CRUSH rule by adding the following section under the `rules` section, generally at the end of the file. Finally, save and exit the CRUSH map file:

```
rule cache-pool {
                ruleset 4
                type replicated
                min_size 1
                max_size 10
                step take cache
                step chooseleaf firstn 0 type osd
                step emit
}
```

4. Compile and inject the new CRUSH map to the Ceph cluster:

```
# crushtool -c crushmapdump-decompiled -o crushmapdump-compiled
# ceph osd setcrushmap -i crushmapdump-compiled
```

5. Once the new CRUSH map has been applied to the Ceph cluster, you should check the OSD status to view new OSD arrangements. You will find a new bucket root cache:

```
# ceph osd tree
```

```
[root@ceph-node1 tmp]# ceph osd tree
# id    weight   type name         up/down reweight
-5      0.02998 root cache
0       0.009995                    osd.0   up      1
3       0.009995                    osd.3   up      1
6       0.009995                    osd.6   up      1
-1      0.09     root default
-2      0.03            host ceph-node1
1       0.009995                            osd.1   up      1
2       0.009995                            osd.2   up      1
0       0.009995                            osd.0   up      1
-3      0.03            host ceph-node2
3       0.009995                            osd.3   up      1
5       0.009995                            osd.5   up      1
4       0.009995                            osd.4   up      1
-4      0.03            host ceph-node3
6       0.009995                            osd.6   up      1
7       0.009995                            osd.7   up      1
8       0.009995                            osd.8   up      1
[root@ceph-node1 tmp]#
```

6. Create a new pool and set `crush_ruleset` as 4 so that the new pool gets created on SSD disks:

```
# ceph osd pool create cache-pool 32 32
# ceph osd pool set cache-pool crush_ruleset 4
```

```
[root@ceph-node1 ~]# ceph osd pool set cache-pool crush_ruleset 4
set pool 16 crush_ruleset to 4
[root@ceph-node1 ~]# ceph osd dump | grep -i cache-pool
pool 16 'cache-pool' replicated size 3 min_size 1 crush_ruleset 4 object_hash rjenkins
 pg_num 32 pgp_num 32 last_change 1142 owner 0 flags hashpspool stripe_width 0
[root@ceph-node1 ~]#
```

 We do not have real SSDs; we are assuming osd.0, osd.3, and osd.6 as SSDs for this demonstration.

7. Make sure your pool is created correctly, that is, it should always store all the objects on osd.0, osd.3, and osd.6:

   ○ List the cache-pool for contents; since it's a new pool, it should not have any content:

   ```
   # rados -p  cache-pool ls
   ```

   ○ Add a temporary object to the cache-pool to make sure that it's storing the object on the correct OSD:

   ```
   # rados -p cache-pool put object1 /etc/hosts
   ```

   ○ List the contents of the cache-pool:

   ```
   # rados -p cache-pool ls
   ```

   ○ Check the OSD map for cache-pool and object1. If you configured the CRUSH map correctly, object1 should get stored on osd.0, osd.3, and osd.6 as its replica size is 3:

   ```
   # ceph osd map cache-pool object1
   ```

   ○ Remove the object:

   ```
   # rados -p cache-pool rm  object1
   ```

```
[root@ceph-node1 ~]# rados -p cache-pool ls
[root@ceph-node1 ~]# rados -p cache-pool put object1 /etc/hosts
[root@ceph-node1 ~]# rados -p cache-pool ls
object1
[root@ceph-node1 ~]# ceph osd map cache-pool object1
osdmap e1143 pool 'cache-pool' (16) object 'object1' -> pg 16.bac5debc (16.1c) -> up ([3,6,0], p3)
acting ([3,6,0], p3)
[root@ceph-node1 ~]#
```

Creating a cache tier

In the previous section, we created a pool based on SSDs; we will now use this pool as a cache tier for an erasure-coded pool named EC-pool that we created earlier in this chapter.

The following instructions will guide you through creating a cache tier with the writeback mode and setting the overlay with an EC-pool:

1. Set up a cache tier that will associate storage pools with cache-pools. The syntax for this command is ceph osd tier add <storage_pool> <cache_pool>:

    ```
    # ceph osd tier add EC-pool cache-pool
    ```

2. Set the cache mode as either writeback or read-only. In this demonstration, we will use writeback, and the syntax for this is # ceph osd tier cache-mode <cache_pool> writeback:

    ```
    # ceph osd tier cache-mode cache-pool writeback
    ```

3. To direct all the client requests from the standard pool to the cache pool, set the pool overlay, and the syntax for this is # ceph osd tier set-overlay <storage_pool> <cache_pool>:

    ```
    # ceph osd tier set-overlay EC-pool cache-pool
    ```

```
[root@ceph-node1 ~]# ceph osd tier add EC-pool cache-pool
pool 'cache-pool' is now (or already was) a tier of 'EC-pool'
[root@ceph-node1 ~]# ceph osd tier cache-mode cache-pool writeback
set cache-mode for pool 'cache-pool' to writeback
[root@ceph-node1 ~]# ceph osd tier set-overlay EC-pool cache-pool
overlay for 'EC-pool' is now (or already was) 'cache-pool'
[root@ceph-node1 ~]#
```

4. On checking the pool details, you will notice that the EC-pool has tier, read_tier, and write_tier set as 16, which is the pool ID for cache-pool.

    Similarly, for cache-pool, the settings will be tier_of set as 15 and cache_mode as writeback; all these settings imply that the cache pool is configured correctly:

    ```
    # ceph osd dump | egrep -i "EC-pool|cache-pool"
    ```

```
[root@ceph-node1 ~]# ceph osd dump | egrep -i "EC-pool|cache-pool"
pool 15 'EC-pool' erasure size 5 min_size 1 crush_ruleset 3 object_hash rjenkins pg_num 16 pgp_num
16 last_change 1181 owner 0 flags hashpspool tiers 16 read_tier 16 write_tier 16 stripe_width 4128
pool 16 'cache-pool' replicated size 3 min_size 1 crush_ruleset 4 object_hash rjenkins pg_num 32 pg
p_num 32 last_change 1181 owner 0 flags hashpspool tier_of 15 cache_mode writeback stripe_width 0
[root@ceph-node1 ~]#
```

Configuring a cache tier

A cache tier has several configuration options; you should configure your cache tier in order to set policies for it. In this section, we will configure cache tier policies:

1. Enable hit set tracking for the cache pool; the production-grade cache tier uses bloom filters:

   ```
   # ceph osd pool set cache-pool hit_set_type bloom
   ```

2. Enable hit_set_count, which is the number of hits set to store for a cache pool:

   ```
   # ceph osd pool set cache-pool hit_set_count 1
   ```

3. Enable hit_set_period, which is the duration of the hit set period in seconds to store for a cache pool:

   ```
   # ceph osd pool set cache-pool hit_set_period 300
   ```

4. Enable target_max_bytes, which is the maximum number of bytes after the cache-tiering agent starts flushing/evicting objects from a cache pool:

   ```
   # ceph osd pool set cache-pool target_max_bytes 1000000
   ```

```
[root@ceph-node1 ~]# ceph osd pool set cache-pool hit_set_type bloom
set pool 16 hit_set_type to bloom
[root@ceph-node1 ~]# ceph osd pool set cache-pool hit_set_count 1
set pool 16 hit_set_count to 1
[root@ceph-node1 ~]# ceph osd pool set cache-pool hit_set_period 300
set pool 16 hit_set_period to 300
[root@ceph-node1 ~]# ceph osd pool set cache-pool target_max_bytes 10000000
set pool 16 target_max_bytes to 10000000
[root@ceph-node1 ~]#
```

5. Enable target_max_objects, which is the maximum number of objects after which a cache-tiering agent starts flushing/evicting objects from a cache pool:

   ```
   # ceph osd pool set cache-pool target_max_objects 10000
   ```

6. Enable `cache_min_flush_age` and `cache_min_evict_age`, which are the time in seconds a cache-tiering agent will take to flush and evict objects from a cache tier to a storage tier:

```
# ceph osd pool set cache-pool cache_min_flush_age 300
```

```
# ceph osd pool set cache-pool cache_min_evict_age 300
```

```
[root@ceph-node1 ~]# ceph osd pool set cache-pool target_max_objects 10000
set pool 16 target_max_objects to 10000
[root@ceph-node1 ~]# ceph osd pool set cache-pool cache_min_flush_age 300
set pool 16 cache_min_flush_age to 300
[root@ceph-node1 ~]# ceph osd pool set cache-pool cache_min_evict_age 300
set pool 16 cache_min_evict_age to 300
[root@ceph-node1 ~]#
```

7. Enable `cache_target_dirty_ratio`, which is the percentage of cache pool containing dirty (modified) objects before the cache-tiering agent flushes them to the storage tier:

```
# ceph osd pool set cache-pool cache_target_dirty_ratio .01
```

8. Enable `cache_target_full_ratio`, which is the percentage of cache pool containing unmodified objects before the cache-tiering agent flushes them to the storage tier:

```
# ceph osd pool set cache-pool cache_target_full_ratio .02
```

9. Create a temporary file of 500 MB that we will use to write to the EC-pool, which will eventually be written to a cache-pool:

```
# dd if=/dev/zero of=/tmp/file1 bs=1M count=500
```

 This is an optional step; you can use any other file to test cache pool functionality.

The following screenshot shows the preceding commands in action:

```
[root@ceph-node1 ~]# ceph osd pool set cache-pool cache_target_dirty_ratio .01
set pool 16 cache_target_dirty_ratio to .01
[root@ceph-node1 ~]# ceph osd pool set cache-pool cache_target_full_ratio .02
set pool 16 cache_target_full_ratio to .02
[root@ceph-node1 ~]#
[root@ceph-node1 ~]# dd if=/dev/zero of=/tmp/file1 bs=1M count=500
500+0 records in
500+0 records out
524288000 bytes (524 MB) copied, 1.66712 s, 314 MB/s
[root@ceph-node1 ~]#
```

Testing the cache tier

Until now, we created and configured a cache tier. Next, we will test it. As explained earlier, during a client write operation, data seems to be written to regular pools, but actually, it is written on cache-pools first, therefore, clients benefit from the faster I/O. Based on the cache tier policies, data is migrated from a cache pool to a storage pool transparently. In this section, we will test our cache tiering setup by writing and observing the objects on cache and storage tiers:

1. In the previous section, we created a 500 MB test file named /tmp/file1; we will now put this file to an EC-pool:

   ```
   # rados -p EC-pool put object1 /tmp/file1
   ```

2. Since an EC-pool is tiered with a cache-pool, file1 should not get written to the EC-pool at the first state. It should get written to the cache-pool. List each pool to get object names. Use the date command to track time and changes:

   ```
   # rados -p EC-pool ls
   # rados -p cache-pool ls
   # date
   ```

   ```
   [root@ceph-node1 ~]# rados -p EC-pool put object1 /tmp/file1
   [root@ceph-node1 ~]# rados -p EC-pool ls
   [root@ceph-node1 ~]# rados -p cache-pool ls
   object1
   [root@ceph-node1 ~]#
   [root@ceph-node1 ~]# date
   Sun Sep 14 02:14:58 EEST 2014
   [root@ceph-node1 ~]#
   ```

3. After 300 seconds (as we have configured cache_min_evict_age to 300 seconds), the cache-tiering agent will migrate object1 from the cache-pool to EC-pool; object1 will be removed from the cache-pool:

   ```
   # rados -p EC-pool ls
   # rados -p cache-pool ls
   # date
   ```

   ```
   [root@ceph-node1 ~]# date
   Sun Sep 14 02:27:41 EEST 2014
   [root@ceph-node1 ~]# rados -p EC-pool ls
   object1
   [root@ceph-node1 ~]# rados -p cache-pool ls
   [root@ceph-node1 ~]#
   ```

As explained in the preceding output, data is migrated from a cache-pool to an EC-pool after a certain time.

Ceph benchmarking using RADOS bench

Ceph comes with an inbuilt benchmarking program known as **RADOS bench**, which is used to measure the performance of a Ceph object store. In this section, we will make use of RADOS bench to get the performance metrics of our Ceph cluster. As we used virtual, low configuration nodes for Ceph, we should not expect good performance numbers with RADOS bench in this demonstration. However, one can get good performance results if they are using recommended hardware with performance-tuned Ceph deployment.

The syntax to use this tool is `rados bench -p <pool_name> <seconds> <write|seq|rand>`.

The valid options for `rados bench` are as follows:

- `-p` or `--pool`: This is the pool name
- `<Seconds>`: This is the number of seconds a test should run
- `<write|seq|rand>`: This is the type of test; it should either be write, sequential read, or random read
- `-t`: This is the number of concurrent operations; the default is 16
- `--no-cleanup`: The temporary data that is written to pool by RADOS bench should not be cleaned. This data will be used for read operations when used with sequential reads or random reads. The default is cleaned up.

Using the preceding syntax, we will now run some RADOS bench tests:

- A 10-second write test on a data pool will generate the following output. The important thing to note in RADOS bench output is bandwidth (MB/sec), which is `13.412` for our setup, which is very low as it's a virtual Ceph cluster. Other things to watch out for are total writes made, write size, average latency, and so on. As we are using the `--no-cleanup` flag, the data written by RADOS bench will not be erased, and it will be used by sequential and random read operations by RADOS bench:

  ```
  # rados bench -p data 10 write --no-cleanup
  ```

```
[root@ceph-node1 /]# rados bench -p data 10 write --no-cleanup
Maintaining 16 concurrent writes of 4194304 bytes for up to 10 seconds or 0 objects
Object prefix: benchmark_data_ceph-node1_26928
   sec Cur ops   started  finished  avg MB/s  cur MB/s  last lat   avg lat
     0      16        16         0         0         0         -         0
     1      16        16         0         0         0         -         0
     2      15        18         3   4.88541         6    2.4189   2.12187
     3      16        24         8   9.21183        20   3.31423   2.59351
     4      16        25         9   8.04351         4   1.90747   2.51728
     5      16        29        13   9.48749        16   5.37976   3.26326
     6      16        29        13   8.02065         0         -   3.26326
     7      16        33        17   9.07075         8   5.23925    3.3801
     8      16        35        19    8.9441         8   3.31397   3.59352
     9      15        39        24   10.0899        20   2.52773   3.98084
    10      16        40        24   9.12944         0         -   3.98084
    11      15        41        26   9.03055         4   4.05948   4.23526
 Total time run:         12.227935
Total writes made:      41
Write size:             4194304
Bandwidth (MB/sec):     13.412

Stddev Bandwidth:       7.60183
Max bandwidth (MB/sec): 20
Min bandwidth (MB/sec): 0
Average Latency:        4.61251
Stddev Latency:         2.54733
Max latency:            11.7108
Min latency:            1.17417
[root@ceph-node1 /]#
```

- Perform a sequential read benchmarking test on the data pool:

```
# rados bench -p data 10 seq
```

```
[root@ceph-node1 /]# rados bench -p data 10 seq
   sec Cur ops   started  finished  avg MB/s  cur MB/s  last lat   avg lat
     0      12        12         0         0         0         -         0
     1      15        21         6   23.7445        24  0.365323  0.517866
     2      15        25        10    19.889        16   1.91165  0.947636
     3      16        31        15   19.9216        20  0.832548    1.1234
     4      16        36        20   19.8804        20   3.81842     1.623
     5      16        41        25   19.9027        20    2.4696   1.94785
     6      15        41        26   17.2372         4    1.4177   1.92746
 Total time run:         6.807863
Total reads made:       41
Read size:              4194304
Bandwidth (MB/sec):     24.090

Average Latency:        2.48104
Max latency:            6.38046
Min latency:            0.365323
[root@ceph-node1 /]#
```

- Perform a random read benchmarking test on the data pool:

```
# rados bench -p data 10 rand
```

```
[root@ceph-node1 /]# rados bench -p data 10 rand
   sec Cur ops   started  finished  avg MB/s  cur MB/s  last lat   avg lat
     0     12       12         0         0          0       -          0
     1     15       22         7   27.8596         28  0.300826  0.468331
     2     16       27        11   21.8062         16  0.237253  0.635548
     3     16       34        18   23.6913         28   1.52991   1.18525
     4     15       36        21   20.7954         12   3.79887   1.53081
     5     16       41        25    19.784         16   2.73283   1.91815
     6     15       48        33   21.6187         32   1.68679   2.20121
     7     16       58        42   23.6049         36   1.84635   2.31201
     8     16       63        47   23.0549         20     4.173   2.33454
     9     16       69        53   23.1574         24   2.31493     2.294
    10     16       73        57   22.4116         16   2.45812   2.32087
    11      4       73        69   24.7012         48   3.27041    2.3137
 Total time run:        11.206381
Total reads made:      73
Read size:             4194304
Bandwidth (MB/sec):     26.057

Average Latency:        2.38341
Max latency:            5.19721
Min latency:            0.188254
[root@ceph-node1 /]#
```

In this way, you can creatively design your test cases based on write, read, and random read operations for your Ceph pool. RADOS bench is a quick-and-easy benchmarking utility, and the good part is that it comes bundled with Ceph.

Summary

Performance tuning and benchmarking make your Ceph cluster production class. You should always fine-tune your Ceph cluster before moving it to production usage from preproduction, development, or testing. Performance tuning is a vast subject, and there is always a scope of tuning in every environment. You should use performance tools to meter the performance of your Ceph cluster, and based on the results, you can take necessary actions.

In this chapter, have reviewed most of the tuning parameters for your cluster. You have learned advanced topics such as performance tuning from hardware as well as software perspectives. This chapter also included a detailed explanation on Ceph erasure coding and cache-tiering features, followed by the Ceph inbuilt benchmarking tool, RADOS bench.

Index

Thank you for buying
Learning Ceph

About Packt Publishing

Packt, pronounced 'packed', published its first book, *Mastering phpMyAdmin for Effective MySQL Management*, in April 2004, and subsequently continued to specialize in publishing highly focused books on specific technologies and solutions.

Our books and publications share the experiences of your fellow IT professionals in adapting and customizing today's systems, applications, and frameworks. Our solution-based books give you the knowledge and power to customize the software and technologies you're using to get the job done. Packt books are more specific and less general than the IT books you have seen in the past. Our unique business model allows us to bring you more focused information, giving you more of what you need to know, and less of what you don't.

Packt is a modern yet unique publishing company that focuses on producing quality, cutting-edge books for communities of developers, administrators, and newbies alike. For more information, please visit our website at www.packtpub.com.

About Packt Open Source

In 2010, Packt launched two new brands, Packt Open Source and Packt Enterprise, in order to continue its focus on specialization. This book is part of the Packt Open Source brand, home to books published on software built around open source licenses, and offering information to anybody from advanced developers to budding web designers. The Open Source brand also runs Packt's Open Source Royalty Scheme, by which Packt gives a royalty to each open source project about whose software a book is sold.

Writing for Packt

We welcome all inquiries from people who are interested in authoring. Book proposals should be sent to author@packtpub.com. If your book idea is still at an early stage and you would like to discuss it first before writing a formal book proposal, then please contact us; one of our commissioning editors will get in touch with you.

We're not just looking for published authors; if you have strong technical skills but no writing experience, our experienced editors can help you develop a writing career, or simply get some additional reward for your expertise.

[PACKT] open source ✤
PUBLISHING   community experience distilled

Pentaho Data Integration Beginner's Guide

Second Edition

ISBN: 978-1-78216-504-0   Paperback: 502 pages

Get up and running with the Pentaho Data Integration tool using this hands-on, easy-to-read guide

1. Manipulate your data by exploring, transforming, validating, and integrating it.

2. Learn to migrate data between applications.

3. Explore several features of Pentaho Data Integration 5.0.

4. Connect to any database engine, explore the databases, and perform all kind of operations on databases.

Data Manipulation with R

ISBN: 978-1-78328-109-1   Paperback: 102 pages

Perform group-wise data manipulation and deal with large datasets using R efficiently and effectively

1. Perform factor manipulation and string processing.

2. Learn group-wise data manipulation using plyr.

3. Handle large datasets, interact with database software, and manipulate data using sqldf.

Please check **www.PacktPub.com** for information on our titles

Scaling Big Data with Hadoop and Solr

ISBN: 978-1-78328-137-4   Paperback: 144 pages

Learn exciting new ways to build efficient, high performance enterprise search repositories for Big Data using Hadoop and Solr

1. Understand the different approaches of making Solr work on Big Data as well as the benefits and drawbacks.

2. Learn from interesting, real-life use cases for Big Data search along with sample code.

3. Work with the Distributed Enterprise Search without prior knowledge of Hadoop and Solr.

Fast Data Processing with Spark

ISBN: 978-1-78216-706-8   Paperback: 120 pages

High-speed distributed computing made easy with Spark

1. Implement Spark's interactive shell to prototype distributed applications.

2. Deploy Spark jobs to various clusters such as Mesos, EC2, Chef, YARN, EMR, and so on.

3. Use Shark's SQL query-like syntax with Spark.

Please check **www.PacktPub.com** for information on our titles

www.ingramcontent.com/pod-product-compliance
Lightning Source LLC
LaVergne TN
LVHW081338050326
832903LV00024B/1202